P9-CRP-039

SPIRIT *of* ADVENTURE

ALSO BY ALVIN TOWNLEY

Legacy of Honor

ALVIN TOWNLEY

SPIRIT *of* ADVENTURE

Eagle Scouts and the
Making of America's Future

THOMAS DUNNE BOOKS ST. MARTIN'S PRESS NEW YORK

THOMAS DUNNE BOOKS.
An imprint of St. Martin's Press.

www.thomasdunnebooks.com
www.stmartins.com

Find out more, share your story, and get involved at www.AlvinTownley.com.

Library of Congress Cataloging-in-Publication Data

Townley, Alvin.
Spirit of adventure : Eagle Scouts and the making of America's future / Alvin Townley.—1st ed.
p. cm.
Includes bibliographical references and index.
ISBN-13: 978-0-312-37898-1
ISBN-10: 0-312-37898-X
1. Eagle Scouts—United States—Case studies. 2. Boy scouts—United States—Case studies. I. Title.
HS3313.Z7T685 2009
369.43092'273—dc22

2008044632

10 9 8 7 6 5

For my two-year-old nephew Will and his generation, to whom my generation will one day pass the torch. I hope our generations, and all generations, find some inspiration herein.

CONTENTS

SPIRIT *of* ADVENTURE

INTRODUCTION

On an ordinary April weekend, I would have been well prepared for a springtime backpacking trip on the Appalachian Trail. My father, brother, and I would have encountered a soft path flanked with fresh greenery, and broken the quiet of the woods often to speak with passing hikers. We would have slept soundly in the cool mountain air, and crisp mornings would have given way to bright days as sunlight filtered through a canopy of new leaves. And for warmth, the three of us would have needed to pack nothing heavier than a fleece. This particular weekend, however, would prove far from typical.

Neglecting Scouting's *Be Prepared* credo, I began the weekend by missing the local weather forecasts. Then I left my well-traveled, zero-degree sleeping bag at home, a misstep I realized an hour into the drive from Atlanta to western North Carolina. I thought I could remedy the second mistake by borrowing a sleeping bag from my cousin when we arrived in the mountains. Once in North Carolina, my cousin Mark graciously lent me a decades-old flannel-lined bag, a green behemoth that exceeded the size of my entire backpack. Despite the bag's size, the manufacturer had clearly designed it for winter in Miami. The antique had a thinning liner, held together in several places by duct tape. I wasn't concerned, however. It was mid-April; I expected warm days and mild nights.

Nature proved me wrong almost immediately. During the short hike to our first campsite near Winding Stair Gap on the Appalachian Trail, the temperature tumbled twenty degrees. It continued to free-fall as we pitched our tents. We lit a fire and kept our hands inches from the coals to prevent the dark night from siphoning off the warmth. Then, nature tossed in a new element: snow. I imagined local meteorologists feverishly reporting the record-breaking cold weather; I was sure that back at home, my mother and sister were chuckling about our predicament. How could it get worse?

The temperature continued to plummet, and I sought protection inside the tent my brother Rob and I were sharing. Rob crawled into the tent after me, carrying our flashlight. The beam lit the tent's interior and we immediately realized we'd chosen the perfect tent for a summer evening—and nothing else. The tent's thin rain fly covered only a mesh dome. Cold had already poured through and snow would soon follow. We groaned, anticipating the long, frigid night ahead.

Snow fell and the temperature dropped relentlessly throughout the night. At six-foot-five, Rob found his sleeping bag too short; mine was too thin. We commiserated through chattering teeth, curled as deeply as possible into our bags while various extremities gradually lost feeling. Sometimes, you have to laugh. Somehow, we managed to.

Dawn finally broke, ending the long and sleepless night. The snow ceased, save occasional flurries caused by treetop gusts. Our father, who had slept soundly in his winter tent and sleeping bag, roused us with hot chocolate and oatmeal prepared on a hissing burner. The hot meal gave us the strength to resist turning back, and so with numb feet and only slightly warmer fingers, we began hiking north, following the white blazes of the nation's most famous footpath. We plodded through an undisturbed white landscape, our boots making the first prints on the snow-covered trail. The muffled silence of a fresh snowfall surrounded us. As the serenity of the scene struck me, I began considering this challenging weekend in a different light; it also held its special rewards.

After four uphill miles, we arrived at the final approach to our destination, the windswept crest of Siler Bald, an Appalachian Trail landmark. An expansive meadow, covered in undisturbed snow, rose between us and a solitary tree that marked the peak, two hundred yards above the trail. For two brothers, it clearly invited a competition. Rob and I raced for the summit, high stepping through boot-deep powder. The wind bit our cheeks and cold air stung our lungs as we plunged upward, hearing nothing but our heavy breathing and the crunch of grass beneath the white snow and our boots.

Winded, we found ourselves standing on the 5,200-foot summit, encompassed on all sides by the gentle ridges and peaks of the Southern Appalachian Mountains that we know and love so well. The wind made the only perceptible noise as we spun slowly around, absorbing the majesty of the view.

For the first time in too long, I remembered how much I had enjoyed the adventure of Scouting, and how it had forever shaped my character. I remembered standing atop Mount Phillips and the Tooth of Time at Philmont Scout Ranch, looking over the Rocky Mountains of New Mexico. I remembered sailing through the Caribbean Sea under night skies crowded with stars. I thought about expeditions down foaming rivers where we burst through lines of frigid rapids, soaking our gear but not caring. Every day of those treks proved extraordinary. I realized too few days since had been the same.

Standing on Siler Bald, I thought about my journeys in Scouting as an ambitious teenager and more recently, as a reflective writer. I thought about the ideal of honor, such a part of Scouting and our nation. I remembered that alongside the more traditional values of leadership and integrity belong the spirited principles of passion and adventure. I wondered if others had forgotten that truth as I had.

I found something moving about standing on that Appalachian peak, spinning around and seeing snow-dusted mountains circling the entire horizon. The powerful sensation reminded me of mankind's place in nature, of our role in the larger world. It recalled the lessons I learned on countless treks with Troop 103. I remembered that the adventure of Scouting didn't end when I reached Eagle. I realized anew how vital the qualities of adventure and passion remain throughout our lives.

We found my father waiting for us on the trail where he had stopped, just below the final approach to Siler Bald. The five miles up had pressed his limits, and prompted a story. "I remember walking in downtown Atlanta with your grandfather when I was ten years old," he said. "He'd be walking ninety-for-nothing down Peachtree Street and I had to run to keep up with him. It's funny how positions shift in life. Now I'm the one struggling to keep pace with you two." He smiled. We laughed slightly nervously in response.

My father's story preoccupied me as we descended the peak. He and I are Eagle Scouts of two different generations, but although we hold the same rank, I think the ways we live and understand the values of that rank naturally differ. The past decades had shown how his generation lived the Eagle Scout ideal and shaped the world. But hiking down the trail, I began wondering about *my* generation's role in the legacy of Scouting. Beyond that, I considered our role in the future. How are those of us in our twenties and thirties shaping our families, communities, country, and world? I wondered if others shared my view of living significantly, making good on our promise to do our duty to God, country, and other people. I wanted to discover if this younger generation of Eagles remembered the adventure of Scouting. I wanted to understand how, or if, my cohorts were living with the same passion and purpose that they had once applied to Scouting. Yet again, I had burning questions that wouldn't let me rest.

When I traveled across the country to meet Eagle Scouts and write my first book, *Legacy of Honor*, I sold my house and left my job, pouring all my energy, money, and hope into that great adventure. The gamble offered no certainties and took its toll over many months and miles. Some days frequently proved more difficult and trying than I like to recall. But after exhausting myself and my savings, I finally found a publisher and a paying job. I also found happiness and some welcome stability in coaching track and working with high school students. I eventually became comfortable, a potentially dangerous state for anyone, particularly writers. Too much comfort can sometimes sap the spirit that drives us to explore and experience life. But after our hike along the Appalachian Trail, I began feeling challenged by these new questions more and more. I knew in my heart that I needed to find the answers. I also worried I might be too comfortable to go seek them if I didn't change the status quo.

Legend tells that when Hernán Cortés reached the coast of Mexico in 1519, he disembarked his legions and ordered them to burn their ships. From the beach, the conquistadors watched flames consume timbers, masts, and all avenues of escape. Cortés and the four hundred men under his command had no choice but to pour their hearts into their mission and succeed; they could not turn back. Taking a lesson from the story of Cortés, I realized the best way to succeed was to leave no option for failure. I understood the value of pursuing a mission with a singular focus. I also knew the sense of raw adventure that accompanies laying everything on the line.

While I was not particularly eager to repeat the uncertainty or risk of writing my first book, I realized only one real choice existed. Once again, I left a job and a life I loved so that I could set out to meet the individuals who held the answers I sought. I started the engine of my ten-year-old Ford Explorer, gambling that it could take one more cross-country journey, and put my hometown of Atlanta behind me. I headed west to meet the rising generation of Eagle Scouts and to continue an adventure that began more than a century ago.

THE ADVENTURE OF SCOUTING

On the morning of July 29, 1907, a local boatman set out across Poole Harbor in southwest England. He found the water still and the air already heavy with summer. His boat, the *Hyacinth*, cut through the water gently as it carried one of Britain's great heroes to Brownsea Island, an isolated 560-acre patch of wilderness in the harbor. From the small boat, General Robert Baden-Powell, hero of the recently concluded Boer War in Africa, surveyed the approaching island. He glanced over the contingent of boys who joined him on the voyage and he considered how his life had changed. No longer did he lead men into battle; no longer were his troops crack soldiers of the British Empire. The energetic boys gathered around him were his latest command, and perhaps his most significant.

He felt a slight unease as the shoreline of Brownsea Island drew near, and he quietly considered his lingering doubts. The trip to the island would rigorously test a daring concept. The general had devoted several years to developing a new program for boys, and had taken a sizeable risk by investing his time and credibility in something entirely untried and unproven. But he felt the youth of Britain needed it desperately. When he had triumphantly returned from Africa in 1901, he found a changed nation. He toured the country during the ensuing years and found poverty affecting millions of families. He particularly noted how the scourge affected children, and his heart ached as he found young boys idle, directionless, and often in trouble. Somehow, he thought, Britain must engage their young minds or lose an entire generation.

Drawing on his experiences in the army, Baden-Powell began formulating a plan that would instill skills, initiative, citizenship, and character in Britain's youth. His initial goals were modest and cooperative: "To help existing organizations in making the rising generation, of whatever class or creed, into good citizens." He hoped his ideas would help young people from all socioeconomic backgrounds, a decidedly novel concept in Edwardian England. He envisioned a program that boys throughout the country could practice together in their respective communities. He realized, however, that boys, just like boys today, would never knowingly volunteer to learn about values and citizenship. So, Baden-Powell added a critical element to his plan: adventure.

He combined the scouting skills he'd honed in the army with the outdoor skills he'd learned as a boy, such as tracking animals, camping, and cooking outdoors. His new Boy Scout program would teach the skills and values young men needed, but would cloak those lofty lessons in outdoor adventure. The general also envisioned a program led by the boys themselves. He designed the patrol method, under which groups of five boys functioned as a unit, led by one of their own. Within the patrol, the boys worked toward common goals, teaching and helping each other along the way. They were entirely responsible for themselves, which, for many turn-of-the-century adolescents, was an entirely new experience.

Before Baden-Powell launched his program nationally however, he had to test it. He needed a proving ground and had chosen the island now ahead of him. The excursion would confirm his vision, or utterly dash his hopes. He was apprehensive, but he also felt electrified with anticipation.

He again surveyed the group of boys who were looking anxiously toward the nearing shoreline. Once on the island, they would make camp and join the other young men who Baden-Powell had hand-selected for his experiment. To assemble these campers, B-P, as he was often called, had reached across highly stratified British social classes and gathered boys from families wealthy and poor, well-educated and not. In all, twenty-one boys, with an average age of fourteen, would spend a week camping together on Brownsea Island.

At nightfall on July 31, 1907, the boys gathered around the campfire that marked the true beginning of their week on the island. The next day, they broke into four patrols—the Bulls, Curlews, Ravens, and Wolves. Baden-Powell designated a patrol leader for each. Then, resurrecting a practice from his army days, the general pinned a fleur-de-lis emblem to their hats. Soon thereafter, the fleur-de-lis would become the enduring symbol of the Scouting Movement.

With their badges displayed on their coats or soft-brimmed hats, the four patrols spent the week under Baden-Powell's tutelage and learned the range of skills that came from the fifty-year-old general's experiences: his game-playing and studying at Charterhouse School, his hunting expeditions, his military training, and his scouting in Africa. He collectively called these skills Scoutcraft, and the boys soon became experts. Their leader understood young men well, and he ensured every lesson maintained an element of adventure or competition to hold their attention. Games played around the island and in the harbor taught the boys animal signs, elements of tracking, rowing, and swimming. They learned first aid, cooking, and camping; how to identify plants and animals, tie knots, and save lives. Baden-Powell also added lessons on geography, history, government, and virtues. To test their newfound skills, every patrol spent at least one night away from camp, fending for itself. The boys in each patrol carried all of their gear and prepared their own food; no small challenge for boys unaccustomed to life outside the city.

The social aspect of the Brownsea experiment also went well, as boys from different backgrounds found themselves thrust together as equals. In their patrols, they learned to work with and appreciate one another, and only occasionally did differences appear. Arthur Primmer, one of the original Brownsea campers, remembered, "One of the upper-class boys in my patrol put his hand up one day and said 'Please, sir can I leave the room?' and one of the town fellows said, 'Silly fool, doesn't he know he's in a tent?' "

At night, the boys all came together and listened intently to Baden-Powell's campfire stories, and perhaps unknowingly witnessed the great general returning to his element. Telling stories and leading campfires, B-P relived many nights spent on quiet African plains. As he explained new skills to the boys and saw them learn and practice, he was reminded of his time spent training soldiers. Camping on this isolated island, the general recaptured the daring spirit of his military days, and instilled his passion for adventure in a new generation.

Baden-Powell did not design Scouting for conformists, the uninquisitive, or those willing to venture little. He had risked everything on an untried idea, and raised eyebrows among the establishment as he brought together boys from different social strata. His campers arrived on Brownsea Island with little experience in camping or living outdoors. Nobody had ever designed a similar week of discovery and learning for young men, or harbored such a sweeping vision for a program to change the lives of youth. From its very inception, Scouting was an adventure.

One hundred years later, I stood on the bow of a boat very different from the *Hyacinth*, watching the Brownsea shoreline approach. Even though it was spring in England, chilly gusts buffeted the modern ferry, which was carrying me across Poole Harbor to the place where Baden-Powell landed his expedition a century before. I stood almost alone on the upper deck, quietly contemplating what he and the boys had been thinking as they transited the bay. To my right, the trees, beaches, and low rise of the island drew closer. The small castle and quaint dockside buildings at the island's southern tip were the only major structures visible from the water, just as they were in 1907; little had changed on the spit of land since. Soon, I stepped onto the dock and began walking inland along the same path as the campers had hiked. Fifty paces from the dock, a canopy of trees closed over the wide dirt road, breaking the chilly wind and allowing the filtered sunlight and still air to provide some welcome warmth. Saint Mary's Church, with its somehow unpretentious gothic construction, still marked the fork that led to the shoreline where Baden-Powell situated the first Scout camp. I turned onto the road's left fork and soon arrived atop the long spine of the island. Grassy fields covered the ridge. Cliffs fell away to the west, wooded hollows to the east. Eventually, the cliffs gave way to a gentle slope and I wandered downward toward the beach. I realized that Baden-Powell had found the perfect spot to launch his ambitious program. Thinking like a Scout, I recognized that the island offered endless avenues for fun, mischief, and adventure. Uncharted woodlands to explore, campfires to build, and relatively little adult supervision would have unleashed the imagination of anybody and offered unlimited chances to hone new skills.

A small trail branched from the dirt road and it guided me through a scrub thicket and across a small bridge that spanned a marshy bog. I emerged from the trees onto a sunlit plain, covered with moss, grass, and white sand. The soft ground led down to the seashore where Baden-Powell's campers had raised the British Union Jack each morning during their week on the island. Beyond the dunes, the cold harbor lapped at the sand beach and the countless pieces of terra-cotta pottery that littered it, remnants of a failed mid-1800s ceramics factory.

I saw the beach and the campsite much as B-P's Scouts had. I felt a quiver of energy and a sense of history in the field. I walked across the grass where they camped, imagining them drawing water from the nearby creek, cooking meals, and taking in the same views of the harbor. A signpost stood amid a pile of round stones, myriad arms pointing in every direction, some weathered to illegibility, others considerably more recent and clear. Scout troops from around the world—France to Korea to Australia to Brazil—had made these pointers showing where and how far the Movement had carried from the English shoreline where I now walked.

Since 1907, the Scouting Movement had spread from that very spot to 156 countries. Today, twenty-eight million young people are Scouts. More than 250 million the world over have joined the Movement during the past century. Quite auspicious for an endeavor that began so humbly.

Robert Baden-Powell initiated something special here on this English isle, and it spread across not just continents, but also generations. Having seen where it started, I felt an even greater desire to know where Scouting was going. And where it would go, I realized, would be decided by my generation.

So I returned to the questions that first formed on the Appalachian Trail, along the snowy path from Winding Stair Gap to Siler Bald. Our generation was beginning to come of age, and Scouting's future now relied on us. More broadly, the world's future lay with us, Eagle Scouts and otherwise. But for those of us who held Scouting's highest rank, I wondered how the program had shaped our lives. Will we be different because of our shared experiences in a khaki uniform? Beyond that, how are we making our communities and countries better places? As Scouts, we're charged to lead lives that are extraordinary, adventurous, and most important, significant; but what does that truly mean for us and for others? What was the purpose we found as we began our adult lives in earnest?

I had enough questions. I needed answers, and I knew exactly where to start finding them.

Late on a summer afternoon, I turned off U.S. Interstate 25 and drove west down two-lane Route 58 toward Cimarron, New Mexico. My truck's backseat held cargo very different from what I'd packed for my previous journey into Scouting, when I'd traveled the country to write my first book. On those trips, I'd met many Eagle Scouts from preceding generations who had carried the values of Scouting to the top echelons of business and government; I often needed suits for Wall Street boardrooms and the halls of Congress. On this new quest, instead of polished shoes and button-down shirts, I packed boots and a fleece. Instead of my suitcase, I'd filled the backpack that accompanied me on my last trip to Philmont Scout Ranch, more than a decade ago. I added my four-piece fly rod, sandals, and lucky fishing hat. Already, this journey was different from my last.

Carrying that load of gear, my truck crossed the grassy plains, hurrying toward their abrupt end at the foot of the rugged Sangre de Cristo range of the Rocky Mountains, which rose higher before me with each passing mile. I finally saw one rocky point rising above the otherwise even ridgeline: the majestic Tooth of Time. The Tooth marks Philmont Scout Ranch and when I saw it, like many Scouts of many generations, I felt that I was home.

Eight hundred thousand Scouts have traveled to Philmont since it opened its gates in 1938, and perhaps more than anywhere else, this famous place inherited the spirit of adventure that started on Brownsea Island. What takes place on Philmont's 214 square miles is one of America's treasured legacies, and it showcases the good that comes from investing in younger generations. Scouting came into being because Baden-Powell believed in the next generation and felt an obligation to it. Likewise, Philmont's former owner, Oklahoma oil pioneer Waite Phillips, understood that he was but a steward of his wealth. Time and circumstance had smiled upon him, and he understood his duty to share his good fortune. He particularly believed in the promise of youth, and passed along his success to the Boy Scouts of America, knowing his gift would leave a mark on generations of American youth long after he had gone.

"That ranch represents an ideal of my youth," Phillips said, referencing the cattle ranch that would become Philmont. "I want to make it available to other boys. I'd be selfish to hold it for my individual use." At the relatively young age of fifty-five, he donated 127,395 beautifully rugged New Mexico acres, along with an Oklahoma City office tower to provide revenue for camp operations. The 1941 dedication reads:

> These properties are donated and dedicated to the Boy Scouts of America for the purpose of perpetuating faith, self-reliance, integrity and freedom—principles used to build this great country by the American Pioneer. So that these future citizens may,

through thoughtful adult guidance and by the inspiration of nature, visualize and form a code of living to diligently maintain these high ideals and our proper destiny.

In Philmont, Waite Phillips found a way to sustain the spirit of America and of Scouting. He provided others the opportunity to learn, discover, and pursue their own sense of adventure. Annually, more than twenty thousand youth and adults embark on treks through the ranch's mountains and canyons. They experience hiking, fishing, rock climbing, horseback riding, roping, fellowship, and lots of trail food. Each Scout who hikes the backcountry of Philmont inherits the legacy of Baden-Powell and of Waite Phillips. The custodians of that legacy are hundreds of Philmont staff, who serve as teachers, mentors, conservationists, and guides. I came to Philmont to meet these stewards.

In Cimarron, an aged frontier town of fewer than one thousand residents, I found the wooden sign indicating the final leg of the trip to Scouting's American epicenter. As I covered the last two miles of road, I remembered Eagle Scout William Sessions telling me about his first trip to Philmont in 1945. "When we got out there, it was just a dream," the retired FBI director had reflected. "Here you were; you were *really* at Philmont . . . It was just a dream." When we met several years ago in Washington, D.C., I had forgotten what he meant. As I passed beneath the shady trees that line the road near the camp headquarters, I remembered.

By the time I crossed under the famous entrance—a simple wooden beam adorned with a summer's worth of worn-out hiking boots hanging by their laces—the sun had fallen below the Tooth of Time casting a shadow that spread rapidly eastward over the camp, ushering an easy breeze through the hundreds of army green tents spread out on the last mile of the prairie. To the east, scattered clouds reflected the sunlight back on the tents and pastures of grazing horses. To the west, darkness fell quickly in the folds of tree-covered mountains. I thought about the four thousand Scouts, leaders, and staff in the backcountry performing the quiet rituals of evenings outdoors: cooking meals, hanging bear bags, bedding down for the night, and reflecting on a day of old limits being surpassed. As the sun threw its last rays onto the eastern clouds, which flashed red, then faded to gray, I honestly sensed a passion for adventure being born in some, rekindled in others.

In the newly fallen darkness, I noticed a light and made my way toward it. I came upon the ranch's campfire ring. There, several hundred Boy Scouts, numerous members of Scouting's coed Venturing program (a fast-growing high adventure program for young men and women ages fourteen to twenty), and quite a few obviously tired leaders had gathered for their closing ceremony. They had spent ten days on the trail, each unforgettable—for better or worse, but unforgettable nonetheless. Now, these hikers were about to leave. As they sang a version of Simon & Garfunkel's wistful "Homeward Bound," I was sure each earnestly planned to carry the lessons and spirit of their trek with them. But I wondered how long they could keep that spirit with them. I planned to find out the next day.

Travis Schreiber and I stood well above the valley floor, looking at a disturbingly sheer forty-foot face of northern New Mexico sandstone. Behind us, opposing forests of pine and spruce faced each other across a grassy valley, split by a small creek and a dirt path, part of Philmont Scout Ranch's 350 miles of backcountry trails. The trail meandered down the valley and eventually reached Dean Cow campsite, where Travis served as a program counselor. He was spending his summer teaching crews of backpackers how to scale the countless crags spread throughout Philmont's current 137,493 Rocky Mountain acres. I had arrived at Dean Cow camp during an afternoon lull and coaxed him off the camp's comfortably rustic porch and down the valley so we could climb the rock before us.

Travis, an Eagle Scout who attended the University of Northern Iowa, pulled a well-worn baseball cap over his short red hair and rolled up the sleeves of his blue staff shirt to allow for full reach across the rocks. He quietly contemplated routes up the face as he held a length of rope for me. I patiently threaded it through the carabiner attached to my harness. The tiny metal ring would save me in case my footing slipped as I scaled the cliff. Without the safety rope, I could fall forty feet from the top, and if I took the right bounce, I wouldn't stop until I met the creek bed another fifty feet below. I took the rope from Travis and paid careful attention as my out-of-practice hands tied a doubled figure-eight knot.

Safely tied in, I raised my eyes. Travis had disappeared. I heard a noise, looked up the rock wall, and saw a pair of legs disappearing over the outcropping at the top. "He's a bit ridiculous," said Kelley Geiser, who had accompanied us. "This is his first summer really climbing and he's amazing. He has the build for it and, like you just saw, he's fast and not afraid of the devil."

"Great," I thought, wondering if my rusty skills would embarrass me. Kelley, one of Philmont's growing cadre of female staffers, recognized the look on my face and laughed. "We do this every day; I'm not expecting you to beat him," she said, then added with a smile, "or me."

Not too long afterward, motivated by pride and the pure challenge, I hoisted myself onto the sunny ledge atop the cliff. Travis had stretched out and was obviously enjoying the expansive view of the valley. "You haven't completely lost it," he said in greeting.

As I unclipped from the belay ropes, Travis said, "Philmont is one of the things that got me past that phase of my Scouting career where I cared what other people thought about Scouts. I went from being a follower to being a leader. Now, it's pretty unbelievable to be back here. This is exactly where and how I got started climbing, right here at Dean Cow, learning from a program counselor. Now, I *am* that program counselor, and you see Scouting in a whole new way."

Travis quickly realized that his primary job had changed. He had always helped other Scouts, but he'd also focused on achieving ranks and awards for himself. As an adult leader, he now had the single purpose of helping Scouts learn skills, including climbing. Some came off the rocks crying, some finished their climbs all smiles, but every Scout that Travis taught carried away something important. Without badges to earn, he could relax and devote himself to these young men. He saw the same in other leaders. "It's amazing to be with these leaders who are just doing things for other people and not asking for anything," he told me. "After you leave Scouting, you realize how unique and awesome that aspect of it is."

As we talked, Travis thought more on a subject he hadn't truly considered from an adult perspective. Barely twenty years old, he observed that reaching Eagle and *being* an Eagle is as much a maturing process as anything else. It went far beyond completing requirements in the Scout handbook. He viewed the rank as a mountain to conquer by constantly practicing the skills and way of life Scouting proscribed. "Use the skills you're teaching everyone else and be able to do it by heart, with your eyes closed," he said. "That's how you become an Eagle: do it until it becomes a way of life."

Finally, we heard a yell from below. Kelley was still waiting to belay us on our descent. Travis slowly moved into action and helped me clip back into the rope. I absorbed the view from the top one more time. "Travis, appreciate this," I advised.

"I do," he promised. "It's an adventure." He struck on the same word that had called me back to traveling and writing. I wondered if he considered adventure in the same way.

"What does that mean?" I asked.

"It's plain fun," he explained. "But the real adventure is being able to get together with complete strangers looking for the same thrill in the outdoors. I see fifty to one hundred people a day—about thirty-five hundred each summer—all strangers. It's like a Scout troop. When you join a troop, you may only know one or two others, but you're all there to have fun and to be in the outdoors and learn something while you're doing it. Anyone can organize a canoe trip, but they don't have the volunteer leaders and others to teach you skills. Scouting is about getting together with complete strangers because of your love for adventure and the outdoors—and learning in the process."

Travis reflected on his two treks to the ranch with his own Scout troop, just several years earlier. "As for Philmont, it's amazing how much you can grow up from ten days in the mountains," he observed "I did two trips, two years apart. It changed me the first time, changed me even more the second time. I matured, I had a different outlook. When we went through Philmont, we began to look at everything differently and appreciate the opportunities this place gives. When you get back to reality, it naturally carries over. You think: Why not get the most I can out of this? That's Philmont or anything. Why not take advantage of your surroundings and everything life has to offer?"

Kelley called from below again, and Travis changed his focus. "Okay, let's head down," he said. He checked my ropes and handed me a pair of gloves. With my feet planted on the cliff's edge, I leaned back until I was perpendicular with the rock face, all my weight on the rope. I felt a thrill I'd missed since the last time I rappelled years before. Several hops later, each longer than the next, I landed next to Kelley. Travis shimmied down the cliff to join us and together we hiked back to the shady front porch of the Dean Cow cabin.

From my first trek to Philmont as a seventeen-year-old Scout, I remembered the gifts that early mountain mornings brought—silence, wildlife, and sunrises—so I rose early the next day. Everything was as I remembered. All that stirred were deer, birds, and the ubiquitous chipmunk. These animals, nearby creeks, and rustling leaves were the only sounds other than the pounding of my Nikes along the backcountry trail.

By the time I'd finished my run, Thurston Drake had been at work for two hours. The twenty-seven-year-old medical student had arrived at base camp's health lodge at 6:00 A.M. sharp. By the time I'd finished lunch, he'd already spent a morning treating the variety of cases found in any community of four thousand people. By the time I'd finished dinner, he'd traveled into the backcountry to treat an emergency, returned to camp, and completed his last rounds. When I met him at 8:15 P.M., he was ending a fourteen-hour workday. As a fourth-year medical student, however, Thurston was already familiar with that routine.

Wearing a stethoscope around his neck, he emerged from the health lodge, stretched, and sat down next to me on the porch. He sighed and soaked up the coolness of the rapidly falling night. "In Mississippi, we'd still be sweating right now," he said, then laughed. "But this is what I love about Philmont, just being outside." He took another deep breath of evening, obviously glad to have escaped the fluorescent lights and sterile environs of the health lodge.

"You know," he reflected, almost as much to the night sky as to me, "Scouting got me outside. Particularly for me, it was being outside and camping and learning that formed the kernel of what the program did for me as a human being. That's not to diminish the things we talk about at meetings and before flagpoles that are of great importance, like the Scout Oath and Law. But it's being outside where those values come out—or don't come out. There were times when I was a participant on Rayado Treks, long before I ran the program, where I wasn't loyal or wasn't hardworking. Where instead of helping clean dishes, I'd just sit there because I was tired. What I'm trying to say is that the opportunity Scouting gave me to be outside in the natural world was what offered me the chance to really live those principles we always recite."

I hadn't realized this fairly soft-spoken doctor-in-training once led Philmont's most demanding and challenging program: the Rayado Trek. The current Rayado coordinator, University of Maine track standout Scott O'Connor, had described Philmont's graduate-level experience to me at breakfast in the staff dining hall earlier that day, so I was well briefed. Over heaping plates of eggs and pancakes, Scott explained that Rayado exists to challenge seasoned adventurers and build future leaders during three-week treks though the backcountry. That's three weeks spent living from a backpack, sleeping on the ground, taking sporadic showers, and eating your fair share of powdered food. As coordinator, Scott created true wilderness experiences for guides and participants alike. He designed crews so that no member would have a preexisting relationship with any other. Nobody would have an advantage and over their three-week trek, participants couldn't focus on their differences. They had to use and rely on each member's unique abilities and talents.

"I'm trying to figure out how I can keep doing something like this," Scott had sighed as we discussed his prospects as an outdoor education major. "It's the best. But I'm graduating U Maine and trying to figure out what to do so I can still get outside and wear boots and shorts on a regular basis! When I leave Philmont, I've accepted that my job won't pay that much, but it'll be what I love to do. I'll be so happy being in the outdoors with other people. You make some sacrifices for what you want to do."

Several years after being in Scott's position, Thurston Drake had yet to make any money that did not immediately disappear into education expenses. Like Scott, he didn't mind. Back on the health lodge porch, Thurston echoed Scott's thoughts, saying, "Rayado takes young people and shows them something new about themselves and about others; about the natural world; and about simplicity and about complexity, both the complexity of human interactions and the complexity of being pushed to the limit. There are physical challenges and emotional challenges. When you have eight teenagers pushed to the breaking point, you definitely get challenges of both varieties! As a participant and moreover as a leader, I realized there's a lot more out there in the world that I wanted to know about—and that there was a lot more about myself that I wanted to understand.

"And that, for me, is adventure," he concluded. "Learning something or doing something that you haven't done before, something that makes you a bit uncomfortable. Adventure doesn't have to have an element of crazy risk. A chief ingredient is doing something unknown that gets you a little unsettled and outside your comfort zone."

Leaving Mississippi and walking onto the prestigious campus of Princeton University certainly constituted one adventure. Thurston found a host of classmates who knew each other from high school and boarding school, whereas he found only one other student from Mississippi in his entire class. He loved college regardless. When he moved to Salt Lake City to enroll in medical school, he walked into the same scenario. He knew nobody, but by this time, he'd begun to relish moving to new places, finding himself in unfamiliar waters, and being forced to make new friends. For someone who genuinely loves meeting people, encountering the unfamiliar was a gift. As a doctor, he realized he'd be experiencing that gift frequently, and would encounter people in every condition that exists—extreme and not. "Life's been a great adventure in that way," he reflected, "so I haven't gotten too far away from Philmont in a sense."

But he had traveled a long way from his home in Mississippi, where until his senior year in high school, he assumed he'd follow his father's path and attend the University of Mississippi, "Ole Miss." He shocked everyone by attending Princeton, where he first aimed to become an English professor, or even a writer, if he felt equal to fellow Mississippian William Faulkner. Then he surprised friends and family again by moving to Utah for medical school—and also to be near the western outdoors he'd grown to love. Even though his family still resides in Mississippi, Thurston can never truly go home again. Hurricane Katrina utterly destroyed the Drake home and everything in it. Fortunately, his family had evacuated to safety. Their Ocean Springs house had been one of the bleak and empty concrete foundations I had seen when I arrived on the Gulf Coast after the storm hit in 2005. His family's church, Saint Paul United Methodist, hosted the camp where I worked as a relief volunteer.

On that trip to Ocean Springs, I discovered that an inordinately large number of Eagle Scouts were involved in the relief effort. One of those Eagles thoughtfully phrased it: "In Scouting, we all learned values. Scouting taught us to give. Now look who came down here to the Gulf Coast to help—Eagle Scouts." His observation along with my experience rebuilding homes in Mississippi reminded me what it means to *be* an Eagle Scout. After Katrina, several strangers reminded Thurston of the same thing.

Six months after the hurricane swept through Ocean Springs, a group of Scout leaders sent a new medal to each of the Eagle Scouts whose homes disappeared during the storm. So Thurston returned to his apartment in Salt Lake City one day to find a box from a complete stranger. Inside was a new Eagle medal. Aside from putting "Eagle Scout" on his college applications and his memories of Philmont, he hadn't thought much about Scouting since he had earned the rank. But upon opening this unexpected box and holding the medal that was enclosed, he found himself a little choked up. "I was really moved and that surprised me," he remembered. "And it made me think about *why*."

Thurston explained how Scouting had, in ways direct and indirect, influenced his life's path at every step. It always offered him a proving ground. "In life," he explained, "you need these opportunities where you're put to the test, where you're outside, where you're taking on these responsibilities as a teenager. That's where you get the chance to live out those virtues. That's where those ideals become real; they're not just words you recite. Scouting gave me the chance to be all those things in the real world and that has been its greatest gift. Now I'm back here to pass that along."

The next day, after a morning spent pulling rainbow trout from the Rayado River in Philmont's backcountry, I went to see the ranch, still much as Waite Phillips had known it: cowboys, horses, steers, and dust. The corral near base camp stables many of Philmont's three hundred horses, and when I arrived the wranglers were staging an informal rodeo. I found Lee Leatherwood in the thick of it.

Wearing jeans, a light blue shirt, and an easy, youthful grin, Lee sat atop his horse, reins held firmly, lasso coiled at his side. Horse and rider stood stock-still and eyed the metal chute to their right. A ranch hand pulled a lever and with a loud clank, a steer shot into the corral. Lee dug his heels into the horse and together, they bolted after the steer, leaving a trail of dust behind them. I could see Lee push the steer toward the fence as another horse and rider closed behind the fleeing bull. Lee stood slightly in the saddle, raised his right arm and began methodically circling his lasso overhead. He closed the remaining distance, lasso still circling. Then he tossed the loop downward and over the horns of the steer. He pulled tight, pushed his horse toward the center of the corral, and brought the roped animal with him. As the "header," Lee's job was nearly done. It was up to his partner, the "heeler," to snare the steer's hind legs. Unfortunately, his partner's toss missed the mark on that round, so the bull won. As much as Lee loves roping and winning, he was too good-natured to let that bother him. When he came back to the fence where I stood with a small crowd, he was all smiles beneath his Stetson hat.

"Heeling's tough; that's why I try to be the header," he joked from his horse. "We're not the best ropers in the world, but we have a lot of fun. I just love roping. Once you take it up, it's such an intense sport that you just can't give it up. It's like the rush you get skydiving."

"Roping is like skydiving?" I asked a bit incredulously.

Lee grinned. "For me it *is* skydiving. This year better be my year. If I have to work or finish college next summer instead of coming here, I want a belt buckle! That's the prize for winning the rodeo, which I definitely didn't win tonight. I've never been a real competitive person, but I want that buckle; I'd like people to know that I can actually catch something!"

Lee dismounted and we began walking his horse toward the stables; horse and rider were done for the day. After handing his mount to another ranch hand, Lee led me to the bunkhouse where he washed his face, hung his hat, and grabbed two drinks from a cooler. We sat down under a shady tree and continued our conversation as we enjoyed the afternoon breezes. I learned that Lee had been a wrangler at the Philmont ranch for three years, and he was hoping for an invitation to rejoin the crew next year. I had little doubt the twenty-two-year-old Eagle Scout from Dublin, Texas, would receive one.

Coming from central Texas, Lee grew up around farms and worked cattle and sheep during high school. He loved managing livestock, and had learned ranch breaking, a style of training horses, but never imagined doing it for an actual ranch. That changed at Philmont. "I'm breaking horses for the ranch, and living like it's 1800," he exclaimed. "We push cattle all day—dawn 'til dusk—and everything we do is on horseback. There're just not many ranches like this anymore.

"But Scouting led me here," he continued. "I really wanted to get out of my town and I was going to work as a wakeboard instructor in Colorado, but my dad said, 'Lee, you know you work harder than that. Why don't you go to Philmont?' I applied and for my three position choices, I listed 'wrangler, wrangler, and wrangler.' I got the job and came out here. It was totally different than anything I was thinking. I thought it'd be all about the Scout sign and teaching merit badges. But I got out here and it's definitely not. It's everything I learned growing up in a small town in Texas."

In that small town, Lee had learned that Scouting built skills. Developing those skills in Scouting and beyond became a lifestyle for him. But real adventure, he explained, involves where the skills take you.

"I've worked every job under the sun," he said, tossing a scrap of food to a bunkhouse cat that was circling us. "And it's all because of the skills I gained in Scouts. Scouting opens doors. It opened the door so I could come out here. I never expected to be riding horses every day, and it's been tougher than I imagined. But I love it. You know, the real adventure of Scouting is in the doors it opens."

Lee paused for a moment, simply watching the late afternoon sunlight wash across the hills and pastures to our east. Then he made an observation I would hear many times over, one that perhaps explained why a Georgia writer could enjoy an afternoon with a cattleman from Texas. Far beyond just learning straight skills, Scouts find themselves in situations—and often in camps and tents—where they end up living with people who they might never know outside Scouting. In those situations, we learn not only to coexist, but to work together and appreciate—even enjoy—one another. In the end, Lee felt he could communicate with *everybody*, not just other wranglers from Texas. Philmont just broadened that understanding.

"This place has just made everything better," he stated. "It gets in your blood and once it does, you can't give it up." He smiled, chuckled to himself, and began a story. "I have a serious girlfriend back home in Texas and I talk about this place all the time with her. We're both getting ready to graduate college in the next year—or maybe two years for me; she's a bit faster then I am! But I was telling her I didn't want to hurt anything between us, so I didn't have to go to Philmont this summer. I could get a good job in Texas. She said, 'No, you've talked about it so much, I'll go home and be with my family. You should go be a wrangler.' I said, 'Okay, good,' and I pulled out my finished application and put it in the mail!"

Lee knew that he might have other responsibilities next summer, perhaps a serious job and others depending on him. That would take him one step closer to being ready for a family. He realized, however, that if he were to start a family, he would have to *feed* a family. "I learned responsibility as a Scout," he said. "I need to be responsible to my family when that time gets around. My dad always taught me that the family comes first and you have to prioritize." Like many other staff and wranglers I met at Philmont, Lee struggled with facing life outside Scouting and far away from the New Mexico Rockies. These young men, in their early twenties, were graduating college, preparing for careers, and facing a daunting task: deciding which path to follow in life.

Earlier in the week, I spoke with Sean Casey, a twenty-six-year-old school counselor who served as head ranger, overseeing the rugged staffers who serve as trail guides for new crews. When we talked at the ranger headquarters, this Eagle Scout from Springfield, Illinois, had confessed to the personal struggle I'd observed in his colleagues. "Growing up as middle-class kids, we're told we can do anything, and I think we sometimes mistake *any*thing for *every*thing," he reflected. "People have trouble making big decisions because there are so many choices they want to think about."

In some ways, Scouting compounds that challenge by providing a true liberal arts education, giving Scouts glimpses into myriad careers and lifestyles. In Scouting, young people can pursue nearly every path that interests them. To earn Eagle, they study at least twenty-one subjects and earn the corresponding merit badges. The 121 available merit badge courses include subjects as wide ranging as astronomy, cinematography, finance, government, horsemanship, journalism, lifesaving, marksmanship, medicine, oceanography, and whitewater canoeing. Only a Scout's time and initiative limit his experiences, and roughly fifty thousand Scouts reach Eagle each year. After leaving their Scout troops when they turn eighteen, however, these young men begin to face very real choices and decisions. Among the Philmont staff, I found many worried about graduating college. After college, they knew they could no longer avoid considering the future and could only escape to Philmont during the summers. I noticed that they all seemed preoccupied with the same question: if, and how, they could sustain the adventure they'd known at Philmont. Beyond that, they wondered how the values of Scouting would guide them in a world without the Scout Oath.

In the shade outside the bunkhouse, Lee voiced the same struggle, but seemed ready to make decisions. Gesturing to the corral and pastures behind us, he said, "I'll probably give this up soon. I'll probably go into banking, but to me, that's being responsible to my family and that goes back to being an Eagle Scout. I'm technically out of Scouting, but you learn so much that throughout your life you use those skills and so you never really get out of Scouting. That's why this place has such appeal. You come out here and see Scouting isn't an organization; you come out here and see that Scouting is a way of life."

At the end of my week's stay at Philmont, staff alumni from the past fifty years returned to Cimarron to celebrate half a century of serving Scouts from around the world. Each worked on staff during their youth, and none ever lost their passion for Philmont's ideals. They came to see each other again and to honor their legacy, Waite Phillips's legacy, and make sure the tradition carried on. As I would soon realize, they also came to find answers.

I joined Bryan DeLaney, a veteran of nine summers on staff, as he led twenty alumni on a hike to the Tooth of Time. The brotherhood that existed among these still-young alumni surprised me. They knew each other well and many had stayed in frequent contact since their days together at the ranch. Bryan knew Thurston Drake, the medical student at the health lodge, and as we set out for the Tooth of Time, Bryan recalled hiking the same trail with the physician-to-be years ago. They both served as leaders for a special needs camper named David who had Down syndrome. During the trek, David's spirit affected everyone he met and Bryan particularly remembered him conquering a rock climbing challenge.

"He was clearly nervous about it," Bryan explained. "You can't even talk about comfort zones with him—*everything* is out of his comfort zone. But he climbed up, rappelled, and finished the trek. It really inspired everyone, and I think he inspired himself. Thurston was important in giving David that experience.

"Despite the Ivy League image he has sometimes," Bryan joked, then turned serious, "he's got a tremendous heart. He talks about being a surgeon, but he probably wouldn't tell you that he really wants to practice in developing countries. He's exceptionally smart, but he wants to use that gift for the greater good."

"But that's why a liberal, Catholic, Marist College graduate from New York and a Methodist, Princeton graduate from Mississippi can have a great relationship on the trail, and stay friends afterwards, right?" I said.

"Exactly," Bryan said. "Everyone here cares about the greater good. It's something that starts in a Scout troop and it carries over to Philmont, and hopefully life thereafter—although I'm trying to stay here as long as possible!"

Bryan was only joking. The twenty-seven-year-old Eagle Scout had already carried those values far away from the ranch. When his season ended at Philmont, he would return to the North Georgia Mountains and resume his post as a leader in the Second Nature Wilderness Program. There, he would spend his weeks and weekends working with at-risk youth and troubled teens, using the power of the wilderness to effect change in their lives. Essentially, he remained a Philmont ranger. On treks through leafy, Appalachian woods, he helped students cope with the unexpected and learn about themselves in the process.

"In a lot of ways, the kids we see at Second Nature are like the Scouts at Philmont," he said. "They may have made some different choices along the way and be facing some real personal challenges back home, but I empathize with them. It's perhaps more challenging in some ways, but it really uses the wilderness to give students what can be a truly life-saving, not just life-changing, experience. But basically, I'm still a ranger!

"They always say 'Rangers change lives,' " he continued, referring to the motto of the staffers who guide crews along the trail. "And I think staffers here do make a difference. The whole place changes lives. You can go to lots of beautiful places to hike, but nowhere else has the community, the fellowship, the history, the adventure, and the learning all together. Nowhere else opens your eyes and makes you appreciate people from all walks of life and all parts of the country. And nowhere else seems to forge the same lifelong friendships.

"Just look at us," Bryan said, gesturing to the column of former staff climbing the trail behind us. "We can't leave this place, and we're all still friends. I hope that never changes."

We continued our hike with everyone doing their best to maintain the pace they kept as staffers years ago. I was sure there would be more than a few aching legs in the morning. One who would decidedly *not* be sore was Chris Sawyer, a corporate auditor with a habit of setting out on long expeditions every few years. He'd hold a good job, save his money, then quit work and pursue one adventure or another until he expended his cash and energy. Then he would return to work and begin the cycle anew. Most recently, he had completed a backpacking trek in Bolivia and climbed Mount Kilimanjaro, the highest peak in Africa. His pace hadn't lost a step. Eventually, Chris began pulling ahead of the main group. I took his bait and followed his merciless tempo up the steep incline that led toward the summit. We stormed up together, breaking at a crossroads shortly before the final ascent. There, we drank deeply from our water bottles and caught our breath in the thinning air.

Chris wiped his mouth and then made an observation about the years he'd spent as a Philmont ranger and Rayado coordinator. "I spent a lot of time here because I always felt like I had a lot to pay back," he explained. "I was a bad kid when I was here—not into serious trouble, but just completely obnoxious. I needed straightening out and to grow up. Philmont did that for me. Although maybe it still has some work left to do!" He laughed and we started for the summit.

The trail soon dissolved into a field of boulders and we threaded our way upward, eventually arriving at the top together. It was magnificent; not just the view but the sensation of standing on the summit of Scouting. To the east were the Great Plains; to the west were the rugged ridges, peaks, and canyons of the Rockies, of Philmont. All around us trail crews perched on rocks and enjoyed lunches and views. Many of these backpackers were preparing to descend the long spine of the Tooth, hiking the final miles of their ten-day trek. By dusk, they would be in base camp. The next day, they would leave for home.

Chris and I stood at the summit, absorbing the vista. "This wouldn't be a bad place to stay forever," I observed, as a warm summer wind rose up from below the peak. The only sounds the breeze carried were occasional chirps from birds on the lower slopes below us. The quiet was majestic.

"Well," Chris finally answered as Bryan and the others climbed toward us, "Philmont is a great place to figure out what you want to do, but Philmont itself isn't what you want to do. You have to move on."

Atop the Tooth of Time that summer afternoon, a group of Eagle Scouts stood enjoying a moment, enjoying the adventure that has always been Philmont. I sensed that these Eagles also wondered how to continue that adventure or, if they had lost sight of it, how to reclaim it. So many lived outdoors during Scouting and their time at the ranch, and as they began careers, got married, started families, and took on mortgages, they either found outlets for their adventurous spirit or adapted to find excitement and discovery in other pursuits.

In a way, I think all of us still looked to Scouting to show us what to become and how to become it. That's why we'd all returned to Philmont, to recapture the perspective of a simpler time and to breathe in the land's not-entirely-tamed spirit. I had wondered how Scouting was helping us address questions about what we will become, what it meant to our generation, and how we were carrying its legacy. I began to find my first answers at Philmont, and the Eagle Scouts I met had unknowingly helped define my coming journey. Travis Schreiber reflected on how our roles shift from learners to teachers as we change from Scouts to adults. Thurston Drake mused about the ever-changing nature of adventure and its many forms. For all his love of rodeo, Lee Leatherwood faced real decisions about responsibility and family. Sean Casey was trying to make life choices in the face of virtually unlimited options. Maybe Scouting can't provide us with the ultimate answers, but those of us on the Tooth that day believed it would at least help us begin to find them. We had, I think, returned for many superficial reasons. At heart, however, we had returned to find guidance.

I moved away from the group and walked to an outcropping. I looked into the heart of the mountains. I thought about the thousands of Scouts and adults hiking beneath the pines and spruce at that moment, and my own time here years ago. I thought about my most recent trip and what lay ahead of me. Slowly, I realized that I wasn't simply standing on the summit as an author observing others grappling with the challenge of sustaining an adventure and finding purpose. I was wrestling the same questions. Like them, I needed Philmont's help to move forward. At that moment, I understood that this quest wasn't just about other Eagle Scouts. This quest was about me as well.

PART I

Adventure Abroad

I knew that places like Philmont Scout Ranch, the Florida National High Adventure Sea Base, the Northern Tier Canoe Base, and countless camps and trails throughout America had instilled in me an appreciation for what the outdoors and the unexplored world offer. These venues also taught me that the world didn't exist solely for my entertainment. As a Scout, I learned that I have a duty to these places as well as the people I encounter, whether along a Canadian river or on a neighboring block in my hometown of Atlanta.

My experiences in Scouting also left me with a bit of wanderlust, and truthfully, I still find something strangely reassuring about putting on a backpack and setting out for a new destination. The open road—or trail—holds a particular allure that I can never seem to escape. In my travels as a Scout and since, I discovered that unlimited adventure awaited me across the country and around the world, if only I was brave and ambitious enough to pursue it.

I also knew that those trips revealed the world's needs in a unique way; you can't venture to new places without being touched by both the place itself and its people. I wondered if other Scouts of my generation experienced my same desire to explore beyond America's shores. And if they did, I wanted to know how they responded to the challenges they faced and the needs they uncovered. In short, I decided to set out and discover how Eagle Scouts were shaping our world.

SEALS

Hours after American aircraft crossed into Iraq to begin the Second Gulf War, four gray Mark V jet boats skimmed across the Persian Gulf toward their target: the Mina-Al-Bakr Oil Terminal, a floating behemoth whose miles of twisting, metal piping carry a vast majority of Iraq's total oil exports. Almost no other target had greater value and importance for the country's future and well-being.

On board the Mark Vs, two platoons of elite Navy SEALs endured the constant jarring of waves and rechecked their gear. Their minds focused on their mission. Orders directed them to secure the oil platform and stop Saddam Hussein's forces from creating an environmental and financial catastrophe by sabotaging miles of pipelines. Blowing the pipes would send thousands of barrels of oil cascading into the Gulf, suffocating marine life and crippling Iraq's ability to recover economically after Saddam Hussein's regime fell.

By the time the SEALs neared the terminal, darkness had settled over the sea.

"It was a beautiful night," Petty Officer Robert Sterling remembered. "Awesome night, no moon, and a beautifully lit target."

The night's beauty did nothing to lessen the seriousness of Rob's mission or calm his nerves. "Deep down inside, going into combat, everyone is nervous," he confided. "Anyone who isn't nervous, isn't really serious. Anyone who tells you they're not scared has become complacent and forgotten the little things. There's not an op I've been on where the hairs on the back of my neck didn't stand up. On this op, the war had basically started early. We were supposed to be the first strike, but the air war had already opened. So we're thinking, 'Great, they'll be waiting for us.' We may get on final approach and get blown out of the water. Or what if the intel was wrong? Or a million other things that could go wrong. Every guy has a scenario running through his head—all different—but every guy is thinking about something."

The SEALs geared up on the Mark Vs, adding more than one hundred pounds to their weight in body armor, gear, and ammunition. Then they transferred to the smaller RHIBs (rigid-hulled inflatable boats) and went quiet. "Once you're in that boat, there's silence," Rob said. "There's no turning back and everybody knows it. You flip the serious switch and rely on training and rehearsals and everything prior to."

Two boats, each carrying a squad of combat-ready frogmen with blackened faces, crept stealthily toward the towering platform, moving from the dark sea into the area illuminated by the rig's lights. "We motored in, nice and quiet," Rob explained. "We didn't see anything, and there was a ladder that came down to the water's surface. I was number-one man, and I stepped onto the ladder, and moved right on up."

Petty Officer Sterling and those behind him remained silent as they pushed their way through the platform's corridors and rooms, not knowing what lay behind each door. The United States was at war. Her enemies would shoot to kill. The SEALs ascended another flight of stairs, opened a door, and surprised their first Iraqi soldier.

"He immediately put his hands in the air and we told him to get down quietly and he did," said Rob. The SEALs bound the soldier's hands and feet then moved stealthily into the next room. They found twenty soldiers staring at them. The sight of the battle-ready American soldiers alone proved enough for the Iraqis to throw their hands skyward. The soldiers' cries and pleas intermingled with the SEALs' shouts until Rob's team established calm. They began interrogating the leaders and learned that Saddam Hussein's government had paid them handsomely to blow up the platform and themselves along with it. Rob noted that the soldiers had carried the money with them, instead of sending it home to their families—a good sign they had little intention of sacrificing themselves. That said, Rob observed crates and crates of TNT and plastic explosives rigged to rip apart the platform. "The charges would have definitely blown all the pipes open," he observed. "Maybe collapsed the whole rig. Disaster."

Rob's two teams cleared the entire structure, five kilometers of decking in all. Thankfully, neither side sustained casualties. The team secured the platform for the inbound Marines who would soon take over; new missions elsewhere demanded the special abilities of the SEALs.

"All that ties right back to this surf," Rob said as we stood together in La Jolla, California, a coastal village a thousand miles west of Philmont. The sun had just sunk into the Pacific Ocean, dragging the day's remaining warmth with it. The Pacific surf crashed onto the darkening rocks below and sent a frigid mist up to where we stood.

"That story happened on the other side of the world, but it all relates to our training here in San Diego," the thirty-one-year-old Eagle Scout observed, unfazed by the spray. "Sitting around in Kuwait waiting to go, people get sick of each other. That's going to happen with a bunch of alpha males like us. But what's funny is that when it's time to work, we revert right back to training. It's like being back in BUD/S—that's our SEAL training program.

"When you're on a mission, everything you went through in training—paddling, Hell Week, running with a boat on your head—it all comes back to you. You put differences aside. Everybody is there for each other. Whatever disagreements were, they're put aside and once the task is done and over with, you don't even remember what those issues were."

Rob smiled, noticing my reaction to the chill. "In BUD/S we got real used to this," he recalled, surveying the rocks below the low bluff where we stood. "We'd be in camies, and they'd run us out into the surf and we'd tread water until we were about frozen. Then, being merciful, our instructors would call us out of the water . . . and then tell us to roll around in the sand! We'd be shivering, exhausted, and entirely caked with grit and sand. We basically spent an entire month like that. It definitely changes your impression of Imperial Beach!"

Later, I arrived at Naval Amphibious Base Coronado, which borders Imperial Beach, California, and houses active SEAL Teams One, Three, Five, and Seven. It also hosts hundreds of confident SEAL candidates each year. Of the hundreds that report for training, however, only one out of every three successfully endures the notorious thirty-week program. Along the Grinder, the bleak courtyard that serves as the center of SEAL candidates' regimented training, a line of helmets confirmed the statistic. Nearly forty green helmets lined the pavement's edge, each placed there by a sailor who had left the current class of candidates. Near the helmets hung an unassuming silver bell, rung by each candidate who withdrew.

On the morning I arrived, I found the Grinder empty and quiet. If I hadn't known the feats of endurance it saw daily, I might have considered it peaceful. But for much of the year, exhausted SEAL candidates fill the air with chants as they exercise and pour sweat for hours on end. White flippers mark the asphalt at regular intervals, outlining the spots where candidates pound out push-ups and perform other creative varieties of PT (physical training) until their arms and legs can perform no more. When that happens, instructors order them into the sea. Trust me, the ocean offers them no quarter.

Less than one hundred yards from the Grinder, I reached the soft, white sand that belongs to Imperial Beach. I crested a large sand berm, and saw the broad beach and blue Pacific stretch out to the north and south. The rhythmic sound of waves replaced the industrial hum of the base. It seemed relaxing and peaceful, but I would hear quite a different perspective of Imperial that evening.

Chief Petty Officer Tom Campbell, a SEAL instructor who reminded me of Tom Selleck's character on *Magnum, P.I.* drove fellow instructor Aaron Reed, two SEAL candidates, and me to dinner at a local Mexican restaurant. As the five of us hustled down Coronado's main thoroughfare in Tom's Land Rover, candidate Lieutenant William Thomas explained, "I love the water and skydiving, so this is just where I wanted to go."

I knew what challenges face SEAL candidates in the Pacific surf. "Still love the water?" I asked William.

"Yes," he answered over the laughter of everyone else in the car, "but maybe in different ways now."

Because of Basic Underwater Demolition/SEAL (BUD/S), SEALs will never view Imperial Beach the way I do. I see it as a vacation spot. They don't. BUD/S training lasts six months, during which SEAL candidates undergo a training program designed to ensure the mental and physical fitness of everyone who graduates and becomes a member of the Navy's vaunted special forces group. When SEALs see action overseas, they are ready. The notorious first phase, Basic Conditioning, lasts seven weeks. Candidates spend about two months training furiously on the base, on the beach, and in the water. They endure long runs wearing boots and full backpacks, two-mile swims in the open ocean, and a ceaseless regimen of calisthenics. Demanding obstacle courses and small boat maneuvers in the crashing surf add important skills to the basic physical conditioning.

Second Phase develops SEAL candidates into combat swimmers and divers, building their stamina and navigation abilities until they can master long-distance underwater operations. The final nine-week Land Warfare phase includes marksmanship, demolition, rappelling, and small-unit tactics. When they graduate and become SEALs, their skills and physical condition are unmatched. Many consider BUD/S the toughest training program in the world, and the general respect non-SEALs hold for SEALs would help confirm that.

The arsenal of tales SEALs use to trump any civilian's stories come from enduring BUD/S and going on covert operations around the globe, like Rob Sterling's attack on the oil platform in Iraq. The civilian's one advantage: most of a SEAL's missions are classified. As the U.S. Navy's special operations group, the SEALs strike first. They typically attack from and return to the sea, but they are also trained HALO (High Altitude Low Opening) parachutists and generally seem willing to ride into a fight by whatever means will take them. Their performance in combat is legendary, but that stems from their training, an arduous ordeal for which many in the public have difficulty believing soldiers actually volunteer.

"The atmosphere is pretty intense," admitted Lieutenant Thomas from the backseat of the Land Rover, "but the people you meet in BUD/S, you stay friends with forever. I've never laughed as much, and I've never endured as much pain—particularly going through Hell Week. But the camaraderie is something you can't experience anywhere else. It's the best training around, and there's not a better proving ground for yourself and your team. It challenges you in every way possible. I knew this was what I wanted to do."

"I just saw forty helmets worn by guys who also thought this was what they wanted to do," I said. "How did you survive?"

"A big part of it is maturity," he answered. "In our class, a good number of guys have quit at one point and come back; this is their second time through BUD/S. If I were eighteen coming through this straight out of high school, I don't know if I'd have had the maturity to do it. But going through school and working your mentality up to accepting that you'll be running four miles with a pack on a regular basis really develops your capacity."

The loaded four-mile runs are only a small part of the training, which has components that test every aspect of a soldier's abilities—and limits. The instructors found their greatest resource is the nearby surf. SEAL candidates hit the cold salt water often, and it's known by all as "getting wet and sandy." Depending on whether the perspective belongs to a candidate or an instructor, this drill adds to their misery or toughens them so they can survive the worst in combat. After drills, before long runs, after long runs, in the middle of the night, and just at an instructor's whim, the aspiring SEALs get ordered into the water. When they're exhausted, near drowning, and nearly frozen, they're ordered out and onto the beach where they cake themselves with sand. They pound out push-ups. Repeat the cycle until utter exhaustion and then do it all again.

The hardest challenge William and each of his comrades face during training is Hell Week, a brutal, five-day training ordeal in First Phase that washes out many candidates. It's a mental and physical marathon where instructors show neither mercy nor compassion. The candidates are constantly moving through the surf, along the beach, around the base, across the bay—anything but sitting still. For five days, they get neither rest nor sleep. For five days, their fatigues remain wet and covered in grit. Their clothes chafe them so much that hitting the salty Pacific electrifies their raw skin like alcohol on a fresh cut. A five-and-a-half mile swim proves the end for many. Those who survive it can count on getting wet and sandy the second they flop exhausted onto Imperial Beach.

"Hell Week was the toughest thing I've ever finished," William said without hesitation. Everyone agreed.

It almost sounds masochistic, but in their own eyes, these young men are proving their mettle. They're proving they're equal to any challenge. In their instructors' eyes, all this prepares them to wear the Trident pin that signifies them as a member of the world's arguably most elite combat force.

We arrived at the restaurant, bailed out of the Rover, and found an empty patio table. Any wariness these Eagle Scouts had about me had disappeared en route to the restaurant, and their individual personalities began to show as their sunglasses came off and their guards came down over dinner. Aaron Reed warmed up faster than most. Aaron was a thirty-year-old Kentucky-born marksman visiting Coronado from his base in Kodiak, Alaska, where he was a SEAL weapons and survival instructor. He viewed enduring any ordeal, and surviving it with style, as a direct personal challenge. His Hell Week offered a perfect example. Every twelve hours, the team would have a medical check to allow candidates to clean their cuts. The process began with a cold shower.

"Unless," Aaron explained, "you figured out how to go around the back of the building and turn on the hot water." His plan succeeded brilliantly until the instructors noticed steam billowing from the shower room. "They'd run in there and yell," he said, "but really, what were they going to do? Run you or give you PT? That's all they do the whole week anyway, so big deal!" Even though he was back in the freezing surf soon, his small victories helped him muscle through the week.

Those examples of spirited creativity and resourcefulness reminded me that these men were not just SEALs, but fellow Scouts. The skills they learned years ago had helped them complete not just Hell Week, but the entire BUD/S ordeal. And they knew those skills would continue to help them throughout their lives. Eric Ramirez, a SEAL candidate from Ohio, explained, "Scouting led me here by giving me the confidence to go out and do something on my own. One particular time, I was hiking in Georgia on a forty-mile trip with some of my old friends from college. One guy got hurt out there and I had to figure out what to do with him and how to get us to where we needed to be. It fortunately went well and I just liked that feeling of being in control, being in the outdoors, taking care of my guys, and functioning on the fly. Everything I did in that situation was based on things I learned in Scouts. That stayed in my mind for years and eventually led me to the military and it'll be with me after I leave it, as well. It's thinking on your feet, being outdoors, being adventurous, doing different things, and not being in an office."

"Yeah," Tom interjected, "wait until you get some more rank, then talk with me about offices!"

After a laugh, Eric continued and observed that he had found relatively little practical application for many things he learned in school, whereas in Scouting, he learned skills that he could directly apply. He studied camping and survival techniques at meetings and before trips, then he'd utilize those skills in a real setting where he'd develop confidence in his capabilities, like his trip to Georgia. When he'd leave for a weekend expedition, he'd consider what he needed to carry in a backpack to survive. For most American teenagers, that is not a typical thought process. Later, Eric had found a unique opportunity in the navy to continue applying those skills in real situations. He spent a month in SEAL survival school in Kodiak, Alaska: fires, shelters, minimalist camping in freezing weather. It was everything he'd done as a Scout.

Eric called his father shortly after returning to base: "Dad, thanks for putting me through Scouting—it actually works!"

"For me," William volunteered, "Scouting was about getting you out of your comfort zone. Early on, any time we'd have a rappelling trip, I'd be terrified to look over the side of the cliff or start down or trust that the rope would hold me. Going whitewater rafting as a ten- or thirteen-year-old kid, those waves can look pretty big and it takes you out of your comfort zone and gets you used to working outside that zone. It's the difference between being afraid of something and not being afraid and being able to face it. Then I'm going to college and getting my skydiving license! That's something Scouting definitely does for you. With backpacking, I enjoyed having everything I needed to survive on my back. I remember walking in the woods on my first trip and thinking what if something goes wrong? Then I realized that I had water purifiers, food, a tent, sleeping bag; I had everything I needed to survive actually on my back—that's a cool feeling."

Aaron was ready to share another story from his Kentucky adolescence. "Richard Walker was my Scoutmaster, an absolutely great guy; a bunch of us still keep up with him," he began.

Then he caught our attention: "He loved me but had to kick me out twice!"

The first time Scoutmaster Walker bounced him, Aaron had brought a climbing rope with him on a backpacking trip and took a group of young Scouts rappelling without informing any of the adult leaders. Aaron was out for a month until he begged his way back into the troop. Not long after returning, he found himself kicked out again. "We had a rival Scout troop in town and they had a campout," his story began, and I knew right away where it was leading. Aaron and his brother, also an Eagle Scout, planned a raid. Their mistake, Aaron admitted, was inviting two guys who were not Scouts.

"Our plan was to raid their camp in the middle of the night and tie their zippers together and do stupid things like that," Aaron explained. "Well, these other two knuckleheads who weren't Scouts thought it was an actual raid and they'd basically cut their way through a tent and sliced their way back out. So, that didn't look good on me and I took the rap and got kicked out again. I had to go to all the families and apologize for their sons' gear being trashed. I had to answer to all of that in my Eagle Scout board of review."

The skills and experiences William, Eric, and Aaron had as Scouts have yielded real dividends on missions. Tom Campbell, who'd seen more action than anyone else at our table, explained, "You know, as SEALs, we're in survival situations in almost any operation and the things you learn from being a Scout, the knowledge you take with you, really helps. One year, we were on an operation in Korea . . ." He explained that his squad had run out of food and water and faced frigid temperatures that they weren't expecting. They found themselves cut off from their extraction point and so they scaled a nearby peak to secure a safe and commanding position where nobody could approach unseen. Near the summit, they realized they were unprepared to stay overnight in the plunging temperatures, but fortunately the men found abandoned fortifications that offered some relief. The fortifications were just trenches lined with logs, Tom explained, but they at least broke the wind. Tom split his men into two groups and told them to light a small fire for warmth. He started his own fire and then went to check on his companions. He found them trying to light huge logs with matches from their MREs—the SEALs had not yet implemented their now mandatory survival training program. Tom showed them how to build a discreet fire for warmth.

"We survived," he said, "but I was shocked that these guys had no idea how to make a fire! I made two fires that night. That's where Scouting pays off directly. These were good American kids and you assume they know everything you know, but that's just not the case sometimes."

Aaron had apparently been quiet too long. "Did any of you go to Junior Leader Training?" he asked. He was referring to the renowned leadership course (called National Advanced Youth Leadership Training since 2003) for upcoming Scout leaders run by older Scouts. It reflects Baden-Powell's goal for Scouting to be "boy-run."

I knew Aaron had asked his question for a reason. "Why? What'd you do, Aaron?"

"Get kicked out of that, too?" Tom asked.

Almost, as it turned out. Aaron and the other JLT participants had spent several days learning skills for communication, problem solving, teaching, leading, and team-building—all things they practiced in the field during the week-long training program. Ultimately, participants would carry these skills back to their troops. Unfortunately, Aaron's particular instructors happened to go off-book, and the campers had to endure several days of overly strict regimen. Toward the week's end, the staff pushed too far and ambushed the entire class with water balloons. Everyone was soaked. "We were at war then," Aaron said.

Aaron went to each camp and recruited a leader and together, they organized an elaborate raid on the instructors. He designed a map of the instructors' campsite and designated points of attack for each squad. The water balloon raid went off and the JLT participants were avenged. Then the staff learned who masterminded it.

"They came after me hard," Aaron said. "They yelled that I didn't learn anything, that I was an embarrassment to have in the course. But really, I thought I learned more than anyone else there; I was the Junior Leader!"

Then Aaron grew serious. "All the knuckleheaded stuff aside, Scouting is your first step in a life of service, and as SEALs, that's pretty much what we do. We serve our country."

With those two simple sentences, Aaron drove home a point about Scouting and about the military. For all the enjoyment and challenges associated with those two parts of Aaron's life, they'd ultimately prepared him for his life and career. He had upheld his country's values wherever duty took him: Iraq, Afghanistan, and other far-flung places he couldn't reveal. Now, almost like a senior patrol leader in a Scout troop, he was preparing new SEALs to serve overseas and uphold the same virtues and way of life. Aaron and all of the SEALs with me that evening were continuing on a trail they started years ago, serving their country, confident that they were changing the world for the better.

After nightfall I stood behind Tom Campbell on the dock at Coronado. He carefully inspected a long line of divers in black wetsuits. He tugged on gear and checked the oxygen flow for each rig, ensuring everyone was prepared for the upcoming night dive. He gave William Thomas and Eric Ramirez a particularly rigorous shakedown, clearly letting them know that since our dinner had ended, he was once again their instructor. Occasionally, he fired a salvo of questions at a diver to ensure he could manage the complex rebreathing system that would keep him alive and invisible during a dive. All checked out, the candidates walked to the nearby dive ramp, waded into the dark bay two-by-two, and disappeared. Once they were all underwater, the dock fell quiet.

Tom and I watched a long line of green buoys slowly crawl across the black surface of the harbor. Beneath each buoy were two divers with an attack board consisting of a compass, depth gauge, and a watch. For many, tonight's dive was their first at night in many months and their first that relied entirely on underwater orienteering. With their oxygen rebreathers functioning, no telltale bubbles broke the glassy surface. SEALs rely on stealth and surprise, and I imagined the many docks and harbors around the world, where on moonless nights like this, SEALs had suddenly broken the surface without warning.

Half an hour into the dive, Tom went to walk along the pier and observe his trainees from another angle. Someone turned on a stereo in the nearby hangar, and its speakers began blaring "Sweet Child O' Mine," by Guns N' Roses, breaking the silence on the dock and providing me with some company. I met the culprit when Jake Baker walked onto the dock carrying a hot calzone and wearing a big grin.

Earlier in the day, Aaron Reed had pointed out Baker as he sat in one of the rubber boats floating by the docks. He was wearing combat boots, camouflage pants, a flop hat and was completely soaked. Baker—nobody seemed to call him Jake—looked back at us with an understandably puzzled expression. Aaron grinned broadly and made the three-fingered Scout sign with his right hand. Then he pointed again at Baker with his left. Jake grinned back, then shook his head and pulled his hat over his eyes. Aaron and I laughed. I'd quickly learned that the fast-talking Eagle Scout had a reputation as a character. He had an ever-present smirk that I imagined had infuriated more than a few instructors during his training. His excuse for missing our dinner was a trip to the local tattoo artist, famous among SEALs, who had added a flying turtle to Baker's side. Despite his slightly contagious carefree attitude, however, Jake had become an expert and dedicated sailor.

We sat down at a wooden table, watching the line of green buoys snake out and back and begin to scatter as the divers struggled with the finer points of nocturnal submarine navigation. Baker had yet to tackle dive qualification, and had three months left until he would receive his Trident. Honoring a superstitious tradition among SEALs, he noted, "That is, in the *un*likely event I graduate." Now, however, graduation looked significantly more likely than it did during BUD/S. Several months after we met, Baker would be wearing his own gold Trident.

"I'm not as excited as I thought I'd be," he confessed. "I've been thinking about how much I still have to do. You train to wear the Trident then spend the next fifteen years trying to keep it. The hard work is just starting, and I'm looking forward to training with SEAL Team Two and doing a mission. It's like being a marathon runner: you spend an entire year training and you want to go out and do it."

When he first joined the military he sought out the most difficult assignment, where he'd have to try his hardest every day. He certainly found that challenge. The training took its toll. Baker encountered several setbacks during BUD/S, breaking an ankle, breaking a foot, and tearing a knee. Either he was particularly fragile under his formidable exterior or training was just that tough. I gathered it was the latter case, although he suffered plenty of ribbing for his injuries.

After thoughtfully chewing a mouthful of calzone, Baker gestured at the water and the base behind us. "All this shows you how much you can do," he said. "You're sore every morning and your boots are still wet when you put them on. You'll wake up for a four-mile run and your legs are creaking and aching from the day before and you think, 'I can't do this.' Next thing you know, you're out there doing it.

"You kinda forget *why* you're doing it while you're in BUD/S. You just know you want it more than anything—this is the one thing in life that you want to finish. We may start it to prove ourselves, but ask a guy who's a couple of weeks into it and he'll say 'I'm just trying to finish this run right now.' You start focusing on the little things that get you through the day.

"You also learn what you can actually do as a team," he continued after another bite of calzone. "Nobody makes it through this program alone. One day someone is pushing and pulling you through the program; the next day you're pushing or pulling someone else."

"You work within a group and learn what you can do," he added. "It's like in Scouts. Not everyone can lead. Someone comes up with a plan and you may not agree with that plan, but you have to go along with it; it may be the best thing you have going. That definitely came in handy in Alaska during survival training. Some of these guys had never spent the night out in the woods in a tent before or started a fire. Knots were also a big help. Some guys didn't know how to tie a square knot or bowline, basic stuff to us after you've done it so long in Scouts."

"Seems a lot like summer camp," I observed, before I snatched a piece of calzone for myself. "Maybe I missed out on something."

"Yeah, it may seem fun," Baker said, "but I promise you, our instructors can take anything cool and make it absolutely miserable—going to a tropical island, skydiving, whatever. You name it and they can ruin it with a heavy pack and PT!"

After Baker turned in, I walked onto the pier where Tom stood observing the divers' progress. Axl Rose had stopped belting "Sweet Child O' Mine." An absolute still hung over the docks. Tom watched the candidates' lights, finding out how well he had prepared his men. He pointed out that even if divers were off course, the telltale buoys moved at the same pace, SEAL pace. All SEALs learn to swim at a constant rate, which allows them to precisely plan missions—one hundred yards will always take three minutes for any SEAL to swim underwater.

"It's been a lot of years since I was doing this for the first time," Tom reflected, looking over the dark harbor. "I probably like being a regular SEAL a little bit better, but instructor is a satisfying job and it's one you generally get as you get older—*more experienced* is the nice way to say it. I get to put my mark on guys who are the future of the SEALs. I hope I'm doing a good job in molding good SEALs and good citizens as well. They'll be out there representing who we are to the public and to foreign counterparts.

"And that's what we need to be doing for our country: serving and representing America well. I came into the military because of the way I felt about this country—and I'm here today because of the way I still feel. This job lets me do directly what needs to be done with regard to our foreign policy and the way we're perceived overseas.

"Look at these guys," he said, pointing to two black figures emerging from the harbor. Water dripped from their black wetsuits. They held their flippers in their hands, and their masks were pulled down to their necks. It was Eric Ramirez and William Thomas. They had completed the dive first, and judging by the glowing buoys scattered around the harbor, many of their classmates would be a long time in joining them on land.

"Both those guys are sharp and will be the leaders in this class," Tom continued, watching them walk up the boat ramp below us. "Yeah, probably in part because they're Eagles, but really because they're still focused and know how to work. What we all learned in Scouts stays with you if you keep working on those skills.

"I'm surprised I'm attributing anything to Baker," Tom said with a wry smile, "but he made a good point to you earlier. Earning Eagle is like earning our Trident. That really just represents the first step . . . and you can't rest there."

The SEAL training program demands incredible sacrifices from the hundreds of fresh candidates who arrive in Coronado each year. Aspiring SEALs commit their entire selves to the goal of wearing the Trident. Beyond earning the coveted gold pin bearing an Eagle, pistol, anchor, and trident, SEALs endure hell to achieve a goal both very personal and, at the same time, very selfless. A genuine duty to others motivates these young men, just as the same ideals drive Eagle Scouts. As Eagles, we want to help others, just as SEALs hope to serve their country and defend millions of people they'll never meet and who might never appreciate or even know about their sacrifice. The goals of Eagles and SEALs are not entirely altruistic, however. We both want to discover if we have what it takes to overcome a challenge and reach a goal. We chose the biggest challenge and toughest test available, but we also recognized a higher purpose in our aspirations. Making sacrifices and passing those tests—completing the trail to Eagle or enduring BUD/S—is a beginning for us, not an end.

I was reminded of another type of sacrifice shortly after parting ways with Tom Campbell that night. I received news from Coronado about another SEAL I had hoped to meet, but never would. Chief Special Warfare Operator Mark T. Carter of Fallbrook, California, a twenty-seven-year-old Eagle Scout and Navy SEAL, had been killed in combat in Iraq, serving his country.

SURVIVORS

I hike fast. I always have, probably due to some combination of too many seasons of cross-country and competing with other Scouts as we hiked the Appalachian Trail on countless weekends. For a while, it had seemed I was as familiar with the trail up north Georgia's Blood Mountain as my own street in Atlanta. I learned to appreciate the view from the front on those hikes and consequently, I'm not accustomed to looking at someone else's boots pounding the trail ahead of me. One mile into a trail several hours north of San Diego's Imperial Beach however, the heels of Burton Roberts's Salomons were seared into my eyes.

I expected as much, and viewed the day's expedition as a particular challenge. Weeks of travel had siphoned away time for staying in shape, and I wanted to see if my muscles had atrophied beyond recovery. In that sense, Burton served as an excellent test. He had a long list of triathlons under his belt, and still traveled the world regularly for mountaineering expeditions, cycling tours, dives, and hiking treks. Clearly, he was in shape. The proving ground for *my* fitness, which was still in question, would be the Santa Monica Mountains near Los Angeles. Burton drove us there in his truck, which bore a small Texas flag on its side; I long ago had learned that Texans forever remain Texans wherever they may live. We stepped out and inhaled the blissfully dry air. Then we listened to the sounds of civilization fade as we set out up a canyon and into the mountains.

Along the trail, I learned exactly why a day-long expedition didn't phase Burton in the least; he was an adventurer. Like the SEALs I had recently met, Burton always sought opportunities to prove himself. But he did so without fatigues and a rifle.

Burton grew up on a Texas farm then moved to Saint Louis, Missouri, where he joined Troop 492. For him, Scouting provided a channel and focus for his overabundant energy, a focus he confessed was difficult to find at school. The merit badges and system of ranks at Troop 492 became great motivators and expanded his horizons immensely. He remembered several summers where he spent more nights outside than inside, and developed a lasting love for the outdoors.

"Our Scout troop pushed us to get out in nature, which is so important these days because television, the Internet, and video games can engulf kids," he said. "To me, getting outside is important because it gets you away from the monotony—or the craziness—of life. It gives you time to think, clear your head.

"Especially out here in California," he added, motioning to the trees around us and blue sky above us. "It's so beautiful. You're out in the middle of nature and it's very peaceful. Even if you're on an extremely physically exhausting trail run, you're revitalizing yourself and you're refreshed and energized just being outdoors."

In addition to getting him outside, Burton observed that Scouting gave him a vast array of skills that became lifelong interests. He'd ridden horses before Scouting, but the week in which he earned his horsemanship merit badge, he learned much more than he ever had before. Not only did he learn to ride better, he also learned how to care for the animals: cleaning their feet, grooming them, feeding them. He learned to be a true horseman. Without Scouts, he never would have developed such an understanding of horses nor the love of riding he still has today. He observed that Scouting's adventure comes in its expansive curriculum and its insistence that Scouts master skills in so many varied arenas: "That was such an amazing experience that so many people miss because they don't have someone pushing this tremendous variety on them—camping, whitewater expeditions, merit badges of every kind, you name it."

Burton's résumé still prominently lists Eagle Scout because, in addition to fostering an instant bond with others who understand Scouting, he believes the rank defines him at a deep level. "You don't *have* to get Eagle," he explained, "but if you work hard enough and you go through all the different levels and ranks, you can earn that and it encourages you to have that desire to reach the high levels and go after things throughout life, not settle and compromise on what you want to do. 'Eagle Scout' says here is a person who is not afraid, very motivated, willing to go out and do whatever it takes to get something done, and willing to take on adventure and challenges and not stop until the goal is reached. Especially when you're young in Scouts, it's not always easy to get all the merit badges and learn all the skills. It's not a job. You're not getting paid for it, it's not a requirement for anyone. It's just your self-motivation. A lot of people settle for the average rather than pushing themselves to be better or achieve a higher goal. Not Eagles."

Burton stopped to negotiate a creek bed, and took a moment to listen to the quiet of the canyon. Occasional breezes and scattered birds provided the only sound other than our boots and conversation. "You know, those skills and the love of acquiring those skills led me straight to *Survivor.*"

For their hit television show's seventh season, CBS producers had selected Burton from forty thousand competing applicants to live on the Pearl Islands off the Pacific coast of Panama. There, twenty million television viewers watched him improvise and persevere against fifteen others. He would spend thirty-six days living like a castaway and competing to "outwit, outplay, and outlast" his fellow contestants for a million-dollar prize. He appreciated—*loved* might be too strong considering the primitive conditions and vicious competition—every minute on the island. When he left, only four others remained.

"You have to understand that it's a cutthroat game where unfortunately there's backstabbing and manipulating and everything else," he explained. "You're dealing with strategic game play twenty-four hours a day, wondering who is in your alliance, who is lying to you, who is going to vote you off. Is my alliance together? Is Alvin lying to me? If he is, what should I do? That's what kept me up at night.

"But beyond all that," he continued, "it was living in the most pure environment you could. You had the resources there and you couldn't get anything else, so if you didn't catch food for a day, you didn't eat. I'd go swim around in our lagoon every day, partly to be out there spearfishing to get food, but really I just loved it. It was our own private Blue Lagoon. A lot of people never put on the mask and snorkeled around to enjoy it, which I thought was just tragic because even though you're in this game, there's this purity and aspect of nature that not everyone gets to experience. Then, here these people are with it in their backyard and they never did it."

On *Survivor*, Burton might as well have been returning to a Scout expedition. Fires? He could start them. Shelters? He could build them. Spearfishing? He improvised—successfully. "Only two of us ever caught any fish," he said. "And it was amazing to see people who had no idea how to make a fire or keep a fire going. Or little things like knowing you have to boil water before you drink it. In one challenge, we had to tie sticks together to reach a certain key. No one else could very effectively lash sticks together, especially under pressure. But I'd done that countless times in Scouts.

"*Survivor* was just unbelievable," Burton said as we resumed our hike on the far side of the creek. "I could have done away with the mosquitoes and backstabbing, but being outdoors and living on your own and *being* on your own was really special. And the older you get, the less opportunity you have for things like that, and the less people do."

Survivor represented one challenge, but Burton joked that fifteen minutes of fame is a very accurate phrase. He knew the experience was a brief moment in life. He enjoyed every second of it, then applied that same spirit to other pursuits. He made a personal mission of creating opportunities to be outdoors and test himself. At every chance, this graduate of Southern Methodist University and Northwestern's prestigious Kellogg School of Management kayaks, scuba dives, snowboards, skydives, skis, hikes, and competes in triathlons. He'd recently completed his fourth Escape from Alcatraz triathlon in San Francisco Bay. He found a real challenge in the notoriously frigid water, and signed up for the Bay's Shark Fest Swim, a one-and-a-half-mile swim from Alcatraz Island to the mainland. He completed the event five times, once without a wetsuit. "Everyone told me it was probably the dumbest thing I'd done," he said, "but I wanted to challenge myself and set a goal and did the best I could to prepare for the freezing water. Of course, I was cold for the rest of the day!"

Certain accomplishments earn guys automatic respect among other guys: being a Navy SEAL or fighter pilot rank among them. So does competing in the Eco-Challenge. The legendary Eco-Challenge adventure races cover more than three hundred miles, and have been televised on MTV, the Discovery Channel, and as part of the ESPN X Games. As we climbed higher into the Santa Monica Mountains, Burton began talking about adventure racing, the grueling cross-country competitions often held over several days that involve almost every imaginable outdoor skill, from climbing to paddling. First aid can also be a big plus. The races became a way for Burton to combine all his outdoor pursuits, and the world famous Eco-Challenge proved to be his most difficult test. In 2002, on the wild Pacific island of Fiji, he and several teammates competed with scores of others, racing through jungles from point to point, and relying on their outdoor knowledge and survival instincts.

"That was a seven- to ten-day, three-hundred-and-fifty-mile race, depending on how lost you got," he explained. "There was mountain biking, river kayaking, trail running, navigation, rappelling and climbing, and kayaking. My team raced for six and a-half days straight, and for every twenty-four-hour period of racing, you slept maybe four hours, so it was one of the toughest mental and physical challenges I've ever done.

"One of the greatest aspects of adventure racing is the unknown. You know the general location and the general events, but that's it. Unknown course. Unknown distances. Unknown order of events. Unknown terrain. Unknown weather conditions. You get my point. There were eighty-one teams in the jungles, rivers, and ocean that make up Fiji and there were eighty-one different paths traveled."

At the start, the teams received their course maps and had five minutes to plot their route to the first checkpoint before a gunshot announced the beginning of the race. Immediately, Burton's team found themselves crossing and recrossing a river. Soon thereafter, they were swimming through a canyon, dragging their packs and clawing for handholds along the cliffs that formed the riverbanks. The next day, the team worked with natives to build bamboo boats to negotiate a twenty-mile stretch of river—partly after dark.

The race continued over the coming days, with the team slashing and trekking their way through jungles and up mountains. Mud, suffocating humidity, and brutal heat were constant companions. Bruises and lacerations received while plowing through the dense foliage added to the difficulty. Unhealed cuts grew increasingly painful as the race continued. Days of sweating in the same clothes left Burton with a painful heat rash, but he kept going. Finally, he arrived at a refreshment stand run by natives. He craved a cold Coca-Cola and arrived just in time to watch the racer in front of him buy the last one. Instead, he bought five butter sandwiches, which are exactly what they sound like. "Best sandwiches I ever had," Burton said smiling proudly.

Sandwiches alone wouldn't feed anyone who raced nearly twenty hours a day, so each day, Burton gulped down a one-gallon bag of food. The bag contained somewhere between four and five thousand calories and included several Snickers bars, a PayDay, two Cliff Bars, a Luna Bar, a bag of trail mix, several packs of sesame seeds, a bag of ramen noodles, one foil packet of tuna , granola bars, string cheese, a Pop-Tart, two packets of instant oatmeal, beef jerky, almond M&M's, and an assortment of bite-size candies. The body cannot digest much more, but it can burn more. Burton was always hungry. I asked how he cooked the ramen noodles while on the run. He smiled and said, "Do you want to know? Before going to sleep, I added water to my ziplock bag of ramen and put it in my shirt pocket close to my body to warm it up. When we woke the ramen was warmed up and was absolutely amazing. Just rip the corner of the bag off and pour it into your mouth!"

After a day of river kayaking, which provided a welcome relief from carrying packs and walking in boots, the team resumed trekking and slashing through damp jungles. Exhausted, they fell into a village hut the next night and found two young guides to take them to a rocky waterfall they would have to scale to reach the next checkpoint. Despite setting four alarms that would allow them four hours of sleep, Burton awoke nearly two hours late. He rallied the team and set out for the waterfall. Passing teams with injured members along the way seemed a bad omen; one had even been airlifted to a hospital. The following day, after nearly seven days of racing, officials pulled Burton's team from the course when their chances of reaching the next checkpoint before the deadline slipped away. His team never quit; they had trekked hard until the last. But despite their rookie team besting more than half the teams in the race, Burton was severely disappointed. With a grin and the perspective of time passed, he jokes about one letdown: "I cannot believe we raced for so long in Fiji and never even saw the ocean!"

Once removed from the heat of competition and the Fiji jungle, the competitors realized the race was about more than just battling other teams and the island's harsh geography. The race had also been a true cultural revelation as he learned about new people and customs when his team met native inhabitants who rarely saw outsiders. "These villagers would come out and let their schools out and line up along the roads and be giving you high-fives and just be smiling," Burton remembered. "They'd invite you into their huts and homes and give you anything they could—maybe some rice or coconut milk. There was this sense of generosity from these people with absolutely nothing. They would give you their bed when you were damp and muddy and so exhausted, and they'd sleep on the floor."

Reflecting on his exploits in Fiji and elsewhere, Burton observed that his love for a challenge links back to Scouting, which taught him to set goals for himself. He had never done a mile-long swim before, but took the challenge one year at Scout camp.

"It might have taken well over an hour," he said, "but you have people there supporting you and keeping you going." By swimming laps around a lake at camp, Burton realized at a very young age what he could accomplish. When he flopped exhausted onto the beach, he had a new sense of confidence. He believed it would be quite difficult for someone to put him in a situation where he had no idea how to respond—and the producers had certainly tried on *Survivor.* He'd learned to value Scouting's *Be Prepared* motto.

"The more you've done, the more prepared you'll be," he said, as we relaxed on a shady log beside the creek that ran through the canyon. "Whether I'm on *Survivor*, going to climb a mountain in Africa or California, or doing an adventure race that's three hours or twelve hours or a week long, it's always about challenging yourself and pushing yourself and seeing where your breaking points are. Knowing how you get there and hit those, then go beyond that. Mentally, I think we can push ourselves through pain and through some places where people would normally quit. Once you've gotten to that breaking point, you might want to back off, but you realize, 'Okay, I've been there before. It's not that bad.' You know it's just a temporary thing and you can get through it and go beyond it.

"In racing, and in basically anything you do, experience makes the difference. Not experience in paddling or biking per se, but experience in attacking a challenge and overcoming it. That's what I mean by *being prepared*. Ian will probably tell you the same thing."

On the other side of the continent, Ian did just that. Ian Rosenberger, whom Burton knew as the *other* Eagle Scout on *Survivor*, met me on a Saturday morning at a Second Avenue bakery in Manhattan. He walked into the shop wearing jeans and a blue ball cap on backward—a trademark of his, I'd learn.

We talked about Burton briefly, then I asked the twenty-six-year-old about his time on *Survivor: Palau*, which took place in the South Pacific island nation of Palau during 2005. A country only since 1994, Palau's tropical archipelago covers 117 square miles of ocean five hundred miles east of the Philippines. Interestingly, Ian's grandfather had fought on the island of Peleliu in the Palaus during World War II. That two-month struggle, which his grandfather survived, resulted in nearly ten thousand American casualties and is considered one of the toughest battles of the entire war. Ian had felt a special connection to his grandfather being in the same part of the world, although Ian was on a mission of a very different nature.

Ian emphatically told me that *Survivor* was by no means a defining experience in his life, but he indulged my questions. I discovered that when *Survivor* called, he'd left his life in the Florida Keys, where he trained dolphins for use in children's therapy. "I was Jimmy Buffett," he said. "I had a boat and a dog and I helped kids." As the legendary musician and former Scout himself would say, "You couldn't beat that with a stick."

When Ian received the phone call, however, he recognized the opportunity. He had learned to rush through open doors as a Scout, so he jumped. Just as Scouting helped lead him to this new adventure, it also helped him once he arrived on that remote South Pacific island. He told me that the television show was a lesson in Baden-Powell's patrol method, and I began to recognize how well Ian understood the philosophy and history of the Scouting Movement. Beneath his lighthearted exterior, Ian was completely serious about Scouting. He understood the theories behind Scouting the same way my college professors understood Aristotle, Locke, and Smith. As a Scout, he developed a real love for the program and joined a coed Venturing crew when he turned eighteen so he could continue on until he reached twenty-one.

He echoed Burton's sentiment, saying, "I did well in *Survivor* because of Scouts." In fact, as a Scout, he'd already done many of the challenges the show posed. He took it for granted that most people had cleaned a fish, made a fire, lived in the woods; he quickly found that wasn't the case. "I've done those things so many times, it's just part of who I am," he explained.

He thought for a moment, sipped his coffee, and observed, "I want to say those hard skills I learned in Scouts made the biggest difference on the island and thereafter: learning how to build a fire, learning how to put up a tent. But it's not those things. It's the first time you *fail* at building a fire or the first time you *fail* at putting up a tent. Scouting is a place where you're allowed to fail and that's the point. We'd walk seventeen miles in the wrong direction so you can learn how to orient your map right next time. We had leaders who were not afraid to let us fail. They guided us instead of telling us."

I asked him which soft skills and ideals were truly useful, and he answered by beginning to repeat the Scout Law, "Trustworthy, loyal, helpful, friendly, courteous . . ."

I cut him off. "Come on, Ian. It was a competition. Were you really courteous out there?"

I shouldn't have doubted Ian, who has an incredibly honest heart.

Ian was one of the final three contestants on the island, but he left on principle after his last challenge made him think about how he'd played the game. "Cutthroat" aptly describes the game; nobody expects honesty, especially from the winner. But that didn't sit well with Ian. He believed the game reflected life and he was unhappy about how he would be winning one million dollars.

"I realized it's not just winning the million," he said. "It's *how* you win it. That's what I learned in Scouts. It's not just accomplishing something; *how* you accomplish it becomes important."

Ian spent twelve hours on an ocean buoy during the longest challenge in the show's history. Alone, Ian thought of the people who would watch his actions, and his twelve-year-old sister was the most important. He'd spent the game lying to people and the constant deceit bothered him. He realized it would be a poor example for his younger sister. "I thought about what that million would mean," he explained. "I thought about Scouting, and I thought about the people who would watch me win. They wouldn't have been proud. I decided to bow out. That was because of Scouts. That was because of the Scout Law . . . and because of my sister."

It was also because of his best friend on the show, Tom, the eventual winner. "I'd been backstabbing people and I was planning to do that to my best friend in the game and realized I would lose that friend if I continued playing the game in the same way," he said. "Every time I pulled money out of that ATM account with the million dollars, it would bother me. It became really apparent what I needed to do. The decision became very easy very quickly."

"Was Tom planning to stab *you* in the back?" I asked.

"Nope," Ian answered.

So Ian walked away from a chance at one million dollars, his honor intact, but his wallet not so full.

"I can't say that the cash wouldn't come in handy right now," he admitted, "but I'm completely happy with the decision I made. I don't regret it at all. It's only a million bucks. I left with pride and a story I could be proud of . . . although if I'd stayed, I wouldn't be eating ramen noodles every day as I am now!"

Holding up Scouting's ideals may have cost him financially, but Ian departed *Survivor* convinced that his experience growing up in Ambridge, Pennsylvania's Troop 414 and Venturing Crew 414 was the best and most important thing to happen to him. He never realized how much being an Eagle Scout meant until he began to face major crossroads in his life, points that prompted important decisions about relationships and the future. As I had realized on the Tooth of Time, life does march on and Ian, like the rest of our generation, was slowly recognizing that we all do have to grow up eventually.

"I've always been Peter Pan," Ian explained, "and as I've gotten older, I've finally realized that being an adult is making those decisions and making the right choices when faced with them. When facing those crossroads, you fall back on the things that are the most important and have had the most effect. I fall back on my family, I fall back on my spirituality, and I fall back on Scouting.

"It wasn't about the badge, just like it wasn't about the million dollars," he continued. "It was about the *process* of becoming an Eagle Scout and realizing that the journey had made all the difference. Realizing how the adventure had shaped me, and that the adventure is not in the idea that you're rappelling, rock climbing, or building fires. The adventure is in the idea that you're learning how to be a human. Looking back, you realize that the process has made you a man. You started as a little kid and then this transformation happened that shaped who you'll be for the rest of your life. That's such a cool thing. What other process out there is there for people to grow that much with? From the time you're a six-year-old Cub Scout until you're a sixty-six-year-old Scoutmaster, there's nothing else out there that has such a profound effect on you and is there with you every step of the way. Nothing in my life has been more influential than Scouts in shaping who I am as a person. It's so much a part of me. Certain things in life happen to you and certain things become part of you. Scouting's a part of me."

To this point, I'd been dutifully pursuing my mission to learn about the Eagle Scouts of my generation, documenting their actions and discovering what values drove them. However, I began realizing that my exploration had so far only scratched the surface. Talking with Ian that day in

New York, I began to understand that the quest was not only about finding facts, but finding purpose. And it wasn't just my purpose, or Ian's; it was our generation's. I had to look beyond what Ian did on *Survivor* or what values defined SEALs like Tom Campbell. Our legacy will be established as we collectively meet the challenges of our era, each of our actions adding to others and creating the record that will ultimately define us.

As the morning moved toward afternoon, Ian and I began contemplating our generation, his enthusiasm and optimism propelling the conversation. I began to consider us as a force in ourselves, with our own responsibilities and character. I began thinking of our legacy as, in some ways, distinct from other generations of Eagle Scouts. As we come into our twenties and thirties, our roles change. The rising generation, we are the next Scout leaders, the next national leaders. We are the future. Our elders may not acknowledge that shift quite yet, but nevertheless it's real. It's our world and our time; we need to seize it. At least that's how I felt after talking with Ian.

"Okay," I said. "Let's talk about our generation. Describe us."

"One word," he replied quickly. "Opportunity."

He smiled and explained. "The impact our generation of Eagle Scouts will have is difficult to see yet," he said earnestly, "but we're on that edge and soon, it'll become apparent. We as a people, Americans, we're in an interesting time. . . . This generation of Eagle Scouts has a responsibility to be the voice of good leadership. It's like that Walt Whitman quote from *Dead Poets Society*: 'The powerful play goes on and you may contribute a verse. What will your verse be?' As human beings, as Eagle Scouts, we're lucky enough to have been given tools to write a verse and make a difference and I can't wait. I can't wait to see where that group of Eagles takes us. I'm so proud to be part of that." To Whitman's point in his poem "Oh Me! O Life!" we do have a verse to contribute. I was watching Eagles across the country write their part.

Like Burton Roberts, Ian relishes a challenge and he had recently completed a thirty-six-mile race in South Africa, where he ran to support Grassroots Soccer, an organization using soccer to teach African children about AIDS prevention. The race made up only a small part of the trip, however. Ian also visited children in South African villages and discovered the vast complexity and personal sides of the epidemic. He found communities with HIV infection rates exceeding 60 or 70 percent, where many people were not using available modern treatments. At first, this American was naturally surprised; after all, governments had made medications and information readily available. But he soon realized that the village poverty rate hovered at 100 percent. People didn't neglect their AIDS medications because they considered them unimportant; they neglected them because they had to choose between food and drugs. On his trip to South Africa and on another expedition to Zimbabwe, Ian left the comforts and filtered news reports of the United States and saw the world for himself. He encountered its spiraling complexities, but harsh reality failed to dull Ian's desire to help. It only increased it.

Africa captured Ian's imagination, and to him, the continent symbolized both our generation's responsibility and its opportunity. It offered a chance to apply the broad tools Scouting gave him: knowledge both practical and conceptual, a predisposition to action, leadership, and a sense of duty that channels it all toward a greater purpose. Couple those tools with the good fortune to call America home, and he saw an unmistakable and unavoidable responsibility emerge for responding to the world's poverty, disease, and inequality. He views being an Eagle Scout as a tool—a set of tools, really—with which to honor those responsibilities.

He explained, "The cool thing about Scouting is that it *starts* at age eighteen. All that time, from the time you begin until you get that Eagle badge is school. Then, that day you become an Eagle Scout is graduation. On that day, you take everything you learned and you put it in action and you use it. That's why you're an Eagle Scout forever. That's why you die an Eagle Scout. You have a responsibility to use the knowledge you gained from that adventure and turn it into something great. There's always a mountain to be climbed, but it's not just for the hell of it, not just because it's there."

Again and again, with Burton, Ian, and countless others, I witnessed the passion my generation of Eagle Scouts seems to hold for Scouting. Honestly, I didn't think I'd find two *Survivor* veterans that positive about their experiences in Scout uniforms. Nor did I think I'd find Navy SEALs willing to open up about the value of Scouting. I was flat wrong. Unless you're me, Scouting might not make the daily or weekly list of conversation topics. When it did surface with these young men however, it brought with it deep-seated emotions and a very real passion. Our generation understands the value of that experience we had as teenagers. We seem to grasp its meaning and with it, our obligations.

In particular, these two veterans of *Survivor* reminded me about life's challenges and opportunities. Burton didn't see the sense in living without a challenge to overcome and he sought them out wherever he could, pursuing adventures around the world. Ian felt the same way, and like Burton and the SEALs, found challenges that pushed his limits. Both Ian and Burton persevered on *Survivor* because of their Scouting background, but also because they had an almost unconquerable desire to test themselves on one of the world's greatest (and certainly most watched) proving grounds. They showed me that part of our generation's legacy would be taking on challenges of every sort and relishing the competition against others and self alike. They also reminded me that our legacy is far from secure or even established. It's up to us to take a step and seize that great opportunity Ian described, and to continue to shape our world, one action at a time.

HEALERS

As Ian and I finished our conversation in New York, Vance Moss strode into the bakery. I say strode because he strode—no uncertainty in his entrance. He had an aura of determination and confidence. People clearly noticed. Ian and I rose to meet him and we all stood together in the bakery and shared a moment of sorts. We were three Eagles of the same generation all using our skills in different ways, but all having a flat-out blast as we careened through life not really sure what would come next. Part of Ian wanted to write like me, part of Vance wanted to pit himself against a desert island—preferably a tropical one, he noted—and part of me wanted to save lives like Vance was doing around the world. But we all respected the paths chosen by the others; we saw how our trails extended naturally from our one common experience: Scouting.

Ian and I surrendered the table we'd monopolized for the past few hours and the three of us walked outside. Ian left, and Vance led me to an Italian restaurant at the corner of Fifty-second Street and Second Avenue for lunch. Before we settled in, Vance received a phone call. "Dr. Moss," he answered. It was his twin brother, Vince, saying he couldn't join us; the hospital had just called him for an emergency surgery. Vance seemed disappointed, but not surprised. "We've both gotten used to life as surgeons," he explained.

The Moss brothers had followed the same dream and both graduated from Penn State, then Temple University School of Medicine. From there, they completed residencies and fellowships before opening their own practices in New Jersey. Remembering their humble beginnings, they opened offices in low-income areas that most doctors—particularly those with outstanding school loans—typically avoid. The two surgeons felt a special calling and have never left these neighborhoods. They treat patients in communities where paying medical bills often presents a serious challenge, and many rely on Medicare and Medicaid. For the brothers, this often means that they only receive reimbursement for a fraction of their actual costs. Additionally, they face malpractice insurance premiums that have sailed well north of $50,000 per year.

"You can see why delivering healthcare to these communities is a challenge for society," Vance said. "But at the end of the day, my bills get paid. I'm certainly not getting rich from medicine, but the richness that's instilled in my mind stems from my patients and keeps me motivated. I love what I do for them and they know I could be anywhere else, but I choose to be there and they appreciate that. But I'm not going to lie about it; it can be a real challenge." I was beginning to learn that the Moss brothers like nothing better.

Years ago as Scouts in Maryland, the brothers had learned that if they decided to take on a challenge, they should tackle it wholeheartedly until they conquered it. Their troop leaders held high expectations and the Mosses lived up to them. Those leaders also noticed that hours spent in forests and on lakes instilled an unusually thoughtful perspective in these two Scouts. With few distractions in the outdoors, the brothers found time simply to reflect and consider life.

"You're very impressionable at that age," Vance reflected. "You think about a lot of things out there and on top of that, you're learning to survive. I mean, you're out there trying to survive with no utensils, cooking a hamburger on a rock! I tell ya, some people may think that doesn't mean anything, but when you're eleven years old and you come home and tell your parents, 'I actually survived out there with no utensils and I ate a hamburger off of a hot rock,' it instills a lot of character.

"We also went to Philmont Scout Ranch. At age fourteen, you're thinking, 'I'm going to be hiking one hundred miles in the Rockies in Cimarron, New Mexico. I've got to get from point A to point B with eleven of my other colleagues, with just our forty-pound packs and whatever we're carrying—that's all we're going to have to accomplish that. I remember getting on the bus coming home. I was the proudest person I could ever be. I made it, you know. It's almost like going to war. You come back home, you're like, 'I made it!' "

It was a credible comparison. The Moss brothers know something about going to war and coming home.

In 2005, Vince and Vance, both Army reservists, were called to active duty while they were working in post-residency fellowships. Vance left a fellowship in renal transplant surgery while Vince left one in cardiothoracic surgery. Both programs allowed the brothers to graduate despite their early exits, but the months away from their new practices took a toll.

The twins' orders called Vince to South Carolina and Vance to Texas. They drove south down Interstate 95 together and stopped for breakfast one morning in South Carolina. When they finished their meal, they walked to the parking lot and stood looking at each other. Something struck them: they had never been separated from one another. In Scouts, in college, and in medical school, they had always been together. They'd always shared meals and a roof. Each was the other's best friend. They didn't say much about the apprehensions racing through their minds. They just shook hands and parted ways, leaving for their respective duties.

During the next months, they learned to exist on their own, although they didn't particularly enjoy the separation. They spent their tours of duty in the U.S. treating veterans wounded in Iraq and Afghanistan. By the end of their stateside service, the Moss brothers had learned from their patients that many of the war's other victims were going untreated. They heard story after tragic story from veterans: military doctors treated only combatants; civilians, especially women and children, went largely unaided. The brothers sensed an opportunity to carry the spirit of service they had learned in Scouting to the far side of the world.

When their tour ended, they were given the option to extend their active service. They needed to return to their practice and careers, but after hearing the stories about Afghanistan in particular, they wanted to care for the civilians who needed help in the war-ravaged country. Vance explained the statistics that drove them: in any war, most casualties are civilians, and many of those casualties are children. So the Moss brothers proposed to their commanding officers the idea of treating civilians in Afghanistan. The military thought the idea was noble, but had no interest in supporting it. The mission was too dangerous and against every regulation. That neither fazed nor discouraged Vince and Vance. On their own time and money, they organized a small force of individuals who provided the intelligence, security, equipment, and supplies they'd need to go into Afghanistan's treacherous mountains and help those who needed them.

The Moss brothers shed their army uniforms, and entered Afghanistan as civilians. With a security detail of local tribesmen and several light trucks, the brothers ventured into the towns and mountains of the notoriously dangerous and rugged nation. They operated in makeshift hospitals, sometimes in homes, and even inside caves under lights from cell phones and candles. They successfully operated on thousands of people, but only after they first earned the Afghanis' trust.

"We were always as incognito and as unintimidating as possible," Vance said. "Well, as much as two six-foot-two African-Americans can be in Afghanistan!" He laughed. "We did not want to file into a village like we're occupying it. They're used to that. They're ready to defend themselves against that. Us? We were going in there to help."

But not everyone received them warmly. As they have for centuries, roving factions and warring tribes still dominate Afghanistan. Governments and conquerors alike have often met failure when they tried to tame the wild mountainous regions of the country where the two American surgeons traveled with their caravan. With no military support, the brothers were vulnerable and their fate entirely attached to providence and chance. They could have simply disappeared into the Hindu Kush mountains; nobody would have ever known what went wrong. That almost happened on several occasions.

Once, a band of militiamen stopped the twins' small convoy and ordered everyone out of their cars. Given the number of rifles pointed at them, the group complied. Although Vince and Vance were dressed like locals, their skin and language immediately told the militia they were Americans. "There's no way they'll believe we're doctors," Vance remembered thinking. "They're going to think we're soldiers trying to infiltrate their village and get intelligence."

The militia thought exactly that and soon, Vince and Vance were on their knees. Grizzled soldiers aimed AK-47 assault rifles at their heads. Arguments raged among the militia members, between the militia and the brothers' escort, then again among the militia. "At that point, we knew we were dead," Vance recalled. "*Dead*. They were going to shoot us execution-style in those mountains and nobody would ever know what happened to us. We could see the lead on *Good Morning America*: 'Twin brothers presumed killed in Afghanistan on the stupidest cavalier mission you could ever think of!'

"Then, they just let us go." More than a year later, Vance still seemed baffled. He shook his head slowly. "I still don't know why; have no idea why. So that was one of our greatest accomplishments, just getting out of there alive."

In other quarters, the doctors received warmer receptions. Their reputation grew across valleys and ridges, spreading from town to town. "By the end of our visit, the people knew us," Vance explained. "They began calling us *Doganagy*, which, in their language, means 'same-face healers.' Wherever we go now, everyone's screaming down the streets, '*Doganagy, Doganagy, Doganagy!*' Kids would be chasing after us; husbands would sometimes be chasing after us carrying a sick wife or child. They wanted us to help."

"Wait," I said. "*Do-gana-gy?*"

"Right, *Doganagy*," Vance confirmed. "That's what they call us: 'same-face healers.' They're very spiritual people, and when they saw my brother and me, they saw that we had the same face and they thought that was not only weird, but it was very mysterious. And we're also probably the first African-Americans they'd ever seen."

For much of their first tour, local leaders would not allow Vince and Vance to treat women or children; custom dictated men should receive treatment first, and others second, if at all. Eventually, the doctors insisted upon treating the women and children, despite long-standing Afghani traditions.

When they finally returned to the United States, their experiences haunted them. They wanted to return, but first threw themselves into their practices, which were struggling as a result of their long absences. Afghanistan never drifted far from their thoughts, however, and they began planning their next mission.

In late 2006, they again left the security of America and returned to the danger, uncertainty, and desperate needs of Afghanistan. On their second trek into the ancient land, they insisted on seeing women and children first. Men were traveling to Kabul for medical care, leaving wives and children in villages with no electricity or running water. The conditions left the American doctors in disbelief. They adamantly stood by their position of helping women and children and local leaders eventually acquiesced.

"We were in some villages where we were the first doctor they'd ever seen in their lifetime, and I'm talking about twenty-eight, thirty-year-old women," Vance exclaimed. The twins treated civilians with every condition or disease they could imagine: cancer, lung problems, chronic illness. "You just name it," he said. The twins worked in a land where life expectancy remains below forty years, and nearly one-third of children die before the age of five. Half of those that survive past that age are malnourished. Estimates place one in three children as an orphan. The brothers' disbelief was never fully dispelled.

Nothing broke the brothers' hearts more than the thousands of crippled children they encountered. Most received their wounds from the millions of land mines still scattered throughout the country, deadly remnants of the Soviet and Taliban occupations. "There are over ten million mines still left in Afghanistan," explained Vance, citing United Nations estimates. "*Ten million*. And these young children would be walking to school, or going to their place of worship, or playing soccer, whatever, and they would walk on one of these mines and it would blow them up. I don't have an exact number, but I would say every family out there either has someone in their family, a child in their family, or they know a family that has been affected by a mine." According to U.N. reports, mines kill or injure roughly two Afghans every day; 80 percent of those injured are males below the age of twenty.

"Let me tell you a story," he said after we had placed our lunch orders. "I remember landing and getting off the plane in Kabul, and it's an image I'll never forget. After hearing about the millions of mines and the kids who are victims of these mines, the first thing my brother and I see on the tarmac is this fence where kids are lined up to watch the plane come in—that's entertainment for them. What do we see? About half of them with missing limbs; amputees with no arms or half a body. I still to this day don't remember walking from the plane into the security building because I was in such shock looking at this, going, 'Oh my God, these guys are running around, managing by themselves in carts and with makeshift devices that act as limbs.' I don't even remember walking into the airport."

At least Vince and Vance could improve life for some of those children and their families. While the doctors couldn't undo the damage wrought by the land mines, they did their best to lift the burdens weighing on those children and their families. The spirit of the young people they treated affected the brothers deeply.

"They were some of the strongest individuals I've ever seen in my life," Vance reflected. "Some of the kids, we had to operate on and take off their . . ." He hesitated. "We could only use a local anesthesia. No, they weren't put to sleep. We didn't have the resources. They rarely cried. They just took it, which was a symbol of their resiliency. They're just really strong people. And the kids were very appreciative. They loved the fact that we were there. It was, it was sign of hope for them that we were there to help them, not liberate them or anything like that, or take over their village or whatever. We were just there to help them. And that was something they hadn't seen in their lifetime. The Russians, the Taliban, maybe even the American military as they see it. Everybody comes to Afghanistan to take over or occupy. They haven't seen anybody that was there actually to help, literally. That's all we came to do."

"Could you communicate with them?" I asked.

"There's some communication you don't need a translator for," Vance answered. "A smile, a grimace, a sign of appreciation. You don't need to say a word.

"Now, there were also other types of communication," he said, smiling. He recalled treating the leader of a local military unit who had cancer. The brothers began an operation to remove the man's kidney, and focused intently on their task. At some point during the procedure, however, they realized fifteen gunmen had filled the operating room. Most of them were smoking, sometimes tobacco, sometimes local drugs. From time to time, one approached the operating table, weapon drawn. He would skeptically observe the operation, asking hostile questions, pointing his rifle, and narrowing his eyes at each new cut the surgeons made into his commander.

"Our professors in med school were never that intimidating," Vance joked. "And when we finish with an operation, we usually take off our gloves and masks and then walk out of the room. We tried to leave and these guys said, 'No.' We weren't going anywhere until this guy woke up. We were just like, 'Are you kidding me?' One thing we realized was that, in America, if you mess up you're going to get sued. Here, if we messed up, these guys were going to shoot us!"

The waiter delivered two heaping plates of Italian food, which I realized neither of us would be able to finish. Vance hungrily dug in. After a few bites, he said, "I've got to tell you, it was an incredibly emotional experience. Sometimes, I wish I could forget, but at the same time, I want to remember. I mean, I didn't sleep much when I was in those mountains, wondering if I was ever going to go home again and see my family. Am I ever going to get married, have a kid? Things like that would go through my mind every day, every day. So, sometimes it's really even hard to talk about it, because when you get too deep into the memory, you start to remember those feelings, and it's really very overwhelming."

Vance also confided that he and Vince carried several items with them throughout their treks. Devout Catholics, they brought their rosaries and

Bibles. They also brought their Eagle Scout medals. "We wanted to have items that, if we never came back, would be with us when we . . ." He hesitated again. "Well, you know, if something should ever happen."

His phone rang. "Dr. Moss," he answered. "Mmm. Okay. I'm on my way." He stuck the phone back into his pocket. "We're going to have to operate on this guy today." He sighed. "The life of a surgeon." He made a heroic effort to finish his lasagna, but his time ran short. We arranged to finish our conversation along with his brother Vince in Philadelphia the following month, then left the restaurant and joined the stream of pedestrians on the sidewalk. We stood on the corner together while I hailed a cab.

Vance and I shook hands. "You know where you're going?" he asked. I did. "Okay, I'll see you next month in Philly." I slid into the cab and closed the door. Vance waved again, turned, and strode down the sidewalk with the same air I'd noticed that morning. He walked how he lived: with purpose.

Since their practices and patients dot New York, New Jersey, and Pennsylvania, the Moss brothers travel back and forth between their homes in Manhattan and Philadelphia. They were still settling into a renovated loft in downtown Philly when Vince met me the following month. Nobody could have doubted that the brothers were identical twins, but I learned that they both very much had their own personalities.

Vince and I met by the Delaware River and walked through a typical northeastern chill to his black F-150 pickup. He tossed several bags into the bed, clearing the front seat. I climbed in and we drove to his loft, where he carefully backed the truck toward the building's main entrance. There, I learned that I'd unknowingly been recruited to help move furniture into the Moss suite. Vince and I muscled a boxed table from his truck, up the freight elevator, and into their well-lit loft. He mentioned something about a Scout being helpful as we struggled with the heavy load. Once in the loft, we looked through huge windows at the downtown skyline and I wandered around a true bachelor's pad: trendy furnishings, the latest electronics, but no tidier than my house in Atlanta—not a particular compliment for either of us, but true nevertheless.

Pictures of the two brothers—always together—filled the walls, chronicling years of accomplishments. I could almost watch the young doctors grow up. Vince pointed over my shoulder to one shot of Vance and him near an airplane and said, "Man, I have to tell you a story." He laughed. "Okay, when we got on the plane, the people are Afghani and are wearing traditional garb, and the reality of going over to this country hit me: seeing these beautiful Afghan kids on the plane, and these proud people. The reality made me so nervous. The plane got off the ground and I stood up to go cool off and that's the last thing I remember. My brother said the next thing he knew, people with accents were coming up to him saying, 'You know that guy who has your same face? He's on the floor back there. He passed out!'

"All I remember was waking up, looking up, and everyone was speaking these different languages—I guess they were asking me if I was okay. My brother loves that story: 'That guy who has your same face, he's on the floor!' " Vince cracked up again.

When they arrived in Kabul on their second trip, the brothers met an escort they thought was their security detail. The men led them to a nearby van, which sped to the other side of the airport, where the men took all their equipment and kicked the brothers out. Welcome back to Afganistan.

"We were lucky we had luggage that we checked in, but a lot of the more expensive stuff we carried ourselves," Vince explained. "We watched the van leave with all of our supplies, syringes, needles, medicines, things like that. The average salary these guys make is about thirty dollars per month, so they had three or four years worth of salary in that equipment. We had to go to Bagram Air Force Base and get refitted. Not the best start."

It was noon, so we broke for lunch and took the F-150 downtown, riding high above most of the traffic. Vince's phone rang. "Dr. Moss," he answered. "Yeah, he's with me. Okay. Capital Grill. Okay, we'll listen for you." He slipped the phone back into his pocket. "My brother Vance just got called into surgery," Vince explained. "He'll try to meet us later. We've both gotten used to life as surgeons." I smiled, remembering Vance had said the exact same thing in New York a month earlier.

While they have distinct personalities, the brothers' similarities go well beyond their faces. They both have a gift for medicine, a passion for helping others, and a dedication to whatever goals they decide to pursue. And of course, they share Scouting.

Like many Eagle Scouts, the Moss brothers had started on the Scouting path well before they ever donned a uniform. Vince recalled rummaging in his basement and finding a box of his father's childhood photographs. In one, he found his father in a khaki uniform covered with patches. A sash with small badges lay across his shoulder. He saw his grandparents standing by, presenting his father with a medal that Vince thought looked like an eagle. He shared the photograph with his brother and for years, they wondered about its meaning. When the boys were eight, old enough for Cub Scouts, Haywood Moss explained to his sons that the award was called Eagle Scout.

"We just had so much respect for my father," Vince said as we sat down for lunch. "I mean, he was such a major pivotal figure in our life. When he told us that Eagle is the most honorable thing you can get as a boy, we wanted to get that. So, he got us into Scouting and the whole journey began there."

In Scouting, Vince and Vance learned about brotherhood, and about brotherly competition. "I'll tell you right now," Vince began, "if my brother came home and he had earned a merit badge and I hadn't, I'd be extremely upset: 'Why didn't you tell me about it?' My brother liked to look through the merit badge requirement book and pinpoint the ones he could do and then he'd go do them. Then he'd come home and say, 'Oh, I just got the Citizenship in the World merit badge today!' I'd be like, 'Why didn't you tell me? Why didn't we do this together?' Those were the early years."

As they moved through Scouting, the brothers began working together more. Most other Scouts had fathers *and* mothers who guided them through the ranks. Largely, Vince and Vance only had each other. They were raised by a single father who worked long hours as a corrections officer. He couldn't give them much time, but he provided for them in a different way. Left with only each other, the twins faced down requirements as a team and achieved each new badge and goal together.

"I really credit the Boy Scouts with teaching the rigor, complexity, and details of trying to achieve a goal because it allowed us to think and work on problems," Vince said. "If it was easy, we wouldn't have turned out the way we did. Becoming Eagle Scouts was a reflection of how we were able to work together to achieve a goal. That started us on things like medical school, starting a practice together, going to Afghanistan. It certainly solidified our relationship and our ability to work together."

In Scouting and school, the brothers faced challenges together. Their parents had divorced and both had time-intensive occupations; often, the brothers were home alone in their modest community. Their father signed the boys up for a Scout troop in a more affluent neighborhood, where he hoped his sons would adopt high standards and ambitions. In retrospect, the brothers agreed their troop helped them do just that. At the time, however, they remembered being the only two brown faces in an otherwise all-white Scout troop. They also were the only Scouts who struggled to afford all the troops' activities. Vince thought many people pitied them. Pitied or not, they proved themselves by reaching Eagle.

Vince remembered others in Scouts and school saying, "You're not going to be this, you're not going to be that, and it's not your fault, Vince and Vance. It's not your fault. You're just not going to be this or that." Nobody believed they would reach Eagle. Their high school counselors told them they wouldn't be doctors; they heard the same from their college advisers at Penn State.

"We'd just say, 'Okay,' " Vince explained. "But we'd keep pushing, always pushing together. That's what drove us. We're going to get it. We're going to get it. When we *did* get Eagle, it was one of the most poignant moments in our lives because it was a reflection of him and me working together to do the impossible."

Clearly, it wasn't the last time they would conquer the impossible together. And, as I was finding in Eagles everywhere, the impossible always brings out our best.

THE MEXICAN FISHERMAN

Vince and Vance Moss had traveled thousands of miles to Afghanistan to follow their hearts and pursue their mission. I'd also traveled thousands of miles on a mission with the same Scouting roots, but of a very different character—I didn't need armed militia to guard me. By the time I met the Moss brothers, I'd realized that simply speaking with those who'd served abroad wasn't enough. I needed to experience the other cultures and places alongside these Eagles. So I took another leap. I left the United States to witness firsthand how Eagle Scouts of my generation were changing the world.

I had never traveled as far away from home as Australia. In fact, I *couldn't* travel any farther from Atlanta, Georgia, if I tried. Australia was literally halfway around the world. To reach the island continent, I flew westward over the blue Pacific Ocean, crossing more open sea and isolated atolls than I'd ever imagined could exist. We passed the islands of Hawaii, Truk, Kwajalein, Guam, and Saipan—all sites of historic World War II battles that had fascinated me as a kid. Near Guam, we crossed the Mariana Trench, the deepest point in all of the world. If our plane fell from the sky to the sea, it would still have seven miles to fall before reaching the seabed. My face never strayed far from the window and I spent hours gazing across the sea, trying to digest the sheer size of the mystically blue and apparently endless ocean. I had a new appreciation for the world's size.

Nearly ten thousand miles southwest of Atlanta, I finally emerged from Saint James Station in downtown Sydney, Australia. The trip had done an exceptional job exhausting me and I stumbled wearily to Deutsche Bank Place. There, I met my friend Andy Young, who gave me the keys to his apartment and pointed me toward the ferry to Manly

Beach; he would follow after work. Thirty minutes later, a ferry carried me past the Sydney Opera House and toward the mouth of the harbor. Before reaching the open sea, we docked at Manly Wharf and after a two block walk, I almost fell into the apartment Andy shared with his wife, Sally. Warm ocean breezes passed through the open windows and helped me fall fast asleep.

The next morning, Andy woke me up at dawn. We each put a surfboard under our arm and marched two blocks to Manly's famous expanse of cream-colored sand. As the sun rose above the horizon, its light revealed a calm ocean with no waves suitable for surfing, so we left our boards on the sand and waded into the ocean. We bodysurfed under a magnificent morning sky until Andy had to leave for work. We walked back to his apartment together, letting the warm air dry our board shorts. He talked about his plans for the future: maybe business school, maybe running a company one day. He seemed a bit restless.

I reminded Andy how lucky he was: a wonderful wife, a home overlooking the beach that drew friends from half a world away, and time to surf each morning before ferrying across the harbor to a job in private equity, which he enjoyed wholeheartedly. Why would he want to change anything?

"Remember the parable of the Mexican fisherman?" he asked.

It was a story we'd both learned as new consultants at Arthur Andersen, years ago before the Enron crisis sunk the venerable firm. Ironically, we realized very few people in the company—or outside the company for that matter—ever took the story to heart.

The parable revolves around a fisherman of poor or modest means who lives on a beautiful beach in Mexico. He fishes each morning to feed his household then enjoys lazy afternoons on the beach with his wife and plays guitar with his friends each night. An American businessman on vacation discovers the fisherman and urges him to expand his business and take out a loan to buy more boats. He could then employ twenty other fishermen, expand his operations along the coast, employ even more fishermen, move his headquarters to a big city, and trade with America. He could make thousands and thousands of dollars.

"But why?" asked the fisherman.

"Well," the American responded, "then you'd have enough money to vacation at the beach, fish away the mornings, relax all afternoon with your wife, and be with your friends in the evening."

The fisherman looked at the American quizzically. He smiled politely and turned away, then walked down the beach shaking his head.

Andy and I laughed as we remembered the story and its lesson. Sometimes we have to pause and appreciate what we have. Sometimes we need a friend to point out that we're leading exactly the life we want. The next day, I traveled north to Queensland to remind another fellow Eagle Scout of that same lesson.

Two days after arriving in the city of Brisbane, I sat on a dive boat off Australia's northeastern coast. Eric Treml, an expert diver, sat next to me as the white catamaran plowed through the tranquil Coral Sea. Ahead lay the southern end of the Great Barrier Reef.

After an hour's ride, the dive master called out, "Ten minutes!" The twelve divers on board responded and collectively moved to the aft deck where we began rechecking our gear and strapping our vests to the air-filled aluminum cylinders stacked in rows along the centerline and sides of the boat. Short bursts of air resounded around the deck as divers checked the airflow in their regulators. Once we arrived at the dive site, the engines stopped and people began slipping on their mask and fins. Then after tightening straps and checking air lines once more, they stepped off the deck into the water, one by one. Each looked back from the water at the dive master who stood on the stern. The dive master flashed an okay sign; the divers returned the sign by placing one fist on their head—okay, we're ready to dive. Two-by-two, they disappeared from the surface and descended to the reef forty feet below.

When Eric and the other experienced divers had vanished, the dive master splashed into the water himself. I followed and began my first open water dive, part of a series that would complete the pool training my instructor Luke Stegall, an Eagle Scout by chance, had begun in Atlanta. Unlike the pool, the Coral Sea didn't end at fifteen feet. I watched the sun's rays play in the water as the sand and reefs on the seafloor drew closer and closer. I equalized every few feet as the pressure mounted the closer we came to our final depth. My steady breathing and air venting from my dive vest were the only sounds. We reached depth and I corrected my buoyancy so that I floated weightlessly in the clear salt water. The laws of physics never change, but I experienced them in an entirely different way underwater. I could roll effortlessly; float upright or upside down with easy kicks of my fins. By simply breathing deeply or shallowly, I could rise or sink.

Churning my legs slowly, I began cruising above the reef, looking down on a strange landscape. Purple sea fans waved lazily in the gentle currents and I descended to explore countless nooks of life among the rocks and coral. Then I swam toward the reef's heart, threading small canyons where brilliant coral formed the walls. White sand, speckled with crustaceans and plants, carpeted the ocean floor. Just above the reef itself, fish passing from one unknown place to another formed a slow-moving artery of color that I rose to join. I swam among them, unnoticed amid the brilliant, living mosaic.

As a Scout, I'd previously visited the Florida National High Adventure Sea Base in Islamorada, and joined a crew of six strangers aboard the *Kanga*, a two-mast sailboat. We spent a week sailing north and south, snorkeling at least once every day. We simply dropped anchor and hopped over the side into the warm, crystalline water of the Florida Keys. I'd seen sea turtles, barracuda, and more fish than I can recall, but I could only stay submerged for a short time. I wasn't part of the world under the waves. That changed on the Great Barrier Reef; for a while, I was part of a different realm.

Forty minutes passed faster than I could ever recall them passing, and too soon Eric and I found ourselves returning to the surface, although we first stopped on the decompression bar at fifteen feet. The bar allowed us to rest while any nitrogen bubbles in our blood vessels dissipated before we fully depressurized on the surface. Not decompressing sufficiently can lead to a host of medical problems, some fatal. After three minutes at the safety stop, we rose and broke the waves together, having experienced something that far too many people miss.

Back aboard the ship, the crew provided a welcome lunch buffet before our second dive, which proved as mesmerizing as our first. After we had completed both dives, Eric and I lay on the bow relaxing in the sunlight as the boat hurried home. We lay there and simply appreciated the gift of being underwater for a day. For me, it was a rare gift. For Eric, it was life. I began to suspect he might be the Mexican fisherman.

Several months earlier, Eric and his wife Renee had arrived in Australia from their former home near Durham, North Carolina. The Tremls had moved to Australia so Eric could research the reefs of the southwest Pacific on a coveted international fellowship. The dive he'd just completed with me fell into the pleasure category, but in Eric's world, the pleasure category didn't differ much from the business category.

"I don't know where the passion came from, but for some reason coral reefs clicked," he explained on the foredeck. "They're fascinating systems and their conservation is extremely important. It's weird. I feel like I have a purpose there. It's what I know I need to be doing.

"As for the diving, it's part of the passion. It's liberating, it's unique. It's almost another world in terms of physics. From a biological standpoint, we know very little about the ocean even though it covers a majority of the planet. Putting on scuba gear and getting a closer look at it is incredible. It's just so peaceful and serene, relaxing and exhilarating at the same time."

He looked away, enjoying the view from the boat's bow, appreciating the warm sunshine that took the chill out of the wind. "It's amazing that a small town kid from Wisconsin could wind up here," he said. "But Scouting was part of that."

In Menasha, Wisconsin, Eric had followed his two older brothers into Troop 3, an active group that camped every month and in every condition imaginable. Despite the rain, snow, and cold that often seemed ever-present in his home state, Eric quickly developed a love for the outdoors. At age fifteen, he worked the first of many summers at Camp Gardner Dam, where he became one of the free-spirited counselors everyone remembers from the nature lodge. He learned about biology, ecology, and generally developed a fascination with wildlife. Scout camp gave him his first opportunity to learn about animals in what he termed a "pseudo-formal" setting. He also learned about Scoutcraft, wilderness survival, cooking, plants, and ecology.

"Between summer camp and the Scouting program, you grow up, get priorities straight, find passions," he observed. "You learn what you like to do, and what you don't care about doing. It helped me focus my life, and it set me on a path to pursuing a career in environmental science and conservation."

After his first semester at the University of Wisconsin–Superior, coral reefs had captivated him, even though the closest reef lay a convenient 1,800 miles south. He strolled into a biology professor's office and announced he planned to study marine biology. The professor looked at the overconfident freshman who carried an attitude more suited for Scout camp than college, and dismissed him. Not deterred, Eric walked down the hall to the office of another professor, Dr. Mary Balcer. Dr. Balcer gave him a chance. In January, after seeing his first semester grades, she called Eric to her office. Eric had admittedly enjoyed the freshman experience a bit too much.

"She sat me down one afternoon," he recalled, "and she laid it out. She said, 'Look, here are your grades. You want to do marine biology? That will *not* do it.' Essentially, she said shape up or go home. She was pretty clear that I could continue on the track I was on and waste a lot of money on tuition or I could start working—which meant getting an A average until the end of time considering where I was starting! Plus, I had to add a foreign language, physics, and labs; marine biology is competitive. But that did the trick. I completely changed."

By the end of his sophomore year, Eric had learned to scuba dive and had begun his first research project. He'd found the closest reef to Wisconsin and, for the next three years, studied how recreational divers affected the reefs near Cozumel, Mexico. His trips to Mexico were his first outside the United States and he discovered that he not only loved the science; he loved diving, meeting people, and experiencing new cultures.

"Diving, travel, and the tropics," he reflected on the boat, remembering the story. "Learned to love them then and that hasn't changed. I was hooked."

I thought of Mark Twain's famous quote: "The secret to success is making your vocation your vacation." Eric seemed on the right track.

His interest led him to pursue a master's degree at the College of Charleston, on the South Carolina coast. While working in the field—and surfing on Folly Beach whenever school permitted—Eric earned a degree in marine biology from the college's highly regarded program. He graduated and took a position at the National Oceanic and Atmospheric Administration (NOAA) where he quickly distinguished himself and received a promotion into the management ranks, which many people would consider a reward. Not Eric.

"I was growing up too fast, if that makes sense," he said. "I started managing other people. I could read about and write about coral reefs, but I wasn't gaining experience *in* the system. The only way I could do that was to enter a PhD program where people pay you to ask questions and go dive to find the answers!"

He entered the PhD program at Duke University. He earned his degree in 2006, and then found another organization to support his passion. As his wife Renee told me—because Eric never would have—he was chosen from several hundred applicants to receive the prestigious

Kathryn Fuller Fellowship for postdoctoral research from the World Wildlife Fund. That grant had brought the Tremls to Australia and the University of Queensland in Brisbane.

The morning after our last dive, we devoured quiche à la Renee then walked to the Yeronga train station and caught the Citytrain to the Uni, as everyone calls the University of Queensland. The train deposited us near the Green Bridge and we walked across it to the leafy campus where Eric worked when he wasn't under the surface of the southwest Pacific. We crossed the central quadrangle and entered the Goddard Building, where the largest crocodile I'd ever seen greeted us from where it hung (stuffed) in the atrium. We turned down a corridor and passed several classrooms and labs filled with science students before taking a staircase to the lower level, that hosted the genetics lab and Eric's office.

We entered a sterile laboratory with counters laden with tubes of genetic gels, centrifuges, microscopes, and a general assortment of scientific equipment that I didn't recognize. Students and professors wore gloves, glasses, and white coats as they worked around the counters. Signs warned against taking anything unsafe out of the lab, and Eric explained that scientists produced genetically altered organisms that could do who-knows-what if they escaped. Okay, I wondered, so what was a reef-focused marine biologist like Eric doing in a genetics wet lab?

I followed him into his office where I finally began to understand the purpose of all his time underwater. He'd mentioned his research several times during my visit, but I hadn't quite grasped what he actually did. I'd been more focused on the wonders of diving. In Eric's life, adventure truly meets purpose in the lab. He shook his mouse and his computer screen brightened. He opened a presentation. "Ready to be a student again?"

Using the slides as a guide, he began explaining his research and purpose in Australia, if not in life. Terms like *connectivity*, *biogeographic patterns*, *hydrodynamics*, *sources*, *sinks*, *larval dispersal*, *phylogeography*, and *genetic differentiation* filled the presentation, which I expect would discourage most anyone without a doctorate degree from investigating further. I'd come a long way, however, so I opened my mind and let Eric assume his role as professor and help me understand the value of his work.

As he guided me through the slide presentation that usually accompanies the lectures he gives—the most recent one was the previous week in Bali—I realized that his research was highly complex from a scientific standpoint, but actually very intuitive for someone like me, particularly when a PhD could explain the concepts in BA terms. Basically, Eric sampled the genetic makeup of coral and marine species from different reefs in the southwest Pacific, including those off Australia, Indonesia, the Philippines, New Guinea, New Caledonia, Fiji, and American Samoa. The entire region, a band running twenty degrees north and south of the equator, teems with life underneath the waves. It provides the best work environment I could imagine. Eric knew he was lucky.

When he traveled to those exotic locales, he planned his dives to gather the samples he would analyze in the considerably less scenic genetics lab. Based on the DNA composition of the specimens, he determined how reefs related to one another. Some reefs impacted few others; common genes or relationships proved rare. In other reefs, often separated by hundreds or thousands of miles, Eric found shared genetic traits, revealing that currents and migrations carried larvae from one reef to another, creating important relationships between the seemingly distant systems.

"Just as individual species aren't independent of the reef that is their ecosystem," he explained, "individual reefs aren't independent of the larger area, of other reefs." To continually assess those interrelationships and predict what happens if conditions shift, he developed unique models that involved more math than I'll relate here; it certainly surpassed my knowledge of algebra and calculus.

Reefs aren't unlike our world on land, however, and they hold a larger lesson for Eric. Just as diversity and connections are critical for the long-term health and sustainability of coral reefs, diversity and relationships are also critical for a healthy global community. "If we embrace and foster this diversity and work harder at identifying commonalities and connections at all levels of *our* community," he said, "our lives will be enriched immensely."

Returning from the philosophical diversion, he arrived at a new slide. The screen glowed with an image of the entire Pacific Ocean, with bands of blue, green, yellow, orange, and red to represent water temperature. He clicked a button and the colors began to move, folding and swirling into one another to reveal the complex currents that characterize the Pacific. Two red jets shot west, running north and south of the equator, while a countercurrent of green ran between them, from Polynesia eastward to Panama. Cool blue water ran from Alaska down the California coast. The graph's colors shifted as a function of time and Eric pointed out years where El Niño and La Niña conditions appeared.

"We can study the currents during atypically warm El Niño years and begin to anticipate the effect climate change will have on currents, and consequently reefs," he explained. "If we're looking to protect reefs in decades ahead, we need to consider those realities. Warmer climates will affect ocean currents and the ways coral reefs interrelate."

As the lesson progressed, I began to understand not only what he did, but why it was important. His sponsor, the World Wildlife Fund (WWF), hoped to conserve the world's coral reefs, but they were unsure which reefs to protect. Enter Eric's research: His data tells the WWF, the Nature Conservancy, and many other conservation groups and governments where to apply their efforts. Protecting one reef may be meaningless unless they also protect other reefs that are part of the same extended ecosystem. So Eric spends his days pursuing his passion so that reefs will continue sustaining the life and vibrancy of the sea, and enriching, as well as sustaining, the lives of human beings. On top of that, Eric is on the leading edge of reef conservation. Global organizations are relying on his data and opinions as they invest millions of dollars to guard the treasures of the Pacific. It's quite a purpose and quite an accomplishment for a young scientist.

On my last night in Australia, Eric and Renee produced another outstanding meal in their kitchen. We ate around a small table, with Renee's painting of the Circus Dog Brewing Company label watching over us as we enjoyed drinks from said home brewery, which was located downstairs next to Renee's studio. A family side business, they explained. We finished dinner and then heard noise from outside. We walked onto the balcony and found an Australian possum climbing down the tree that dominated their yard. The "tree monkey," as Renee called it, looked nothing like its American cousin. If a possum can be cute, this one was. We sat down on the corrugated metal stairs to watch it watch us, and Eric joked that he hadn't traveled far from Scout camp.

Beyond ecology and wildlife-watching, however, Scouting gave Eric what he called a liberal arts perspective on life. It was an education in countless areas, which helped him understand and appreciate more people, places, and ideas than he ever would have otherwise. But Scouts didn't just provide a theoretical education. Eric gained a wide range of skills and perspectives he could truly *use*. He still relies on knowledge from his citizenship badges, as well as his cooking and wilderness survival coursework. When he taught underwater navigation to students at Duke University in his supplementary job as a scuba instructor, Eric pulled out his Boy Scout compass and used the orienteering skills he learned in Troop 3.

"It's the whole deal," he mused about Scouts. "One aspect of the adventure is learning all those skills, learning wilderness survival and camping skills from your peers. Another aspect is going polar bear in the winter!"

Yet another facet came from his adult leaders, Hugo Petters in particular. Hugo served as the ranger at Scout camp and Eric served as his assistant. At age sixteen, Eric found himself charged with more responsibility than he'd ever handled. Hugo would load Eric with tasks for a given day. Then he'd take off for other parts of the camp. When he came back, Hugo expected Eric to have the tasks completed. Eric rose to the challenge. He found new confidence in knowing that he could see things through.

"The Scouting program is such a very broad spectrum of education mixed with the high-adventure activities, Scout camp, fishing, camping," Eric said. "It all opens your mind, gives you a taste of what the world has to offer. It does different things for different people. For me, the whole package gave me what I needed to convince myself that if I wanted something, all I needed to do was go for it. It gave me the courage to try new things."

Eric hadn't left those lessons and experiences in his Scout troop or in college. He had carried them into each phase of life, although perhaps he applied them in different ways. Like so many of the people I was meeting, Eric hasn't lost his passion for fun, exploration, and constant learning. He explained how that passion enriched his life in every way, and gave him a guiding purpose. To him, it was no less important at age thirty than at twenty, and he fully expected that passion to shape his life at every age hence. I asked him how he had sustained the adventure thus far.

Eric laughed and said, "Man, I just kept on runnin'! I look at the Scouting program as a well-formed springboard. It introduced me to skills that I could roll up into a nice package, take with me, and keep on cooking. What I do now is a continuation of what I learned through

Scouts. For me, it's always been find your passion, follow it, and rock and roll!"

The next morning, Eric and Renee were up early—5:30 A.M. early—to say good-bye. I insisted they go back to bed, and then walked to the neighborhood train station. Along the way, I reflected on the simple gift of friendship that Scouting bestows. Eric and Renee hadn't known me at all when I asked to come visit them in Brisbane. They certainly hadn't needed to surrender Renee's studio to me and my gear for nearly a week. Yet the Tremls had welcomed me into their life without hesitation.

During my stay, I had learned that it's not all roses for someone living like the Mexican fisherman. Eric lived at the beach, but he still worked at an office. He loved his jobs at the Uni and on the nearby reefs. Brisbane provided Renee with a fresh supply of birds and other subjects for her paintings. But they were still a young couple concerned about the future, carefully watching their Internet minutes to avoid extra charges, paying as they went on their cell phones, and finding specials at the grocery store. They knew wealth wouldn't find them—unless more people began recognizing Renee's abilities as an artist. Their one-bedroom apartment—two bedrooms if you include the studio in the converted garage—wouldn't accommodate a family, which would likely become a consideration in the not-too-distant future. But they seemed to take it all in stride.

I'd found that Scouts seem to handle the simple life just fine. Years of spending weekends, and sometimes weeks, with all our gear in a single backpack taught us how to get by with the minimum. A heated shower of any sort qualifies as a luxury at Philmont, and having a worn mattress to soften an antique cot often qualifies as first-class bedding at Scout camp. We can't necessarily lead our whole lives as if we're still Philmont staffers, especially once families become a consideration, but as I saw in Eric, Eagle Scouts can enjoy life without all its finest trappings.

There is something important in that. As Scouts, we learned how to appreciate simple things: evening campfires, morning sunrises, and a day's walk in the woods. We learned to cook on open fires and overlook the flecks of ash that occasionally garnished our eggs or pancakes; on a chilly morning during a long trek, nothing could taste better. We found weekends in state parks by the beach or in the mountains far more intriguing than a week at a plush resort. We had a purpose as we completed service projects and enjoyed watching others benefit from our work. On weekend trips, leaders could enjoy fellowship with their sons, with whom many regretfully spent too little time during the workweek. In Scouting, our concept of wealth expanded far beyond money and material. The challenge, I think, becomes holding on to that standard as we move through life.

The morning sun warmed my side of the cabin as my plane sped down the runway at Brisbane Airport and rose into the air. I flew north from Australia, and once again, gazed over the blue Pacific, looking down at the only type of office Eric Treml has ever loved. The Great Barrier Reef stretched out below me, white-bordered islets of jade on an azure sea. I thought about Eric's passion and unwillingness to let life's adventure fade. He knew what he loved and never let his passion take the backseat. He lived an adventure with passion and purpose. Like Lord Robert Baden-Powell and so many of the people I was meeting, Eric planned to carry that spirit of adventure with him forever.

CHINA CARE

When Matt Dalio visited Beijing, China, in 2000, he found a city undergoing almost unbelievable change at an even more unbelievable pace. In the city, scores of increasingly sophisticated shops, western and Chinese, were lining famous Wangfujing Street. Not far away, skyscrapers were growing furiously in the Central Business District. Businesspeople crowded sidewalks while modern cars and busses outnumbered bicycles and rickshaws on the streets. Beijing was the nation's cultural, educational, and political capital; less than a decade later, the city would represent China to the world as it hosted the 2008 Summer Olympic Games.

But as sixteen-year-old Matt traveled southwest from Beijing, away from its modernity and commerce, he realized China's explosive prosperity had not touched all areas equally. West of the Taihang Mountains, he entered Shanxi province and found a different scene. Heavy industry dominated the economy and offered workers poor and frequently dangerous conditions. The province also operated 3,500 coal mines, a fact evident enough from the people Matt saw. Their eyes, tired from days and nights spent in the mines, looked out from faces stained with black dust.

As bleak as work in the mines appeared, life seemed even worse for the more than eight hundred orphans Matt found at the orphanage in the capital city of Taiyuan. All the children were abandoned; some were even rescued from Dumpsters. Most were girls. Many had birth defects or deformities. Due to China's one-child policy, aimed to control its surging population, families sometimes rejected a disabled child or a girl. Handicapped girls often fill the beds of orphanages across China.

"I went to the poorest orphanages in the area," explained Matt, recalling the trip he took eight years ago. "You walk into these orphanages that are desolate. There's just nothing. The food is poor, the children are dirty. You see kids who can't walk. They're walking with their hands, crawling, basically lifting themselves up with their arms because their legs can't support them. They're dragging themselves across the floors. They're dragging themselves into these bathrooms where there are holes on the ground. I can barely walk into these bathrooms because of the stench. And these are the older kids who have made it. Then you see the babies and kids who are not going to make it."

Matt recalled that many had cleft lips, a condition where their upper lip never fuses, leaving an unsightly gap between mouth and nose. The condition can take a baby's life. "It causes them to breathe and eat improperly," he explained, indicating the suction and airway problems that afflicted children confront. "Fluid can get into their lungs, they get pneumonia, and they die. It affects their swallowing and their speaking. The corrective surgery only costs three hundred dollars, but that's too much for them."

What Matt found in the orphanage made all this worse. "The orphanage would have fifty infants lined up and they'd go down the line and put a bottle in their mouths and prop it up with a napkin, let them feed, then go back down the line and take out the bottles—*pop, pop, pop*—like an assembly line." Children with cleft lips had little chance. There simply weren't enough staff and resources.

Other children suffered from spina bifida, hydrocephalus, clubfoot, heart problems, and a host of other conditions. Most only needed simple treatments common in America but doctors, technology, and funds were often unavailable in Shanxi. The reality struck Matt squarely in the face: If he didn't help them, these children might never find homes, and many would not even survive infancy.

"You realize you can literally save people's lives," he said. "When I saw that I could do that, how could I not?"

With this thought in mind, the sixteen-year-old returned home to the United States from his first trip to Shanxi and began an Eagle Scout project that continues to this day.

Now twenty-four, Matt met me in Greenwich, Connecticut, where he showed me how very far he has traveled down the road that started in Shanxi. When he returned from that particular trip, he was a Life Scout, one rank shy of Eagle. Like most Life Scouts, Matt had been searching for an Eagle project—a community service effort that he would develop and lead, managing fellow Scouts throughout the entire undertaking. The projects aspiring Eagle Scouts choose are infinitely diverse and include landscaping public areas, repairing and improving schools and churches, organizing food and clothing drives, and starting community programs. Most projects, however, don't touch people halfway around the world.

But at sixteen, this Connecticut native had developed a special affinity for China. He viewed the faraway country as part of his community. His first visit had come at age three when he accompanied his father on a business trip. More visits followed during spring breaks and summers, Matt always tagging along with his father. During one excursion, father and son had looked out over the lowly single-story buildings that covered Shanghai. "Dad said, 'Twenty years from now these will all be skyscrapers,' " Matt remembered. "Nobody believed him. Now that's all you see."

At age eleven, Matt left America to spend an entire year living with a Chinese family. His understanding of the country, its language, and its people deepened and more journeys to Asia were in his future. Back home in Connecticut, he met a couple who had adopted two children from China and his general curiosity gained a focus. He asked them for all the information they had on Chinese orphanages and the adoption process, and he talked with everyone who might have new information for him. The investigation ultimately led to his trip at age sixteen, when he visited the Shanxi orphanage. Upon his return, he started the China Care Foundation with the goals of supporting orphanages and foster care in China, helping needy orphans through medical programs and special children's homes, and facilitating China-to-America adoptions. Five dollars a day would fund a child in foster care. Five hundred dollars per year would support a child in an orphanage. Everybody agreed China Care was a nice idea, but it wasn't a reality without funding.

During the autumn of 2000, Matt spoke with his two mentors, Scoutmaster Bob Neilson and assistant Scoutmaster John Stratton in Troop 37. He shared his two goals: earning Eagle and helping Chinese orphans. The three began debating how this high school junior could work toward both. After thoughtful discussion with his Scout leaders, Matt decided to raise $50,000 for his new China Care Foundation, and use the money to provide supplies for the Beijing Welfare Institute and the foster care program under its management.

"When I first started, my dad said, 'You're going to do *what*?' " Matt remembered. "Granted, it was a little bit different. I had to make my case for why this should be my Eagle Scout project. I got the support of everybody. Bob Neilson and John Stratton were absolutely wonderful. They took up the cause and rallied behind me.

"Then I turned to my troop and said, 'Will you support me?' We printed mailers, had bake sales, did everything we could to raise as much money as possible. The community of Scouting was very supportive, my troop in particular."

Troop 37 pitched in to help make flyers, organize events, and ask for support from friends, businesses, and neighbors. Matt led roughly twenty Scouts in the effort, which lasted from January through May 2001. "Some people gave twenty dollars and then I remember when we got our first seven-thousand-dollar donation. I was dumbfounded: 'Seven thousand dollars? Where did that come from?' We raised seventy-five thousand dollars that first year. I remember setting the goal at fifty thousand dollars and I thought *that* was crazy. We passed it by fifty percent. There was something people liked about the cause."

Indeed they did. People kept giving, and China Care kept growing long after Matt received his Eagle Scout medal.

He appeared on *The Oprah Winfrey Show* in 2002, just weeks before he graduated from high school. Coverage followed in *People* magazine, on *ABC World News*, and on CBS's *The Early Show*. E-mail, gifts, and phone calls inundated the tiny foundation—but that was a good problem to have.

Matt's Eagle project continued when he entered Harvard University in Cambridge, Massachusetts. By the winter of his sophomore year, he had founded the first China Care club on a college campus.

"I wanted to help kids in China but also empower American youth," Matt explained. "At sixteen, I realized, 'Wow, I can raise fifty thousand dollars and change fifty lives.' The idea behind the China Care clubs was to empower American youth—which has now become China Care's second mission."

The Harvard China Care Club attracted more and more members and Matt turned over club leadership to a good friend while he focused on the foundation. Soon, Harvard students were raising money, volunteering in local play groups for adopted Chinese children, and flying to China to help firsthand. The play groups, Matt explained, put Chinese children together in an environment where they could develop a healthy Chinese identity yet also embrace their new world. Orphanage walls constitute the only memories many Chinese children have of China. China Care play groups help engender a positive identity and pride. Play groups flourished along with trips and fund-raising, and the idea has already spread to thirty campuses in the United States and Canada, including Brown, Yale, UCLA, Northwestern, McGill, the University of Texas, Duke, and Emory.

"The cool thing about it is that each school makes it what it wants it to be: play groups, fund-raising, volunteering, advocacy," Matt said. "We've turned China Care into a youth movement. Every year we throw a club conference for our thirty clubs. This year we'll have two conferences; West Coast and East Coast. And every year we throw a great party."

As clubs formed across the country, Matt started an annual benefit concert in Greenwich. He has convinced the likes of B. B. King, Carlos Santana, the Gipsy Kings, Eric Clapton, Marc Anthony, and Sheryl Crow to headline over the years: everybody seems to believe in his cause. The concert helps China Care meet its $1.5 million annual budget. Thinking how far he's come from raising the first $50,000, Matt just shakes his head and laughs.

"The irony is that the choices were much tougher when we had a budget of fifty thousand dollars," he explained. "Then, I was in the position where I was almost choosing which kids live and which kids die. Are we giving this child surgery? No? Then what's going to happen to him? When you're making those sorts of decisions, it becomes so real. Now, the questions are 'Do we want to start a children's home?' It's much more conceptual. It's larger, which is cool because it has a much bigger impact, but it doesn't have the same tangibility. I've realized there is a spectrum. As you do more, it's less tangible."

While Matt appreciates the benefits of having a $1.5 million budget for China Care, he wasn't always sure if the organization would survive. He remembered being in one orphanage—the only one they knew at the time—when conflict erupted between the Americans and Chinese. Matt's leading Chinese board member stormed out of the room and Matt had to trail after her, hoping to repair the relationship with the orphanage. No such luck. They had $60,000 to donate and Matt recalled that the situation deteriorated so much that he thought he would have to return the money to donors.

"I was ready to start calling donor by donor and say, 'I'm sorry, but it didn't work out and here's your check back,' " he said. "Then amazingly there was this fortuitous thing and we were able to do it for another orphanage and we started a great program there. But for that week, we were done. That was the one time I thought there was a cliff. You manage though and there are still times you don't know quite where it's going.

"Sometimes it's like you're in the fog and you have no idea where anything is but you can see ten feet ahead of you. You know you can walk ten feet ahead and you can then see ten feet farther. Every step you take forward, you can see a step farther. Any mission is taking steps in the right direction and you see more as it comes."

"I remember when Matthew first came back from China, talking about helping these orphans," Scoutmaster Neilson recalled about the beginning of Matt's mission. "He was set on helping these orphans, but I didn't think it'd fly. I told Matthew that it was an overwhelming project and I wasn't sure how it'd work since it was out of the country. But he wanted to do it. I was still afraid it'd be too big. You don't want to tie the boys into a project that's too big and they can't complete. Well, it worked and now Matthew's tied down for life!"

Matt said something similar about his Scoutmaster's life choice. "Bob Neilson has served for twenty-eight years. I can't imagine someone saying I'll volunteer for one hour a week and twenty-eight years later, his son is gone off in the world and married, and Mr. Neilson is still at it. He'll probably be Scoutmaster for his grandchildren! What sort of commitment is that? Why? It says something when someone finds a reason to help generation after generation—literally—of kids."

Scoutmaster Neilson, like all Scout leaders, gives far more than one hour a week, and Matt and I did the math together: three hours per week at Scout meetings, one weekend each month on campouts, one week a year at Scout camp, all volunteered freely over twenty-eight years. Scoutmaster Neilson had, very conservatively, given more than twenty-five thousand hours to his Scouts. That's more than one thousand days of his life; almost three entire years.

"He is so committed to his kids," Matt observed. "I've seen multiple kids in my troop have their lives *changed* because of my Scoutmasters. One guy came back and looked at the assistant Scoutmaster and said, 'You changed my life, no doubt. I'd be a mess otherwise.' "

Matt explained that this particular Scout had some serious problems and the assistant Scoutmaster stepped in like a father and said, "No, you're not going to do this." The assistant Scoutmaster buzzed the Scout's head and convinced him to enroll in military school. Matt reported that the Scout now works for an investment bank in London.

"People say that kind of care and commitment makes a difference," Matt said. "It does. Not only does it make a tangible difference in one life, *everybody* looks at that leader and thinks about the commitment it takes. I'm going to do that—be a Scout leader when the time is right and have that commitment to the kids in my troop. And that's something you should take into all your relationships with everybody, that loyalty, devotion, sacrifice.

"Scouting teaches you the importance of commitment. It teaches you the importance of community and having this family; Scoutmasters are like fathers to me. Beyond that, Scouts teaches you what really matters and that that requires a little bit of sacrifice and a little bit of commitment. Everybody is there for everybody else. You see that in an Eagle Scout project where everyone comes out—Scouts and otherwise—and they're there supporting you building a park, restoring cemeteries, or helping Chinese orphans. Everybody is there to help your cause. It becomes a family of its own. It creates a bond among Scouts and that bond extends out to your community. You're always there for your community."

In our technologically advanced world, however, communities are being defined far more broadly. The Internet's wealth of instantaneous news and information has brought younger generations of all nations closer together by creating an awareness, if not always understanding, of current events and culture. At the same time, applications like Facebook and MySpace have created important personal relationships that span hundreds or thousands of miles. More and more people, particularly those online, don't recognize physical borders. And in the real world, international travel seems a hallmark of our generation; we travel far and often. We have few good excuses for not knowing what's happening throughout the world. As Matt's example shows, once we're aware of people in other places, they become part of our community in a sense. When that happens, we can't ignore their needs.

Matt added an emphatic caveat: "It's essential to remember that communities are also the people who are around us and it's essential that our generation maintains a sense of community at the most local level. Scouting does a great job of that. Whether it's kids painting fire hydrants or talking to the mayor about how they can stop people from pouring oil into the ocean, or when they're cleaning the town's cemeteries, or the town's trails, there's a contribution to your close community. One of our generation's challenges is maintaining a close sense of community with those around us."

When we first met, Matt was undergoing another familiar ritual of the mid-twenties crowd: searching for the right job. He still served as the face and president of China Care, but at twenty-four, he wanted a career in business, while also continuing his ongoing Eagle Scout project. Private equity and real estate topped the list and he hoped to have a job lined up within the next month. "China Care taught me that I love building—building companies, building anything," he explained. "I'm a believer that the way to have an impact is through a company that can contribute something to the world . . . That's where advancement in society comes from. If you can find a way of advancing society while making money, your access to capital is infinite. You can raise a lot of money, which means you can do things on a larger scale, which means you can have a greater impact on people. When people can make money, it's easier to raise money. You raise it and you can do something with it again and again, that's why I'm a big believer in doing something noble in this world through investments. I'd like to pursue that."

Given his polish and accomplishments, I told him his major challenge would probably be deciding between offers. He laughed and we began talking about decisions.

"I'm going through the job search," he said, "and I'm making choices that will inherently get rid of options. Every time it's tough. I'm getting rid of an option, the door is closing, and it's tough. I was a psych major and they say that psychologically humans can't deal with choice. It's very difficult for us to say, 'No' to things. Take a game show with three doors. When people see a door closing and the opening getting smaller and smaller, they don't want to get rid of the choice to open that door. They always want the option."

At some point, however, we must surrender options and make choices. Scouting, our parents, and many other influences give us a framework of values and experiences to help us make decisions. Eventually, we need to measure possibilities against that framework and choose. Part of the difficulty I saw many people experiencing lay in the futile pursuit of the *perfect* choice. Through time and hard lessons, I'd realized that perfect choices rarely exist. There are many good choices, and we've been well prepared to make any one of them. We need to review the options, make a smart, informed decision, and move on. The never-ending struggle to make the perfect choice can be terribly debilitating.

As Matt weighed his options, I shared that perspective with him. It elicited another laugh: "My dad told me that verbatim yesterday!" I suddenly felt smarter—or a bit older; I wasn't sure exactly which.

At the end of the day, we all need to choose and let life continue. While career choices may have antagonized both Matt and me at times, neither of us had difficulty choosing our passions and making the required commitments. Matt had doggedly pursued his mission in China, and was deservedly happy with the good China Care had contributed to our world. Clearly, there are plenty of young people in China who believe Matt has made many good decisions, and I know he'll make many more.

Today, China Care runs eight children's homes, which are located near local orphanages across China. The homes receive children who need the most care and whose lives are at greatest risk. Staff and nannies in the homes care for the children—often infants—until they receive needed treatment or are healthy enough to return to the orphanage or a foster care family. The homes typically accommodate six to twelve children or babies each. Two homes serve as the northern and southern medical hubs, and have access to the best available care for the weakest children.

Most children remain in orphanages, so China Care provides many with direct support. Matt remembered visiting an orphanage in Tianjin, near Beijing. When he first saw the facility several years ago, its conditions were decrepit. On his last visit, he found a markedly different place.

"The staff improved and the facilities have been remodeled," he recalled. "Ninety-five percent of the children are physically or emotionally handicapped. You walk through the halls now and it's a better place. The kids are happy. We want to bring that to more orphanages in China."

In addition to working with orphanages, China Care supports foster programs, so children will have family-based care in China. And while adoptions were not an original focus of China Care, Matt has seen how helping American families adopt Chinese children creates a bond between his two communities and benefits both the children and parents.

Matt became godfather to one adopted Chinese child, Cheyenne. Her parents also adopted two blind children, one of whom is also autistic and epileptic. The parents returned to China and rescued a third girl with heart problems, who would have likely not survived without treatment in America. *Then*, the couple returned to bring home her best friend.

"Adopting four children, each with special needs? Who does that?" Matt asked rhetorically. Then he gushed, "But those people exist! One of the things I realized doing this was that *amazing* people exist. And I had no idea."

I would certainly include Matt among those amazing people; people I likewise never knew existed until I began my journey. I had never imagined what one enduring Eagle Scout project can bring about. Both Scouts and not, the passionate individuals I have met give so freely of themselves to so many causes that it can strain credulity. As Matt had asked, "Who does that?"

Well, Matt and I were finding more answers than we ever expected, and we both have a growing, boundless optimism about the future as a result. We understand the power of passion and what one person can accomplish for many.

PRISONER OF WAR

Perched in the front seat of his Apache Longbow attack helicopter, Ron Young flew north into Iraq. It was March 23, 2003, two days after the commencement of Operation Iraqi Freedom. Silver light from the Arabian moon illuminated the suburbs surrounding the town of Karbala and painted the landscape with the shadows of eighteen American helicopters, which were skimming treetops and pounding homes and fields with the downwash from their rotors. Ron's group followed a scout unit of Apaches that had identified targets on the ground, but that had also alerted the Iraqi defenders. The first group just stirred up the enemy, Ron explained. His heavily laden second group would hammer them with ordnance. Loaded with weaponry and its two pilots, his Apache weighed just shy of its maximum weight of twenty thousand pounds.

As the helicopters flew farther north, red tracers from Iraqi antiaircraft installations began streaking upward, sporadically at first. Then everything changed. "All of a sudden, all hell broke loose," Ron explained. "I don't know how else to describe it; just a wall of lead. They'd seen other aircraft move through this zone and knew they'd have to come back, so the Iraqis had moved guns there already and from the moment they started shooting, it didn't let up for twenty-five solid minutes—twenty-five minutes of flying around super-heavy, where just staying in the air is a challenge when you're that close to the limit of the aircraft."

A bullet punched into the fuselage and the Apache lost its weapons system, but Ron and his pilot, Dave Williams, decided to stay in the area in case other airmen were downed and needed a lift home. Ron guided the backseat pilot through the maze of tracers as best he could. "I'm screaming at Dave, 'Turn left, turn left! Okay, turn right, turn right!' " The twenty-six-year-old combat rookie remembered, "I'd look out at the tracers and they'd shoot up in certain patterns and you have to weave yourself in and out of those patterns. So, I'm yelling at Dave which way to turn, just *screaming* at him."

Finally a radio message came through: the units were rallying at a checkpoint to the south. "All this time," Ron continued, "the Iraqis are getting better and better. Bullets are getting closer and closer. I said, 'Hey Dave, we gotta go south.' He was *more* than ready, so we turned around, and I'm still yelling at him, 'Faster, faster, lower, lower!' All of a sudden these tracers come up to us and the aircraft shakes, shudders, yaws to the left, and leans back. I said, 'Dave, what are you doing? Don't slow down!' He screamed at me that we lost an engine. I look up at the instrument display and it's just scrolling through stuff—just flipping through warnings and malfunction indicators, so much is going wrong. I start smelling smoke and powder. Dave screams out, 'They got me in the foot!' At that point, I pretty much knew we were going down."

Their Apache slammed its tail into the field below, then its nose came crashing down, mercifully leaving the aircraft upright. The two crew members scrambled out of the cockpit and started running. "We're pilots and we're on the ground," Ron explained. "That's a *baaad* situation! We probably ran twenty feet and Dave screams, 'My foot, my foot!' Dave's five-foot-nine, I'm six-foot-four and I grab him by his vest and started screaming at him and tried to instill the same fear of God in him that I've got in me. There ain't no 'I can't run' at this point!' "

The two pilots sprinted through the chaos around them and dove into a ditch as an American jet laid bombs into a tree line close by. Ron and Dave found themselves in the middle of a major engagement. Shooting and explosions were everywhere as Iraqi forces aimed up at American aircraft and the aircraft rained ordnance down at the ground. The two fugitives knew the Iraqis would soon find the empty Apache and begin looking for the crew, so they hurtled through fields and waded across irrigation ditches, trying to put distance between themselves and the search parties forming at their disabled helicopter. At every turn, they ducked into ditches and behind buildings, narrowly avoiding Iraqi troops. They could find virtually nowhere to run where they wouldn't encounter large numbers of the enemy.

"Finally," Ron said, "I heard something and hit the ground and looked up and saw a bunch of Iraqis moving toward us. I've got this nine-millimeter pistol and I remember thinking that I didn't want Dave to be mad at me for getting him killed. 'What do you want to do Dave?' I asked.

'Want to take off running, want me to start shooting, or want to give ourselves up?' They'll kill us if we start running, I have fifteen pistol rounds against an Iraqi patrol with automatic AK-47s so I really couldn't work with that, and we felt the only way to live through it was to give ourselves up."

The patrol didn't give the Americans much time to decide.

"They started yelling at us, but didn't come any closer. I said, 'Dave, I think they want us to get up on our knees.' We did and they kept yelling. I said, 'Dave, I think they want us to stand up.' We did, and then they shot at us so we hit the deck!" Minutes later the patrol reached the downed aviators. A boot connected with Ron's head and he blacked out. When he came to, he found himself bound, lying on the ground, and looking at Dave. A soldier had pulled Dave's head back by the hair and had a knife pressed against his throat. Ron instantly understood what they were facing.

The patrol dragged their bound captives from one house to another, trying to avoid the bombings. The treatment was rough and the interrogations sometimes brutal. The Iraqi troops—often young boys or older men, Ron said—were scared and angry. Regardless of what decisions had been made by Saddam Hussein or others to cause the war, the reality staring at these men was this: their hometown was under attack. American bombs endangered their families, their homes, their businesses, and their lives. The two airmen they had captured had been dropping those bombs. Yes, they were angry.

To make them even angrier, the bombing became more intense over the next week. Ron felt his odds getting lower and lower. "Finally, I was thinking this is it—the real *it*. Being in the cell after getting interrogated, realizing we're getting close to these guys just executing us and walking away from the situation. Every day the bombing was getting worse and worse and we were in the middle of the fight every day just waiting for a bomb to be ours. Everything was going up around us."

Ron remembered the low point of his captivity when bombs awakened him on one of the few nights he was allowed to sleep. He began feeling concussions from gunners who were on the roof directly above him. He felt the compound shudder from a nearby bomb hit and he realized if the Iraqis didn't take his life, American bombs likely would. He started to pray.

"I started praying," he said. "And I mean *praying*! Praying like I've never prayed in my entire life. Praying and praying. But when I was praying I began to feel like it was selfish for me to pray. I knew that there were a lot of soldiers out there in the battle that were losing their lives and, you know, I was just praying that God would take the fear from me and that the Iraqis wouldn't torture me and that if I died that it would be swift and mostly painless. But then I thought about the other soldiers out there. Then the thing that came to me in a situation like that where you're waiting to die or lose your life, all I could think about was my mother and my family and the fact that they would never see me again."

Ron shared his harrowing story with me as we ran together on a wooded trail alongside Georgia's Chattahoochee River. The distraction provided by the scenery, Ron's Labrador retriever Mabry, and our steady pace helped him talk about the ordeal. The stress of the situation had dissipated with the passage of time, and Ron's southern-accented voice had a certain energy as he spoke. Part of him still seemed in disbelief that he'd survived. But as he spoke, he remained relaxed and matter-of-fact, confirming that Ron was every bit as laid-back and genuine as he seemed when we first met. He was a simple soldier who relished every minute of life and took everything in stride—even becoming a prisoner of war. As we took a break in the shade of riverside trees, I asked him, "Really, did you think you'd make it out alive?"

"Oh, no," he said without hesitating. "I was just hoping it'd be quick."

Fortunately for Ron, death never came, although he spent twenty-three days as a captive, each day feeling sure he wouldn't see the next sunrise. Between his captors' anger and the American bombs that seemed to follow them from house to house as they moved through small towns surrounding Baghdad, he placed his odds at one in ten on good days, one in a thousand on others.

Finally, locals sympathetic with the U.S. forces became suspicious about the activity at a house where captors were holding Ron, Dave, and five other POWs. The locals called in the United States Marines. Hours later, a squad of armor-clad Marines crashed through the door of the compound, screaming for everyone to hit the floor. The captives dropped. The Marines secured the room then realized the prone figures were Americans. "They were just as surprised as we were," Ron remembered.

Later that week, Ron had landed at Ramstein Air Base in Germany and saw his family again. "I just wanted to be realistic with myself," he said of his time in captivity, "and so I didn't think I'd ever be able to see my family again in my life so when that moment finally came for me, it was the happiest moment ever to be able to put my arms back around my family and my mother and my dad.

"You know a lot of people would think that it was enough adventure for anybody for a lifetime," I commented, looking out at the river, knowing full well that Ron has only picked up his pace since returning from Iraq.

"No, what you find is exactly the opposite," Ron said, giving Mabry an appreciated rub behind the ears. "Being over there was almost like being on some type of drug, because it was amazing that your body could produce those types of endorphins and adrenaline. And it's the same feeling I get just before I go headfirst over the handlebars on my mountain bike!"

In a sense, Ron became addicted to challenging himself, whether on a bike, wakeboard, or snow skis; in new careers or new experiences. Soon after he returned, he received a call from Los Angeles asking him to participate in a reality television show. From the description, he expected to encounter an Eco-Challenge-like showdown with the likes of Burton Roberts. He trained heavily, with long bike rides and night runs with a full backpack. His partner in the venture, Miss South Carolina Kelly McCorkle, also joined in the preparation. When he arrived in California, Ron learned that a full production team would accompany him on an around-the-world competition. "You could only move as fast as the camera crew," Ron said, "so *The Amazing Race* wasn't quite what I expected. Maybe I should have known that, but I hardly ever watched reality shows."

Very much like Ian in Africa, Ron discovered new people as he raced across the world in the seventh season of CBS's hit reality program. It carried him and his partner to Peru, Chile, Argentina, South Africa, Botswana, India, Turkey, the United Kingdom, and Jamaica. The race challenged his ingenuity and spirit; the native people challenged his perceptions about the world. He rode horses in Argentina, just Ron and a true gaucho; he encountered lions in Botswana with a local guide who showed him a different culture; and people in India shared kindness amid poverty. He now viewed the world's people as individuals, and that forever changed his perception of his community and the human race.

Ron and Kelly began the last leg of the competition in first place, but a wrong turn in Puerto Rico sentenced them to a third-place finish, which was still respectable by my estimation. Ron just wished his Spanish had been better.

The former POW aw-shucked being on *The Amazing Race*, and subsequently being selected as one of *People* magazine's most eligible bachelors. Attention, offers, and fan mail, especially from young women, poured in but Ron never changed. He considered himself a regular guy who took advantage of opportunities that came his way. From our time running together on the trail, playing guitar at his home, and having dinner with his friends, I realized that few people are more down to earth than Ron Young. So, I support his claims to being a regular guy. I will not, however, concede his point about opportunities. They did not simply come his way. He made them.

With his good looks, sense of humor, and athleticism, Ron ran with the proverbial popular crowd in high school although he admits a penchant for decidedly unpolished sports like off-roading. As widely liked and well accepted as he seemed, he never felt he quite meshed with others in his high school group.

"I never felt like I totally fit into their world," he said. "I didn't want to lead a normal life. From the time I was young, I really saw my life being about the quality of experiences I'd have. It was a philosophy of life I'd always have with me. You know, you hear that you can't take money with you. The only things you'll always carry are experiences, so you always need to challenge yourself."

"Speaking of challenging yourself," I started, "let's get going again." We stood up from a riverside bench and ended our break. "But why is it important to challenge yourself," I asked as we untied Mabry and turned to run back toward Ron's truck. I'd found Eagle Scouts seem never to give themselves a break. They always push the next goal, the next challenge. I wondered why.

Ron took a deep breath before we both took our first stiff strides on the trail—our break had clearly been too long. As our tempo slowly increased and our legs became limber once again, he explained that he had veered away from the norm by joining Scouts, a choice not always considered the coolest by his peers. He didn't care. He loved every minute of the experience. Through camping, hiking, whitewater rafting, and rappelling, Ron developed a lasting love for the outdoors and a passion for pushing his limits.

"As you're coming up through the ranks as a Scout, you have to achieve the whole way. You're going to camp, you're earning merit badges at meetings, you're hiking, you're learning more, and you're making yourself better. That's the design of the Scout program.

"Of course I also remember showing up on Wednesday nights, and we'd have our Scout meeting, then we'd play the most god-awful game of basketball you have ever seen in your life! But doing that, I developed this camaraderie with a bunch of guys that, outside Scouting, I would probably not have had much to do with. I learned a lot about what their lives were like and their families. You learn to interact with other people in different circles. And some of those guys actually had more in common with me than my group at school."

Then as a sixteen-year-old high school student, he ventured far beyond Scouting and surprised everyone by studying abroad in China. "Talk about changing your perspective on the world," he exclaimed as Mabry eagerly pulled us along the wide path. "I'd never been out of the South before that!" Ron loved exploring the culture of China and returned with a new sense of freedom—he understood that he could lead a life far from ordinary. He simply had to choose it. He entered school to study engineering and then spent his summers as a whitewater rafting guide on the fast-moving Ocoee River in Tennessee.

"I always had that streak where I had to have something to keep the adrenaline going, you know," he explained. "When I was in China, I felt like I was alive. When I was on the river I felt like I was alive. When I studied engineering, I felt like I was alive because I was achieving something and pushing myself forward. Then I go in the military and that's the same thing, we're pushing ourselves and serving the country. That's an Eagle Scout trait, I think; wanting to be alive like that. It's pretty telling that less than one percent of the U.S. population are Eagle Scouts, but around fifteen percent of students at the military academies are Eagles."

Ron was right. Nearly two million Scouts have earned Eagle since 1910, and they regularly comprise between 12 and 16 percent of the student bodies at the U.S. service academies. Nine of our one hundred U.S. Senators are Eagle Scouts. Five of the nine Supreme Court justices joined Scouts as boys. I had found similarly impressive statistics in a host of places where the values of service and integrity were paramount.

Ron's experiences in Scouts had shown him what life could offer and reminded him how he wanted to live. He could take responsibility for his life and not follow traditional paths. He never thought he'd fly helicopters, but he remained open to the idea when army recruiters placed the possibility before him. He viewed it as another opportunity and jumped. I'm sure at the time, neither he nor his family ever imagined the ordeal that awaited him.

"Sometimes people are scared to take advantage of opportunities," he said. "They feel comfort in doing some routine, but that doesn't allow you to have experiences like I've had. This'll sound weird, but I do things based on the question, 'Will my grandkids want to hear about this? Will they be intrigued by this person who is their grandfather?' If you're too comfortable where you are and you're not pushing, you're never going to experience anything different or worth retelling forty years down the road."

Then he turned to me. "Why am I telling you this? That's basically what you're doing."

I couldn't lay claim to risks or adventures like Ron's, but I realized that I'd been living my own adventure in a way. I had put tradition and convention behind me to become a writer and had embarked on a path with few guideposts. Actually, there were no guideposts and not much of a trail at all. I had to figure it out as it came. Sometimes, my friends didn't quite understand. Sometimes *I* didn't quite understand. Life without a steady paycheck or a nice benefits package gets scary at times and injects an element of constant uncertainty into everything. In a way, the experience was exhilarating; relying on yourself to leap the next chasm or scale the next mountain; having incredible experiences in southern California one day and then in New York the next—always discovering something or someone new. It also took balance, something I still grappled to achieve. I hoped Ron and others would begin teaching me how to manage both passion and practicality.

As we moved down the trail toward the run's end, I thought about how close Ron had come to dying. He almost didn't live past the age of twenty-six. After Iraq, he became one of those people who can truly appreciate each day. So his example becomes important, and I thought more on his observations about living with intent and adventure. He views each day as a gift. I hoped that I and other young Eagles could learn to do the same.

Thoroughly winded, Ron and I emerged from the woods at the trail's end. Mabry seemed bitterly disappointed in us when we eased to a shuffle, then finally ground to a walk. We headed toward Ron's truck, walking slowly to recover and enjoying the midday sunshine. He returned to the subject of challenges.

"In our society you *have* to challenge yourself," Ron observed. "I think people underestimate the need to challenge themselves every day." He'd realized, quite clearly, that competition in business and life often drives Americans. The hardest working and best prepared move ahead. Competition determines who gets a job or keeps a job in the long run. Those who don't challenge themselves won't remain sharp. They'll grow stagnant and for Ron, stagnation equates to falling behind since others in society are constantly pushing themselves forward. He has always been driven to make himself better.

"The big point is that there is a whole world, a whole endless amount of possibilities of what I could be in life if I work, if I try to make myself succeed. And I'm just a regular guy. I think that in a lot of ways that's exactly what my story is, you know?

"That was a whole lot about me back there on the trail," Ron said as we arrived at his 4Runner and he opened the back gate for Mabry. "Now let me tell you about real sacrifice." He told me about a friend from flight school, diagnosed with cancer. The friend had combat experience in other theaters, and when his unit was called to Iraq, he wanted to be with them. He was supposed to stay home for treatment, but asked to go.

"He was shot down near Baghdad on his way to his last cancer screening," Ron said, with a somber look that I hadn't seen on the trail. "He was taken away from his wife and two kids and everyone else. At the time he was shot down, he was thirty. It's not just my story. There are a lot of people in our armed services that are willing to make those kinds of sacrifices on behalf of people who will never even know or understand the sacrifices people make for them on a daily basis. And the reason they do that is because they grew up with certain values like what we take from the Scout Oath and Scout Law."

For the first time, I realized that like many of us, I too frequently took the sacrifices of the military for granted. I felt guilty and slightly angry at myself for not thinking more about our servicemen and -women and being more grateful for the protection they provide at personal cost. Millions of Americans don't fully understand or appreciate the individual sacrifices our soldiers make. Yet Ron and his comrades signed up and did their duty regardless. His friend lost his life. Ron almost lost his own. But he'd do it all over again.

The Geneva Convention bars former prisoners of war from returning to combat, however, so Ron couldn't do it again. He wouldn't be returning to the Middle East, but thousands of his fellow soldiers remained there. Thousands more would be joining them, and sadly, many would return home wounded or disabled. Others would not return at all. Nearly five thousand Americans have died in Afghanistan and Iraq, more than half of them never saw the age of twenty-five. The politics surrounding the conflicts in the Middle East had always been complicated, and I doubted that would change anytime soon. But I knew that young men and women would continue to volunteer selflessly to do their duty and serve their country. Many people in our country and in my generation seemed only vaguely aware of the conflict, and often nearly oblivious to the real sacrifices being made on the ground. Honestly—and mercifully—I didn't understand the real nature of war. I had never lost a friend or family member in the line of duty. I had not taken up a rifle and stood a watch. Others had volunteered on my behalf. They didn't know me. I didn't know them. But they were my peers—Eagle Scouts and otherwise—and they were engaged in a conflict that would mark not only our generation, but our country. I needed to meet more of them and understand. Soon enough, I would. But first, I was about to meet others who reminded me there are many ways to serve our country abroad.

PEACE CORPS

My first African sunset came somewhere above Algeria. I had never imagined that I'd watch the sun sink westward into the unending Sahara Desert. Like many Americans, I had never thought that I'd set foot in Africa at all. I looked out over the wing of my plane. We were thirty-five thousand feet above the desolate landscape, which was rapidly cooling with the onset of dusk. I sat quietly, amazed at the surprising new places this journey kept taking me and how it continued expanding my horizons, both literal and figurative.

I'm certain that all this would have immeasurably pleased Scouting's founder. Baden-Powell's program had ultimately brought me to Africa, where he made his name as a young soldier and found the sense of adventure that guided his life. Africa to him represented a continuing voyage of discovery, and he chose to be buried there. Outside Nyeri, Kenya, a simple tombstone now bears the inscription "Robert Baden-Powell, Chief Scout of the World." Engraved above his name is the Scout fleur-de-lis; below, a circle with a dot in its center, the Scout trail sign for "I have gone home."

My journey had brought me to Baden-Powell's beloved Africa, where I felt the shimmer of his passion for life. Or maybe I just recognized that it was already inside me. It was his vision that had lit the spirit of adventure driving me along this quest. Because of Scouting, I learned to love adventure and the sense of fun and fulfillment that comes from being on the trail, being independent with everything you need in your pack. Because of Scouting, I learned to cherish the rewards of discovery that accompany forays into the unknown.

As a Scout, I once spent ten days paddling through the Canadian wilderness at the Northern Tier Canoe Base. Our crew of nine encountered only one other group of people during the entire expedition. We survived on the lakes just as trappers and voyagers had centuries ago, learning to live from the land and appreciate the vast forests and expansive lakes. Off the Florida Keys, I learned to catch the wind in canvas sails and send a ship plowing through the open sea. Beneath the waves, I learned countless lessons in history and biology as I dove at encrusted shipwrecks and brilliant coral reefs teeming with creatures of every sort. Along countless trails in the Rockies and Appalachians, as a Scout and young adult, I learned to survive cold, rain, snow, and general misery, and emerge more confident, with a better knowledge of myself. Of course there were plenty of sun-filled days as well. The examples are endless, and as my flight touched down in West Africa, I realized the adventure of Scouting may never end for many of us. It certainly hadn't ceased for the Eagle Scouts I found in the country of Benin.

Ninety-seven Peace Corps volunteers call the West African nation of Benin home. The former French colony, sandwiched between Nigeria to the east and Togo to the west, holds 6.7 million people, most of whom need the help the Peace Corps offers. Like their eight thousand counterparts in seventy-four other countries, Benin's Peace Corps volunteers chose a job with a mission. Most came straight from a college campus. They are uniformly gifted, and I'm sure passed over many more lucrative and less stressful opportunities back in America. Instead, they volunteered for two years, helping the citizens of developing nations overcome their myriad challenges. Not that it's all for the benefit of others; whether talking with Peace Corps volunteers, Scouts, educators, or nonprofit groups, I learned that those who serve others often receive at least as much as they give. Everywhere I went, I found service work leading to richer lives.

Several months before I landed in Africa, I had learned about Alex Litichevsky, an Eagle Scout beginning his assignment with the Peace Corps in Benin, and I envisioned an easy interview via e-mail or Skype—if Alex could find Internet connections near his post in the not-so-metropolitan town of Gogounou, some 350 miles north of Cotonou, Benin's largest city. Within a month of arriving, however, Alex found a computer and e-mailed me: he had uncovered four other Eagle Scouts posted in-country. More than 10 percent of Benin's male Peace Corps volunteers were Eagle Scouts. Perhaps I should have expected that. At any length, I began looking for cheap airline tickets. I was headed to Benin.

I arrived in Cotonou late in the evening. The next morning, my good friend Lauren Robbins, a fellow alum from Washington and Lee University, dragged my jet-lagged self out of bed at Hotel du Lac. Fortune had smiled upon me at several junctures of this trip, and Lauren, my one friend on the entire continent of Africa, happened to live in the same country where I discovered this group of Eagle Scouts. Despite the help of the Peace Corps, I would have been lost without someone who could speak French, Benin's predominant language. Lauren's French saved me; nobody in the country's rural interior speaks English.

Our driver Carlos met us at the hotel in the Toyota Land Cruiser that would soon serve as our roving home. Gear loaded, we pushed through the rivers of traffic flowing through Cotonou, passing roadsides jammed with vendors selling everything imaginable: blue jeans, bottles of gasoline, cellular telephone cards, jewelry, animals, fresh crops, not-so-fresh crops. Some conducted business from small shacks, others from baskets on their heads, and still others carried goods slung over their shoulders or in their hands. Retail activity covered the city as thickly as the blue smog brewed by its legions of mopeds. Eventually, we left Cotonou and drove toward the town of Lokossa to meet Paul Oxborrow.

After two more hours, we turned off the paved road and I asked Carlos, "Are you sure this is the way?"

Lauren laughed: "Alvin, in Africa, a dirt road doesn't mean a bad area—almost all the roads are dirt!"

We found Paul sitting under a thatched roof at Café Le Colin. He wore a khaki painter's cap, jeans, and a flannel shirt despite the heat. The thirty-year-old volunteer was already enjoying a large glass bottle of Coca-Cola and listening to a rhythmic pounding that seemed never to subside in West Africa: the *whump, whump, whump* of two women pounding yams with heavy wooden pestles and mortars. The sound never left the background of our conversation.

Unlike the other Eagle Scouts I would soon meet, Paul came to Benin with a partner, his wife, Anastasia. For years, they'd toyed with the idea of working overseas together, but they couldn't decide what to do. They had considered teaching English in Japan or Latin America, then learned more about the Peace Corps. They quickly realized they'd really be helping people, and helping an entire nation for that matter. They'd get the adventure they wanted, but by doing something constructive and positive at the same time. To ensure they received assignments in the same area, they had to be married, so that's what they decided to do.

"We both knew we'd found the person we wanted to be with," explained Paul. "It just happened a little sooner and a little less romantically than people would expect. So we wouldn't be lying, the same month we turned in our applications, we went to the justice of the peace, signed the paperwork, and went out afterward—that was our wedding!"

When Paul and Anastasia arrived, they immediately realized their luck. Their home, a three-room concrete house set in a courtyard filled with chickens and goats, had three rarities in West Africa: electricity, a spigot in the wall for water, and an actual shower. "So we don't have to take bucket showers," Paul exclaimed. I'd discover what those were like soon enough.

Paul and Anastasia also realized that their neighbors needed their help. While children attend primary school free of charge, secondary schools cost ten thousand to twenty thousand CFA francs per year, somewhere between twenty-five and fifty U.S. dollars. It's called a contribution, but it's not voluntary. Many people in Benin can't afford an education for their children. If they can only afford to send one child into higher education, they'll send a son, not a daughter, which only adds to the struggles many African women face. Paul and Anastasia sponsored two local girls, who did laundry and other jobs for them in return.

As the yam pounding continued, a waitress dressed in green and blue cloth interrupted our conversation to take our order: pounded yams, fried cheese, and peanut sauce for all. That was a typical breakfast, lunch, or dinner in Benin.

"I was pretty ignorant about Africa when I came," Paul confessed after the waitress left. "I knew generally about the poverty and bad government and some of the wars going on, but I was pretty ignorant of culture and geography. One of the things I've really learned is that if and when change comes here, it'll come from the people themselves, not outside forces. We can help out with development and materials, but with things like gender roles and equality and education issues, that's cultural and needs to come from the people. And I think we're seeing that. More girls are going to school, people are realizing women are capable of doing more. There's hope.

"Those of us in the Peace Corps are here to help other people out, and for me, that translates to Scouting. I did a lot of service projects, especially my Eagle project. You're really taught the idea of service and that defines you as a Scout. You know how important it is to help your community and be involved. For anyone who has been a Scout, that's a familiar concept."

Growing up in the Arizona suburbs, Paul had found adventure in trips to local museums or hikes in the nearby Superstition Mountains. "I realized my friends not involved in Scouting missed out on that," he said. "We were getting exposed to things we'd never get exposed to normally.

"How did that help here? It helped me be resourceful and have a better understanding of different people and places. I was never dropped in a foreign country and forced to fend for my own as a fourteen-year-old, but I think being exposed to the world and realizing there's more out there than your own little neighborhood and circle of friends sets a framework of being open-minded and prepared to go live in a third-world country and continue the adventure. I'd describe that experience as challenging, rewarding, sweaty, exciting, and fascinating. But it can be really tough and there are times my wife and I lay awake and wonder, 'How long is the flight home from here?' "

Our waitress arrived with the meal, which Lauren and Paul hungrily attacked; I explored the dish warily. In the end, it tasted mostly of the peanut sauce that saturated it.

"But you know," Paul continued after a few mouthfuls, "honestly, the only time I've thought about Scouting since I was eighteen was when I debated whether to put it on my résumé. At least until I heard you were coming, Scouting had been something I did growing up. Thinking about it, there are so many things that are ingrained and that I use on a daily basis that I got from Scouting. I really hadn't thought about it before now."

Paul told me that most of the volunteers in Benin knew about my visit with their five fellow expatriates. A general surprise had surfaced when others learned how many Eagle Scouts were serving in Benin, and who those Eagles were. Paul explained his fellow volunteers' shock, saying they only thought clean-cut politicians and military generals were Eagle Scouts. These five rough-and-tumble young men did not match their stereotype.

I reassured Paul that most people I'd met, particularly among our generation, were not on the CEO or congressional track. Similar values? Yes. Similar interests or personalities? Decidedly not. Accomplishing something for others seemed a common theme, but Eagles of our generation pursued a dizzying variety of paths. Take the Navy SEALs in San

Diego and Peace Corps volunteers in Benin; very different paths, but very similar core values.

"I think it's up to our generation," I said to Paul, "to keep defining the Eagle Scout image, or maybe revising it. I'm still wondering how we'll shape the world in a different way than those before us."

"You know," Paul replied, "our generation has grown up in an age of unlimited information, and access to news and what's going on in the world, and I think, at least in my immediate circle and people my same age, there's a lot of international involvement or at least interest in issues going on around the world. That could be just my circle of friends, but I'd like to think that our generation is broad-minded and that we think about what's going on in the rest of the world.

"Beyond that, everybody is pretty laid-back," he said. "We have fewer prejudices and are open to seeing the world in different ways, which is refreshing. You know, the world will be a better place with each successive generation, and we're part of that."

We paid for lunch and Carlos drove us to Paul's school, five minutes away, but well outside the urban areas of Lokossa. We bounced down another dirt road through an open field until we arrived at a grove of trees that shaded Paul's school. Some buildings were tan concrete bearing painted-on flags from countries that donated materials and labor. Thatched roofs and sides covered other buildings. Paul led us to his classroom, a wooden pavilion with partially thatched walls. It was unlike any classroom I'd ever seen.

"The first year here was incredibly difficult," Paul explained as we entered the shade of the hut. "But once you learn the ropes, it's really rewarding. I teach seventh, ninth, and eleventh grades more or less. The main difficulties of teaching here are results of poverty. You teach in a thatched-roofed building like this with dirt floors and a painted piece of plywood being the blackboard. Nobody has textbooks. Textbooks are what students copy off the board. Our class sizes in Lokossa are around fifty or sixty per class. In the north, they'll have seventy or eighty students in a tiny little dirt-floored room with one wall at the end thatched up to the roof where the blackboard is. We come from a society where everyone has a textbook with activities and laptops and multimedia. Here you have a piece of chalk, a terrible chalkboard, and the kids have their notebooks, and so you just go for it!

"They're in here for four hours at a time, but if you teach good lessons and make them want to learn, you can keep them going. I'm getting a lot better at it. I use a lot of visual aids and gestures; I make things relevant to them. Right now, we're talking about health a lot. We'll talk about technical terms like *malaria* and *diphtheria*, but you have to make it relevant: 'If I drink water out of the river, is that good, class?'

"They'll respond, 'NOO!'

" 'What should I do?'

" 'Teacher, you should boil your water first!'

"You have to get them involved," Paul continued. "I'm a clown in class. I trip if I say, 'Fall down.' If I say 'Run,' I sprint out of class. If I'm doing prepositions, I stand *on* the desk, or climb *under* the desk, or stand *behind* the students: 'Class, where is teacher?'

" 'Teacher is *under* the desk!'

"They love the fact their teacher is involved with them," he concluded.

Paul enjoyed himself in the recent semester, but had not forgotten the difficulties of his first year of teaching. Year one of teaching is a challenge anywhere, he noted, but it's particularly so in Africa with a classroom of sixty students who don't speak the teacher's native language. He remembered letdowns, when students seemed not to care about his subjects or did poorly on tests. Good days when students were motivated would always lift his dragging spirits and he would walk home believing, "Okay, I can do this. I'm not a bad teacher."

We left the shade of Paul's classroom and he saw two of his students milling around the campus, enjoying a leisurely Saturday. They brightened upon seeing Paul out of class and he introduced them to us. Their cheerfulness struck me, and I could see that Paul was bringing them hope.

Soon, Lauren and I left Paul and Lokossa behind us, driving north into the rural interior of Benin. Buildings grew sparse along the roadside. Traffic of all sorts—trucks, cars, mopeds, and pedestrians—gradually dissipated. Vast plains opened up to our east and west. Plateaus and scrub brush marked the horizons and the Land Cruiser carried us rapidly into another world.

We arrived in Kandi, with no clue where to find our next Eagle, Michael Portegies-Zwart, who was also into his second year as a volunteer. He had become affectionately known countrywide as "Dutch" or even better, "Dutchpants." We found a local official and asked, "*Où est l'américain?*" It turned out there was only one, and a man soon guided us down dusty roads to Dutch's concession. A concession, I learned, was a walled compound with an open courtyard surrounded by several buildings where two or three families typically live and raise livestock. While Lauren and Carlos waited in the Land Cruiser, I pushed open a metal gate and walked through a yard of swept dirt not quite overrun with chickens, goats, and roosters. I found Dutch waiting inside his surprisingly cool concrete home, packed and ready. "Ben Fouti, another Eagle Scout, wanted to join us," Dutch explained, after our greetings, "but he lives several hours north and couldn't find a bush taxi." The news disappointed me, but at least Ben avoided a long, hot, and dusty drive in the infamous bush taxis, ancient cars filled with people, goods, and livestock. As we had passed bush taxis earlier in the trip, I'd learned that maximum capacity in Benin and maximum capacity in America are vastly different things.

Dutch, a 2001 Eagle Scout from Troop 236 in Rome, Italy, noticed a raw cut on my finger, earned while climbing rocks at a waterfall-fed lagoon that morning in Pendjari National Park, Benin's primary wildlife preserve. He broke out a first-aid kit. After making sure I treated the cut with ointment and covered it with a Band-Aid, he was ready to leave. We hauled his bags to the car, and Carlos drove us toward our next destination as Dutch reveled in the rare air-conditioned comfort. After two hours, we arrived in Sinande and found Collin Gerst, who met us on his mountain bike, one of the few two-wheeled vehicles I saw in Benin without a noisy motor attached.

Collin, a sturdy, six-foot-five Iowan, stood at least a foot taller than most of Sinande's population. Like Dutch, he wore his hair buzzed. He also sported just enough scruff to constitute a beard. His good nature was infectious and our group soon moved to the local restaurant to continue the light conversation and exchange of jokes. Collin had made special arrangements for dinner: yam ragout with chicken. In a stroke of fortune, the restaurant's cooler worked, so we enjoyed cold drinks, which washed down our five pieces of chicken. An enterprising local mutt enjoyed the sixth.

"So how did you get here?" Collin finally asked me.

"Well, Alex uncovered you, Dutch, Paul, and Ben, and I thought it was fascinating that there were five Eagles in a little country that I'd never heard about until Lauren was assigned to come here last year," I said. "So I had to come."

"Only two percent of Scouts become Eagles and five percent of the volunteers here are Eagles," Collin said thoughtfully, running the figures in his head. "That's more than ten percent of the guys!"

"Hmmm. I wonder if that's true Peace Corps wide," Lauren wondered aloud. "Or is Benin just a black hole for Eagle Scouts?"

We all laughed. "It's so rough, we're the only ones who can take it!" Collin replied. "It was nighttime in Cotonou when I arrived three months ago, and I just remember thinking, 'Wow, this is a third-world country.' People were doing everything by candlelight and selling gas out of bottles on the side of the road. Now, having been out here on post, I go back to Cotonou and think, 'Cotonou is a metropolis!' Arriving here was a complete shock."

"I had the same experience," related Dutch. "I took the bus from the airport to downtown, and thought, 'Wow, there's *nothing* here.' Then coming back to Cotonou after being on post for months, I think, 'Wow, there's *everything* here!' "

"This isn't necessarily where I thought I'd be in my early twenties," Collin confessed. "I'm from Oakville, Iowa, population three hundred. I always assumed I'd be living in Des Moines, Iowa, because that seemed like a big town; I'd have been moving up."

"You did move up, Collin," I shot back. "Sinande is a lot bigger than Oakville!"

Dutch, who earned his Eagle in Rome as a member of the Boy Scouts of America's Transatlantic Council, grew up with parents who'd lived and traveled abroad. "I definitely knew I was going to be in Africa," he said. "My dad spent time in Niger and his life turned out well, so I figured it wouldn't hurt to have this experience and get to live like most of the world. Much of the world lives at more-or-less this level of poverty." Collin, a University of Iowa economics major, added for comparison that roughly one-third to one-half of the world survives on two dollars per day or less. Estimates place half of Benin's population living on less than one dollar per day. Average Americans get by on roughly $130 per day.

"But I think Benin is progressing, whether its people want to or not," Collin continued. "In some ways change is being forced upon them. There's electricity. There are a cyber cafés; granted, they don't always work, but they're there and people want to use them. People are progressing whether they want to or not because once an idea is created, you can't take it back. Now, they can call their relatives in Cotonou on a cell phone. Before, it was a once-in-a-year trip that they'd have to save up for. One girl, roughly eleven or twelve years old, is my neighbor and she's always washing dishes in the front yard with water she got herself from the well, and she sweeps the ground by hand. Then she goes to school all day."

With a wry smile, Dutch interjected, "You have to ask yourself, 'Why would someone sweep dirt on the ground outside?' But man, everyone here does it!"

"The girl speaks French," Collin went on. "I can talk with this eleven-year-old girl in French. I couldn't talk to her mother; she doesn't speak French. But the new generation knows French and now they want to learn English and go to Nigeria and Ghana. Even here in Sinande, a Beninese backwater by all accounts, they still are progressing while keeping their traditional tasks and living the life they always have lived."

Soon, we left our spot on the restaurant's porch and went back to Collin's home, where we met the young girl he'd spoken of at dinner. Her family owned many of the animals that roamed freely about the yard. We dropped our gear in Collin's empty concrete living room, adorned with a mosquito net and an Iowa Hawkeyes flag, then stepped back outside. We looked up at a sky full of stars. All of us remembered camping trips away from home where the city lights faded and stars shone. With no electricity flowing through Sinande at that late hour, we saw the skies just as African tribes viewed them centuries ago. We tried to imagine the sense of wonder the ancients felt as they gazed at the stars, planets, and meteors of the heavens. Even with our modern knowledge, we still felt that wonder at the vastness of space and our relative smallness. It was humbling to say the least.

After talking astronomy and reminiscing about camping trips, we followed Scouting tradition and retired to a campfire—of sorts. On Collin's floor, we lit a bucket candle for light. The glowing pot reminded me of the smudge pots that marked trails to Order of the Arrow ceremonies, but without the choking black smoke.

The Order of the Arrow is Scouting's honor society, and its ceremonies and ideals honor Native American culture. I shared my memories of those late-night campfires held at Bert Adams Scout Reservation, just outside Atlanta, Georgia. Ceremonial teams from the Egwa Tawa Dee Lodge, attired as tribal chiefs and warriors, inducted new members and then led them into the adjacent dark woods to begin the secret ordeal that would qualify them for membership, if they completed it successfully. The tasks weren't easy, but they were uncomplicated and made sense. Just like the ideals that underlie all of Scouting.

"It's the simple things that you take from Scouting," Dutch said. "Being prepared—having Band-Aids in my wallet, so whenever someone needs a Band-Aid, I give them the Band-Aid—like I did for you earlier today," he said, gesturing toward me. "People will look at me like, 'Why do you have this?' Well, for situations just like this!

"Scouting gave me the chance to get together with my friends and do things we all enjoyed," Collin said. "That's really what the Peace Corps is; you find a lot of kindred spirits, a lot of people who value the same things you do. It takes a lot to give up your life in America and come over here. We all have a common vow, so it's good to know others like that are here."

"I know leadership comes in there somewhere," added Dutch. "By being forced to act as a leader throughout Scouting, I'm sure that has shown in my life. But it's strange; since getting Eagle, I haven't thought about Scouting that much. It's not something you bring up in conversations often, so it's strange finding a bunch of Scouts here. But when it does come up, you find a lot of people have been touched by Scouting in a certain way."

"It's interesting how you intrinsically use all the laws," Collin said. "I was sitting here going over them in my head, seeing if I could still name them."

"So, what are they?" I asked, taking his bait.

"Trustworthy, loyal, helpful, friendly, courteous, kind, obedient, cheerful, thrifty, brave, clean, and reverent," he said proudly. "I don't think I've said that since I was seventeen. But it's still with me. They're good rules to live your life by. They're always intrinsically there; you don't necessarily think about them every day, but you can't be here and be a leader in your community without using them."

Collin admitted not knowing many Eagle Scouts from other generations, but like me, he had found that few people seemed to fit the stereotype that many—even other Scouts—expected. He had found a diverse and interesting mix with wide-ranging interests beyond Scouting and a broad worldview. "I'd like to see that be the mark of our generation," Collin said, "people who are very accepting, open to new ideas and new thoughts."

"I'd agree exactly with that," contributed Dutch. His eyes darted craftily from Collin to me and back. Then he said, "I didn't know anything about you before you came, Alvin, so . . ."

Collin knew where Dutch was heading and laughed. "I was thinking the same thing!"

"I wondered if some stuffy old guy was going to come talk down to us. I had no idea. That's not who I am, so I thought, 'I'm not who he's looking for.' I didn't think someone like me fit with the mold of the good old classic American Eagle Scout. I'm glad to see that you've also found there are other types of Eagle Scouts out there."

We all laughed easily. I'd found that initial expectation before, many times. And on my end, I would have been unimaginably bored were there only one variety of Eagle Scout. I shared how I'd been encouraged by the idealism of everyone in our generation, and how we seemed more open to different ideas and different paths. We seemed to recognize the value that accompanies differences. I just hoped we'd be able to hold on to those perspectives and that optimism as we grew older.

Early the next morning calls to prayer from loudspeakers at three local mosques echoed through Collin's home at 4:30 A.M. Then the animals added to the noise. I thought roosters crowed at dawn. Apparently, the sun has little to do with it, and their cries resounded from various corners of the neighborhood from four-thirty until we left at eight. I'm sure they continued straight through lunch. The volunteers seemed used to the chorus and didn't stir, but my day started with that first prayer call and the roosters made sure I never fell back to sleep.

Once daylight broke, I quickly visited the outdoor shower, which was a small concrete room. On the floor were a bucket of well water and a cup. I was back at a primitive Scout camp. But for the volunteers and villagers, this was every day. After my bucket shower, we all left for Alex Litichevsky's post in Gogounou, a two-hour drive. As we were leaving Sinande, several children waved to Collin. He explained that he'd spent part of the previous day playing soccer with them. When he saw their game, he'd hopped off his bike and called, "*Ecce, ecce,*" meaning "Here, here!" The makeshift ball soon arrived at Collin's feet and he deftly lofted it onto his knees and began juggling. A firm pop from his right knee sent the ball skyward and Collin headed it back to the children. They laughed and ran to the towering American, forming a circle around him. The few children who could speak French translated Collin's words into the local Bariba language and happy laughs assailed him from all sides. Collin has a good sense of humor that apparently wasn't lost on the children in Benin. "It was just fantastic to know that they were friendly and they wanted to know me and I wanted to know them," he reflected. "Now in the future, I can know them and keep in touch with them and show them that the world hasn't forgotten about them."

"But it can be frustrating," Dutch said, drawing on his eighteen months experience on post. "It's not always easy to show them that and get them to trust you. You have to convince them that it's in their interest to use you and that you're here to help. The most frustrating thing is to see the potential available to them, but see them not accessing it. You really have to work hard and put yourself out there."

Unlike Kandi and Sinande, Gogounou at least had one paved road. Our driver Carlos grabbed the opportunity and pushed the Land Cruiser hard down the ribbon of asphalt that led into town. Soon, the traffic of goats and merchants on foot slowed us down again and we turned off the pavement and rolled a short distance to the concession where Alex lived. We piled out, anxious to stretch our legs, and walked into yet another livestock-filled courtyard, meeting Alex halfway to his concrete home. He almost rivaled Collin in height, although he had a more trim build. He had outdone both Collin and Dutch, not simply buzzing his head, but shaving it. If I hadn't known him as an Eagle Scout and the party responsible for our gathering, I might have been intimidated.

Leaving our gear with Carlos, we walked to meet Emily, the other Peace Corps volunteer stationed in Gogounou. She was bright-eyed and had a buzzed haircut that mirrored those of Collin and Dutch. "It's easy and keeps me cool," she explained. She welcomed us into her concession. Chickens and swept dirt, at this point I knew what to expect. We pulled chairs together beneath a thatched-roof porch and spent the afternoon in conversation, making sure to cover the three staples of on-post conversation: what they'd been eating, what they *wished* they'd been eating, and latrines. Again, I felt like I was on a Scout trip.

The sun finally began to drop in the west and we left for dinner. The six of us walked the half-mile to Restaurant Trois à la Puissance de Quatre, which sounds much fancier than it is. No white tablecloths here, believe me. On the way, we drew attention from every side; we doubted if anyone in Gogounou had ever seen six *batouri*, white foreigners, together.

We began the night with ice-cold drinks, courtesy of another rare, working refrigerator. We sat at a table situated behind the main restaurant and under a thatched roof. No walls enclosed us, so we watched children pass and play on the dirt street beyond the porch. A late afternoon breeze rustled the nearby trees and ushered in a moment of reflective silence. Collin wiped the beaded condensation from his glass and thoughtfully observed, "The big journey we're all on is about finding out where life takes you. We all have different things we're good at, but we all want to do *great* in something. To do that you have to push yourself a little bit further than you think you can go.

"'Doing great' is always relative; it's certainly not just joining the Peace Corps!" he joked. "It may be running a small business. Maybe 'doing great' is going to law school. It's all about wherever life takes you and what your strengths are. Scouting helps you begin to figure that out and teaches you to push yourself."

By earning merit badges, completing projects, and holding leadership positions in his troop, Collin advanced through the ranks of Scout, Tenderfoot, Second Class, First Class, Star, and Life. Then to reach Eagle, he had to push a little more and complete his final service project. From what I'd seen, I realized he might be pressing himself even harder in the Peace Corps, as he met difficult challenges in a particularly trying environment. But I knew he'd enjoy his full two-year tour. In all of the Eagles with me that evening, I saw the satisfaction that came from achieving something extraordinary. Now, they were just seeing where life would lead.

For some time, a crowd of local children had been gathering outside the patio where we ate, listening to the jukebox and intrigued by the handspring displays put on by Lauren and Emily. The children had been showing us local dances—dancing briefly, then running away giggling. Someone eventually suggested we show them a dance from the States. I grabbed Lauren's hand at the beginning of the next song, and we spun onto the dirt road. Clearly, nobody in Gogounou had ever seen Americans dance firsthand, nor had they seen the swing. After several minutes of furious spins, steps, and twirls, Lauren and I bowed to the cheering and laughing crowd that had gathered. As we walked back to our table where clapping Peace Corps volunteers awaited us, I saw young village girls spinning each other, with smiles as big as you can imagine. We had made a connection with these young people. We came from entirely different worlds, spoke different languages, yet for a moment I'll always remember, we understood each other perfectly.

"We showed them something they may never be able to see again and took something we will certainly never be able to find anywhere else in the world," Collin happily observed as we left the first restaurant and walked down the road for our second course: pounded yams and stew at Mama's (every older woman in Benin seems to be called "Mama," just as every meal seems to include yams of some sort). "We touched people in a way that they'd never find otherwise, and we're never going to find again. One night in Benin it all came together, and that's a magical moment."

The magical moment apparently left Collin quite drained and he quickly fell asleep on Alex's extra guest bed, his feet dangling over the footboard. Dutch felt similarly exhausted and lay down on his sleeping pad to listen quietly as Alex and I talked while we enjoyed the day's final minutes of electricity, before power was shut off around midnight.

Sitting at his simple table, Alex, like me, identified Scouting as what had led him to Africa. It had kindled a love for adventure that we both hoped would always remain with us. Earning Eagle entailed overcoming challenges and Alex learned that while those challenges might prove taxing, he could always surmount them by giving his full effort. "Moving here to Benin, West Africa, I knew it would be a challenge," he began. "I knew it would be difficult learning a second language and at my post, practically a third language—the language of the Bariba people. I knew it'd be a challenge here. It also felt like a great opportunity to represent my country. I'm very proud of my country and proud of what we stand for. This was a chance for me to do something to help someone else and influence them and also show them what the truth is about the United States of America. We are a nation of caring, compassionate people who want to make the world a better place."

He explained that Troop 180 in Branchville, New Jersey, emphasized citizenship and taught Scouts to improve their community. Service to self never made Scout meeting agendas. "You leave the campsite better than you found it," Alex remembered learning. "That's really the influence I want to be in my life. No matter exactly what I do, I want to make sure that everything is better off after I've been there."

Based on the conversations I'd been having with Eagles along my trail, I suggested that, perhaps, our generation's calling had something to do with that. He thought for a minute then lent me an interesting perspective. During the short time he'd spent in West Africa, he had already recognized the misunderstandings that many Americans have of Africa.

"The biggest misconception by Americans, and actually westerners in general, is that sub-Saharan Africa is essentially a homogeneous continent. We see and hear commercials and reports that display malnourished children, epidemics of AIDS and malaria, and brutally violent civil wars. Many individuals unfortunately see 'Africa' as a place and not a continent with numerous countries and tens of thousands (at least) of ethnic groups. I have yet to stop being surprised by the amount of diversity—ethnic, language, religious beliefs—that exists just in Benin.

"One other huge misconception westerners have is that Africa is full of incompetent people who will never understand development. This is simply not true. The nations of West Africa are young. Ghana was the first one to get independence, making it just fifty years old. Benin was freed in 1960. Many people expect these cultures and people to simply develop overnight. Forty or fifty years is one generation. Development takes time. But I guarantee you if you went back even ten years ago, Cotonou would be an *entirely* different-looking place. You can't say that about New York City, Paris, or London."

Alex hoped that our generation would think critically, examine the alternative sides of stories with our own perspectives, and form our own opinions. Too much information exists for us to rely on assumptions. "Our generation has had more of an opportunity to grow these skills given our knowledge of technology in particular," Alex added. "I definitely feel that to be a successful citizen you have to know how to think critically and understand the world around you; how it interacts and what you can do your best to improve upon, be it here in the Peace Corps or back at home doing community service in your hometown. Or it could be just leaving a campsite better than you found it."

The day's adventures and the early wake-up at Collin's had left me worn out. Alex felt equally tired and we both yawned. "Tomorrow will be interesting for you, I think," he observed as we turned off our flashlights and began retiring to our respective spots for the night—him to his bed, me to my sleeping bag on the pleasantly cool concrete floor. "Even before we get to class, you'll see an eagerness, an excitement. You'll probably see students come up to me and greet me in English—just for the sheer thrill of speaking another language to a foreigner. No matter who I am, the student values the fact that I'm here and wants to say hello to me in my native tongue, and wants to learn. 'Good morning, good afternoon, good evening.' It's stimulating his understanding that there is a world outside of Gogounou and a world outside of Benin. That's a problem here. Many students do not value education because they don't understand that there is a world out there. They've simply lived in one town their whole life. The fact that I'm here, and that I speak English as my native language, they get a really, really big smile on their face and get a thrill when they greet me and it's not even in school and they say, 'Good morning,' and I say, 'Good morning' back to them. They can communicate with me and it means a lot to them and it means a lot to me. They want to learn; they want to know me."

At 4:30 A.M., predictably, a rooster began crowing. Soon crows sounded from almost every surrounding concession. The volunteers slept away, the author not so much. After an exhilarating bucket shower at first light, I joined Collin, Dutch, Lauren, and Emily in accompanying Alex to work—a four-minute walk down a dirt road. Some students milled about in the field adjacent to the school, buying simple breakfast foods from the motherly vendors who served the children in their equivalent to an American school cafeteria. Their beignets reminded me of ones I'd had in New Orleans, minus the powdered sugar. As Alex had predicted the previous night, students called out in English: "Good morning, teacher!" Alex responded in a particularly enunciated manner, "Good morning, how are you doing?" He explained the exaggerated pronunciation helped the students learn English, which for many was a third, fourth, or sixth language. Most spoke French, along with an assortment of local dialects.

In contrast to Paul Oxborrow's thatched Lokossa classroom, Alex conducted class in a concrete building with a real blackboard—no painted plywood. We sat among the students at small wooden tables. The students clearly enjoyed watching Collin and me cram ourselves into the tiny desks.

Alex walked in, diverting their attention. A booming "Good morning, teacher," welcomed him to the room. Soon, he began working with the students to pronounce *th*, not a natural sound in their native languages. Since it was a Thursday, the lesson fit well. Some questions elicited loud responses from the entire class. Alex aimed others at individuals: "Who can tell me . . . ?" Even if they weren't sure of the answer, students battled with one another to be called upon. Hands flew upward and waved furiously with each of the teacher's questions. He possessed tremendous presence, and the other Peace Corps volunteers marveled at his ability to engage the students and maintain their focus. For his three months of experience, Alex taught the course like a veteran.

When the time came for us to leave, our crew tried to exit the classroom discreetly, but captured the attention of every student. Caught, we turned in the doorway to face a sea of gleaming eyes and white smiles.

"What do we say, class?" asked Alex.

"Good-bye," they thundered happily in unison.

We smiled and waved, then left Alex to his work and his students to their learning. As we walked across the dusty schoolyard, I fell behind and began taking photographs with the camera I'd borrowed from my father. Children at recess immediately responded to the camera with waves, jumps, and acrobatics. I marveled at their joy. From my point of view, their circumstances did not warrant such optimism, but their spirit reminded me that my perspective as an American doesn't always matter and isn't always right.

I saw these Peace Corps volunteers giving new hope to the children and adults of Lokossa, Kandi, Sieninede, and Gougonou, and I knew the scene was replicated through Africa and wherever the Peace Corps sends its volunteers. They are not alone in their work, however, and other organizations share their mission. One group in particular had been working to kindle hope in Benin's young people since 1932, half a century before Africa became a popular destination for aid groups.

Their names were Joel, Christian, and Mathias, and I met them in Cotonou. Their dark skin contrasted sharply with the light khaki of their uniform shirts, and each wore a perfectly tied striped neckerchief. Tourists who'd only seen local youth hawking goods in the streets turned to watch the three well-dressed young men walk smartly onto the riverside deck of Hotel du Lac. They were Scouts—pronounced "Scoots" in French—and members of Scoutisme Beninois. Meeting them helped me understand something important about Scouting. I'd certainly known that the Movement flourished in 156 countries. I'd heard the phrase "international brotherhood" bandied about. My understanding existed only at an academic level, however. My own experiences in the Boy Scouts of America, I was fairly certain, had little to do with boys an ocean away in the developing nations of West Africa.

But then I shook hands with Joel, Christian, and Mathias. When they spoke about Scouting, their perspectives mirrored responses I'd heard many times over from American boys. They were brother Scouts; we believed in the same ideals. We clearly respected each other, even though we came from different worlds. The connection I felt—and the one they seemed to feel in return—gave me a real appreciation of the Scouting Movement, one I hadn't had until that moment. I realized what Baden-Powell's dream had achieved. I understood what he meant when he said, "The uniform makes for brotherhood, since when universally adopted it covers up all differences of class and country."

The boys were in their young teens, and one already led a group of younger Scouts—a position denoted by his blue and yellow striped neckerchief. When I asked about their favorite aspect of the program, Joel answered, "Being outside," while Mathias responded, "The variety. We study so many different subjects and work on projects of all types." Among their projects were AIDS awareness, malaria prevention, and health programs conducted in conjunction with the United Nations. They fought against poverty through microfinance ventures and career training. Scouts in Benin—some 6,500 young men and young women—have wisely used their infrastructure to deliver varied programs throughout the country to benefit youth and communities overall. I was impressed with how these Scouts responded to their country's needs and forged partnerships with larger organizations to accomplish their mission of service.

When I asked the Scouts if they planned to remain involved after they reached the age of eighteen, they replied like Alex's students: "Yes, sir!" I felt good about Benin's—and Scouting's—future.

As the Scouts who would shape that future left, I turned to Jeremie Houssou, Commissionnaire Général, Scoutisme Beninois, who had made the introductions. "Do you think they'll stay involved?" I asked.

"If they can find jobs, yes," he replied. Even he was a volunteer, spending his days working with Population Services International, a nonprofit firm promoting public health in the developing world. "It's hard to volunteer time without having money and a job, and that challenges many adults. In Benin, when Scouts turn eighteen, they join our fourth tier. This is made for Scouts age eighteen to thirty who serve as leaders. Just like in your country, we always need leaders."

He paused, then smiled. Like a true Scouting organizer, he asked, "Now who is the Eagle Scout in Gogounou? We need good leaders in our program there." I revealed Alex's identity, sure that a partnership between an Eagle Scout Peace Corps volunteer and Scoutisme Beninois would lead to good things.

When Monsieur Houssou and I parted, I stood on the hotel's deck with Lauren, believing Benin's Scouts were in the hands of someone who lived the ideals of Scouting. I was also encouraged that the young men involved in Scoutisme Beninois were carrying on Scouting's legacy in their nation, serving others in community after community. Beyond them, twenty-eight million of their brother and sister Scouts were doing the same, all the world over. It was an overwhelming example of the vast potential of the Scouting Movement.

There were no air traffic delays at Cotonou's airport on the evening I departed. In fact, there were no other flights that night at all. My midnight plane thundered down the runway and soon lifted me over vast, darkened swaths of Benin where the electricity slept along with villagers. Three hundred miles into the flight north, I looked down onto what I suspected were the plains of Pendjari National Park, where several days prior I'd had one of the trip's many unforgettable experiences. I came face-to-face with a full-grown male elephant, his ivory tusks nearly as long as I am tall. We stood with just thirty feet of grassland and shrubs between us. We were in the wild, *his* wild, not a zoo. Nothing separated us as we faced off and looked deeply into each other's eyes, not in a threatening manner, but each studying the other. No barriers stood between us; I had stepped beyond any boundaries I'd previously known.

Flying over those plains where the elephants roamed, I realized how I'd truly stepped outside normal limits—both personal, and anything related to animal safety that the *Boy Scout Handbook* contained. Crossing boundaries leads either to trouble or broader horizons, and I considered my new world. I felt like a sailor who climbed from the deck of a Clipper ship, up its endless web of rigging to the crow's nest. The sea—the world—spread out, almost limitless, before me.

Over the preceding months, I'd seen how Eagles had carried their values outside the United States—Vince and Vance in Afghanistan, Matt in China, Eric in Australia, SEALs in a host of undisclosed locations I'll never know. Clearly, our generation is no longer held back by national borders. In another sense, we reject limits on our aspirations. We're willing to pursue the dreams in which we believe, as nontraditional as they may be. The volunteers I met in Africa had turned down a host of other opportunities. I can only imagine my parents' reaction if I'd decided to join the Peace Corps after spending four years, and a considerable amount of tuition dollars, in college.

But while I'd seen, heard, and experienced their stories over the past months, I'd somehow missed two things. Until I began reflecting on my days in Africa as I flew home from Benin, I didn't realize, truly, what inspired these Eagles, and perhaps what was inspiring me. Nor did I understand how much they affected the lives of others in foreign lands. It took me venturing into a world as remote and foreign as Africa, and stepping outside my *own* boundaries, to comprehend what it means to carry our values to other places and people. I had now reached beyond old limits. I'd set foot on continents I'd never imagined visiting, and met people whose situations and perspectives I'd previously neither known nor considered. Once you take those steps, you can't cross back. You realize the world's size. You grow to understand new people, with their own concerns, ways, and aspirations. You witness their struggles and their victories firsthand. You see what they're accomplishing and how others, like these Eagle Scouts, are helping. You'll always be different because your concept of potential and purpose changes forever.

The plane continued north across the vast Sahara and I fell asleep to the static rumble of the plane's engines. I had breakfast in Paris the next morning, then dinner with my parents in Atlanta, less than twenty-four hours after I'd been enjoying a preflight meal with a family of Canadian expatriates in Cotonou. The days had blurred; had it even happened? Had I really just been in a third-world country, where running water and electricity were luxuries and where simply reaching the age of twenty often qualifies as success?

I spent a restless weekend at home recovering with my family; I knew a long trail lay ahead, and the adventure of the road called. Africa had changed me. Being immersed in such a different culture, where my viewpoint was clearly not predominant and often not right, made me realize how much the world had to teach me. I also saw how easily personal connections can grow across cultures; everyone in Benin held their own lesson for me if I could take time to listen. Beyond Benin, Scouts and people throughout the world held their own lessons. That was as challenging and daunting as it was exciting and alluring. My love for discovery was rekindled, and the spirit of this adventure consumed me. The expanse and reach of the Scouting Movement and the lessons my generation held about purpose moved me forward. I needed to see more, understand the needs of our country and our world, and discover how we answered them. I knew then that this journey had no boundaries.

PURPLE HEARTS

One Monday, I accepted an invitation to a local Rotary Club lunch. After negotiating the buffet line, I sat at my table and then noticed two soldiers in uniform near the head table. I figured a member had brought them to add some patriotic flair to the lunch. I imagined a round of cheering would come at some point when the president recognized the servicemen. When that time came, however, one of the soldiers—his dark beret fixed smartly and green uniform pressed immaculately—rose and carried himself on crutches up a ramp and onto the stage. His right leg was missing. I don't remember any applause—although there may well have been some. Like most others in the room, I sat transfixed. I only heard the soft thump of his crutches against the carpeted ramp.

Along with everyone else, I sat silently for the ensuing fifteen minutes as the young specialist told us about the conflict in Iraq—not about the ever-complicated politics or always-debated progress, but about the men who fought there; who fought for each other and did their best in a challenging situation. Then he talked about coming home without his leg and being treated at Walter Reed Army Medical Center. He spoke about the battles he already faced and those he'll continue fighting throughout his life.

We don't often consider this side of war. Many of us don't frequently see, let alone know, veterans who served in Iraq or Afghanistan and received severe wounds in battle, although there are more than thirty thousand of them so far. News stories on the wounded are relatively few; sadly talking heads debating policy receive far more attention. Sometimes it feels easier that way, but we need to understand.

The specialist at the podium that day, resting on his crutches, represented far too many other wounded soldiers. He represented our armed services and he represented my generation. I never learned if he earned Eagle, but I knew that many of his compatriots who passed through Walter Reed had. And I knew that I had to meet them.

A cloudless sky greeted me when I stepped off a Red Line train onto the outdoor platform at the Takoma Metro station in northwest Washington, D.C. I walked several blocks, crossing a schoolyard, before I reached the gates of Walter Reed Army Medical Center. Major Steve Gventer waited for me just inside. Wearing camouflage fatigues, the army's standard beret, and a pair of nonstandard cavalry boots, he looked every bit an imposing solider. He welcomed me with a grin as broad as his shoulders.

After clearing security, we made our way through the century-old campus, spotted with both old brick buildings and modern concrete and glass facilities. Since 1909, the hospital has cared for sick and wounded soldiers and now serves thousands of military personnel and veterans. Walter Reed has become the epicenter of "warrior care," providing treatment to the army's wounded and support to their families. Steve had arrived several months earlier, he explained as we made our way across the campus, the winter sun keeping us moderately warm. The army needed an experienced commander for Able Troop, Warrior Transition Brigade—those recovering from combat wounds. The army knew Steve had been wounded twice and had a unique ability to relate to soldiers. He'd been dragged, wounded, off a Baghdad street by his soldiers, and he had dragged his own soldiers off the streets, as well. He'd been where they were. At Walter Reed, he would help wounded veterans transition back to active duty or, in other cases, to very different lives as civilians. "Some guys come here and can transition back to active duty fairly quickly," he said. "Others will never be able to serve on the front lines again. Their lives are totally turned upside down by their wounds. They have to learn to function again. I try to make it easier for all of them."

On the way to meet two other Eagle Scouts, I learned more about this Scout from Grapevine, Texas. After graduating from Baylor University and teaching and coaching high school students, he had joined what seemed like the family business. His father was a lieutenant colonel, his brother an army captain, and his sister a West Point graduate. As a teacher, he had missed the sense of camaraderie and teamwork he felt in Scouting and saw joining the army as a way to reclaim that spirit. He submitted his Officer Candidate School application and shortly thereafter, received his commission.

Like most active army personnel of the twenty-first century, a deployment to Iraq loomed in Steve's future. He served two tours, receiving two Purple Hearts for taking wounds in the line of duty. His first came from action on August 28, 2004. A captain at that time, he commanded a company of soldiers in the 1st Cavalry Division, and their unit had just moved into Sadr City, Iraq. Though only a seven-by-ten kilometer rectangle, Sadr City houses nearly one-tenth of the Iraqi population. Steve noted that Saddam Hussein had built Sadr City as a Shiite slum. It was laid out as a grid, but with wide roads that were useful in quelling riots with armored battalions. Planners designed the area for three hundred thousand to four hundred thousand people; by 2004, it housed more than two million. Steve described it as "just humanity on top of humanity." Insurgents still controlled much of the area at that time, and the army planned to stabilize the city so its citizens could vote in upcoming elections.

"On the morning of August twenty-eighth," Steve explained, "Bravo Company took pretty good contact and we—Charlie Company—relieved them and started catching grenades off rooftops and RPGs—rocket-propelled grenades—from the alleyways. I've got three platoons and sixteen Humvees. We went in with Red—first platoon, White—second platoon, and Blue—third platoon. Red platoon to the left, White to the center, Blue to the right. My medics and snipers were behind us, back-securing our position. I went out with the patrols and we were really getting pounded from the rooftops and I got out and on the ground. We knew where we were, but we didn't have visuals. You know that a platoon is two rows over, but you can't see them and they can't see you. The tanks were on the main roads but couldn't get into the alleys where we were. Tanks were taking hits from RPGs like crazy. We locked down the entire block where we were. I put second and first platoons on either side of a row, and we went down the two alleys and systematically cleared the block and pushed out the insurgents. You go in one stairwell, go up, and cross over. We're catching rounds from the other side of the street this whole time. We finally got to the other end of the block, just unbelievable amounts of RPGs hitting, but no wounds for us. Insurgents were setting tires on fire everywhere and doing anything else they could to create distractions."

The platoon finished the job and secured the block. Steve requested permission to move north, but was denied. Then insurgents began firing RPGs from a school down the road. Blue Platoon returned fire. Steve ducked behind his Humvee to make a radio call and an insurgent popped up to his north and fired a burst from his AK-47. The bullets stitched across the truck's hood. Steve dropped and moved right toward a wall. Too late, he discovered the wall was a chain-link fence covered with ivy. It offered no protection. Steve moved back, but came into another insurgent's field of view. He fired and Steve saw everything in slow motion: the muzzle flash, himself rolling for cover, concrete exploding in bursts toward him. He caught a round squarely in his left leg.

Steve stumbled back to his Humvee and bandaged the wound. It continued bleeding, but he told nobody, except the staff sergeant at the truck. Knowing he'd have to disrupt the operation to pull himself out of the engagement, he stayed and directed his platoons for the next five hours. "I didn't want a battalion commander to come check on me and distract everyone from the objective," he explained about his decision to keep quiet and not leave. "It was my wound anyway. I was the one who was slow in this case. Also, my fifty soldiers were out there fighting. I wasn't going to leave them and if I'd left, I'd have taken at least three Humvees with me and Alpha Company wouldn't have had anybody covering their flank and keeping insurgents from hitting them with RPGs—that was my company's mission. I would have jeopardized Alpha Company and two of my own platoons. I didn't need to see a doc that badly, so I just bandaged it up and stayed for the fight.

"That was Purple Heart number one. It's really not very glamorous. I should have been smarter and quicker. I'll tell you about the other some other time, the one that knocked me off the front lines and left more pieces of shrapnel in me than I want to think about. But now, you'll meet some guys who've really been through a lot. They're the ones you came to see."

By that time, we had arrived at a modern building that seemed to serve simultaneously as a medical office building, a dormitory, and an activity center. Two floors up, we met sergeants Brent Matchison and Bruce Dunlap. Steve introduced both by their last names, so that's what I called them. Matchison was dressed in his fatigues, beret in hand. He wore glasses and a close-cropped haircut. Dunlap wore jeans and a Washington Nationals sweatshirt. He would leave for his home in Kansas that afternoon. In the past two months, a new medicine had added forty pounds to his formerly athletic frame, but he hoped to be done with treatment and back to his old build soon. As he would tell me, he had a marathon to run.

We walked to Steve's corner office, which looked out over the park-like campus and at the stately administration building. "The reason I took this office is that with the right soldiers, I could defend here a long time," he said jokingly, though I'm sure he could. In fact, I think this self-assured Texan would relish the chance to don his black cavalry hat and defend the office by himself, hand-to-hand. I have no doubt that he would hold the line.

The four of us deposited ourselves onto the chairs and couches arrayed in the office, and I soon learned that both Steve and Matchison were sons of Scoutmasters. "My father led my troop and my Venturing crew," Matchison explained. "I'll do that for our kids later on in life. It never leaves you; it's always there. After I earned Eagle, I figured the army and Scouts have the same set of ideals to live by and the same sense of values, and I wanted to keep going at it like that."

"I came from a single-parent home," Dunlap said. "Scouting was my family and I moved around quite a bit. Scouting gave me stability. I was also shy and it gave me confidence, gave me more confidence than I got anywhere in my life. We went to Philmont, and I was a member of Mic-O-Say in Missouri." The Tribe of Mic-O-Say, as I'd learned several years ago from 1930s inductee Ken Rook, is a secretive Scouting honor society built around Native American folklore. The tribe still regularly inducts Scouts from two Missouri councils, bestowing them with ceremonial eagle claws as they advance in rank.

"And I also earned thirty-six merit badges," Dunlap added.

"Impressive," I said. "I think I squeaked by with twenty-two."

"I got twenty-one," Matchison said. "That was all you needed! But Eagle is a title you can always wear no matter what you do. I took a sense of accomplishment, a sense of belonging. I know it's always going to be there and be something I can live by. It also makes you aware of your community and nation on a different level. Eventually, it makes you aware of the world. Of course in our case, Iraq helped with that as well."

"Tell us your story," Steve suggested from his position on the couch. Matchison edged forward and began.

"We were in the Anbar province," he recounted, "in the city of Ramadi, with the First Brigade, Thirty-second Regiment, First Armored Division. It was one of the worst cities in Iraq and we were invading it." Matchison's platoon established a control point in the city's center, where they were exposed to attacks from all sides. They built a guard tower on top of their building, and soldiers alternated four to six hour shifts each day. Nobody looked forward to guard duty. On December 6, 2006, a pair of snipers ambushed the sentinel. A flash of light hit his face from one location, followed by a sniper's bullet from another location. Twenty minutes later, the young North Carolina sergeant was dead. Three days later, the same sniper found Sergeant Matchison with a .762 caliber bullet from a Dragnuov rifle.

"The initial blow is not even comparable to getting hit in the head with a hammer," Matchison explained. "It was so much more, it can't be described. There's the initial shock of 'This can't be.' Then, 'Snap!' You're out."

Fortunately, the bullet had traveled through two sandbag walls, a pair of two-by-four beams, and Matchison's Kevlar helmet. The sniper had seen Matchison's shoulder and estimated where his head would be behind the guard tower's walls. He guessed well. The bullet lodged in Matchison's forehead at his right eyebrow. "It was that close to taking out my eye," he said, indicating an inch distance with his fingertips. I couldn't believe he'd lived. And his story wasn't over.

"That was Purple Heart number one," he noted. "As they were evacuating me, we took contact from the west and we got ambushed again. We were getting shots from AKs while they're evacuating me. My squad leader picks me up and says, 'Okay, let's get you out of here.' Then, *pop!* He yells, 'You just got shot in the hand!' Believe me, I already knew."

He stuck out his hand. "You can see where it scraped along my finger, then went in right where it's webbed," he explained. "Then it exploded out right here." Shattered bullet and bone had left Matchison's hand littered with small scars.

He withdrew his hand, and smiled. "Then I got hit a third time by an IED on the way back to the base," he related. "Everyone thought I was generally terrible luck!"

"You probably are, Matchison," Steve chided, before becoming more serious. "But everyone here, even though we may not have had as good luck as others, we all have something to be thankful for. We all know people who didn't make it back at all. We all have friends across the Potomac buried in Arlington National Cemetery."

"I was almost one of them," said Dunlap. "I call December 10, 2006, my 'alive day.' It's my second birthday because I was clinically dead. I had no pulse, no heartbeat. I was dead.

"It was around nine o'clock at night," he remembered. "And we were looking for IEDs and talking about what we were going to do at home. I planned to drive to eight different cities in eight days to see eight different baseball games. Then all of a sudden, I heard an explosion and I didn't know who was hit. Then I looked down and I'm on fire! They put fuel in these IEDs sometimes and it shoots flames out. I'm calling out, 'Hey, I'm on fire!' I couldn't hear anybody. There's smoke, chaos. I started laughing hysterically. 'I'm on fire, this is pretty funny, I'm on fire!' I'm out of my mind. I remember blacking out laughing. I couldn't move. I couldn't hear anybody, thought everyone else was dead. I thought okay, 'I'll see you guys in a minute on the other side.' This was all split-second thinking. I woke up. I was on the road and I heard a sergeant say, 'He's pretty messed up.'

"Oh, I guess that's me," he remembered thinking.

When I met Dunlap, I noticed he walked slowly, but I hadn't seen any other signs of injury. Then he lifted his left sleeve, revealing a gouge in his arm. "I had my arm broken here," he said simply. "A metal rod is holding it together." He moved to his left hand. "Another metal rod is holding these two fingers together. This finger was reconnected. I'm missing the tip of my left thumb." Then his right hand. "This finger was reattached, I'm missing the tip of my ring finger, this knuckle is split in half, and the end of this finger was reattached."

He then showed me his legs, which had faithfully carried him through many races as he competed as a collegiate runner. "My left leg had a compound fracture," he noted. "Totally out of my skin. I had seven bolts screwed into my leg to make an X-fix so it can grow and my legs will be the same length again. I'm missing part of my calf on the back. My right leg was the real problem. My heel was shattered, I have a hole in my foot. My kneecap was completely fractured. I have nerve damage from the knee down to the toes; if I touch the middle of my shin, I can feel it down to my toes. It's like touching the whole leg at once."

Matchison and Steve knew that condition well. Both had nerve damage in their arms.

When Dunlap first arrived at Walter Reed, his functions were limited to breathing and chewing. The explosion had devastated his body. His family arrived from Kansas to help him recover and he still remembers his aunt and sister walking into his room for the first time. His wounds shocked them; they had no idea how to respond.

"I said, 'Give me a hug,' " remembered Dunlap.

His family hesitated.

"No," Dunlap had said emphatically, "Give me a hug! I'm not dying."

After he recalled his first days at Walter Reed, where he first had to accept his new circumstances, he noted how the realities facing others were often far more traumatic.

"At least I'm not married with kids," he confided. "I couldn't imagine having kids and a wife and having them go through this. But plenty of guys here do."

Dunlap had the most severe combat wounds I'd seen in person, and his thirteen months at Walter Reed had moved him significantly toward recovery, but he still had many proverbial miles to travel. I couldn't help admire his spirit. Dunlap didn't know how to quit. Like me, he was an Eagle Scout and a runner; a compulsive goal-setter who wouldn't stop until he'd reached his next target. As soon as he could move, and against doctor's orders, he began working to get stronger. He started with hand exercises, then added simple leg lifts. Before long he was putting muscle back on his arms and legs. "I was always busy in my bed," he said, "so when I was strong enough to get out, my muscles would support me walking. That's why I could walk so quickly.

"Several months afterward, I wasn't walking completely yet," he said, "but I did a soldiers' ride from Gettysburg to D.C.—a hundred and ten miles. I still had my X-Fix on and I rode a tandem bike with a marine. In June, I did a half marathon on a bike. Several months ago, I completed the Marine Corps Marathon here in D.C. with a hand-crank bike. This year, I want to run it."

"When you first arrived, did you think you'd ever walk again, let alone run?" I asked, trying to imagine how I would have felt, particularly as a runner, coming to and learning that both of my legs had been torn apart.

"I ran in college and I'm athletic, but I didn't know for sure," he answered. "When I was laying there for a month and couldn't do anything, I had no idea. Once I started walking, I knew my therapist and family would get me back to that point. In fact, I began walking before I had clearance—Scouting, you know what you can do. I'd walk in my room from bed to dresser, things like that. When it was time for me to officially walk, I went from wheelchair to crutches in just three days."

"Unfortunately," said Steve, taking command of the conversation, "getting the physical problems fixed doesn't equate to recovery." He explained that both Matchison and Dunlap had symptoms of traumatic brain injury, TBI. A bullet's impact or the concussion from a roadside bomb are so powerful that they literally rattle your brain. The shock waves can jostle the front lobes of a soldier's brain and loosen the connecting fibers. That leads to TBI. Soldiers can recover from it, but its effects differ from case to case, some experience headaches, loss of memory, and insomnia. With more veterans returning home having experienced attacks, TBI has become a larger problem for the military and public. Often soldiers find little understanding.

Dunlap and Matchison had listened quietly, almost without expression or reaction, as Steve explained their condition and prognosis. When Steve finished, Dunlap spoke up. "Last night I slept three or four hours," he said. "I get headaches when I work out; big headaches when I get stressed."

"I have a broken sleep cycle," Matchison added. "I'll get two hours here, four hours there. It's just a broken cycle and that hurts your recovery. You really need sleep."

"Couple TBI with post-traumatic stress disorder and you're adding dreams to it, depression, or other symptoms," Steve explained. "It can be very difficult for soldiers to recover from. It's frustrating. Mentally, you know you could do things before. You don't know why you can't sleep. Everybody comes back from Iraq with some form of PTSD; it's how you cope with some of those symptoms that determines how you survive day in and day out."

Matchison emphasized that it's especially difficult for soldiers who deploy more than twice. Today, that's most soldiers and average deployments last fifteen months. Many servicemen and -women can cope with reality and symptoms while they're in the military, but once they leave, real problems begin to surface. Often families and relationships suffer severely. "Everybody has it," Matchison added. "Everybody who has been over there has seen something or gone through something they'll never forget. One of my guys died and I was right there. Three days later I got shot in the head. I wondered why I lived and he didn't. I still wonder."

"It's all so random," Steve confirmed. "The second time I got wounded, eight of us got hit; others didn't. Who knows why? We were in Sadr City again and had come around a corner—this is about three A.M. We dismounted and then from a mosque fifty meters away across the street came a huge *pop*, and a flash and a fireball. To see an RPG at night is amazing. It looks like a meteor coming at you. There's a fiery sparkling effect behind it, and the warhead is dead black. It looks like a solar eclipse.

"I yelled, 'Down! RPG!' Everybody ducked and the RPG hit the wall behind us at eight feet; sprayed shrapnel everywhere. We had eight wounded. I dove to the right and when I did, my left side was exposed." He showed me a pair of scars on his side and an assortment of others scattered about his torso. "I've got a bag full of metal from these two holes. I still have three pieces right here above my waist," he said, pointing to his lower back.

"But as that happened, I hit the ground and laid there and briefly wasn't sure what had just happened—I'm going, 'Where am I?' Dust everywhere, unbelievable amounts. At this point, I start hearing gunfire. Things are pinging and tracers are flying above the street. I'm lying on the ground, looking up and thinking, 'Get up, get up, get up,' and not being able to get up. You're stunned. I remember trying to get up and my right arm wouldn't work and so I rolled to my left and started yelling, 'Get out of the alleyway! Get out, get out, get out!' My sergeant major is lying next to me, we're trying to get up. My driver is lying on the ground screaming, and the sergeant grabs him by the shoulder. I couldn't use my right arm, so I used my left arm and grabbed him by the other shoulder and dragged him out of the street. The sergeant and others began returning fire. My colonel was up against the wall, wounded. Other guys were down."

Steve called in help and eventually several trucks arrived. The executive officer (XO)—who was second in command—and first sergeant walked with Steve to gather the wounded and load them into the waiting trucks. Steve painfully lifted the colonel on his left shoulder and with the XO's help, put him in a truck. Red platoon and White platoon were still securing the area; Steve took his Blue platoon and got out. The one escape route took them past the mosque from which the RPG had come, so he ordered his gunners to lay down a carpet of fire toward the insurgents' location until the convoy cleared the danger. Once they were speeding safely toward the nearest aid station, a gunner in Steve's truck looked down and asked, "Sir, are you okay?"

"I'm ticked," Steve fumed.

"You wounded?"

"I took some shrapnel."

"Raise your right arm," the gunner said.

"I can't," Steve answered. Despite his now habitual tendency to ignore wounds, he had taken a serious hit.

"We hauled tail back to our base and got out of there," he recalled. "Everyone made it." They made it because of Steve, who never lost control of his unit. Amid the chaos, he stepped into the void left by his wounded colonel, assembled his men, and organized their escape. Thousands of miles removed from the battlegrounds of the Middle East, Steve still exuded the confidence and presence of a leader, the type of man soldiers would follow into battle.

At this point, Steve turned the conversation to Scouting. He recalled getting intentionally lost in the Pecos Wilderness in New Mexico while backpacking with Troop 700. He camped under the stars before finding the troop the next day. Dunlap recalled his experiences as a Scout in Missouri, under the leadership of Scoutmaster Bob Jones. Matchison, the youngest Eagle in the room, talked about his time with Venturing Crew 6717 in Kentucky, where he earned Eagle in 2002.

"We all have Scouting in common," Steve observed. "We learned how to build those bonds early on. We learned to achieve things and set goals and all of us continue to strive. You're taking a journey and writing a book," he said to me, then continued. "Matchison wants to RTD [return to duty]. Dunlap would RTD if he could. We'd all stay with our units if we could. We're not guys who ever allow a tough road to slow us down. Being an Eagle Scout? Not easy. It takes a lot of commitment and a lot of time. It takes getting twenty-one merit badges, going to meetings, going on camping trips, doing a project. Becoming a sergeant, getting your degree, being accepted to OCS [Officer Candidate School], those are goals you set and continuously pursue and they're based on foundations we built as kids, and those foundations are partially from being Eagle Scouts, being Boy Scouts. Every kid who doesn't make Eagle may still have gotten a ton out of Scouting. They may just have not gotten an Eagle medal pinned on their chest and had a court of honor, but they still gained an immense amount of value from being part of a team and part of a goal-oriented system where they had to be 'physically strong, mentally awake, and morally straight.' "

"That's how boys become men," Dunlap said. "There are still a lot of people in our age group who aren't men. Just because you're eighteen, that doesn't make you a man. To be a man, that's taking care of your responsibility. That's being morally straight, physically fit. Our bodies are temples and therefore if you're not taking care of yourself, you're not a man. If you have kids, you take care of them. You're part of a team, you're a team player. I think Scouting is a rite of passage. Scouting is an avenue to becoming a better person, a better man.

"It teaches you discipline, and when I was in my bed at first, I couldn't do anything for myself, but like I said earlier, as soon as I was able to do anything, I did it. I did physical therapy without the therapist there. I didn't feel sorry for myself. I'm twenty-eight years old. I shouldn't be in a hospital bed not walking. I had too much that I wanted to do and that was motivating. I plan to get active in my old Scout troop again when I move back home: go to Monday night meetings, go on campouts again, go back and hike Philmont. I need to get involved in something that'll help me keep my discipline."

"I think we all want to give back at some point," added Steve, "because Scouts did set a foundation for each of us. As long as you're participating and as long as there is positive leadership, it's tremendous. There's very few people who are involved in Scouting that aren't there to help kids gain qualities that are good qualities for our society. Bottom line, it's all those things in the Scout Law: 'Trustworthy, loyal, helpful, friendly, courteous, kind, obedient, cheerful, thrifty, brave, clean, and reverent.' And the Scout Oath: 'On my honor, I will do my best to do my duty to God and my country and to obey the Scout Law; to help other people at all times; to keep myself physically strong, mentally awake, and morally straight.'

"I'm thirty-something now but I still remember it like it was yesterday. I can't say the Gettysburg Address, I can do Sonnet 116 from Shakespeare about halfway through—there are so many things that I can't remember now that I knew cold when I was younger. Scouting's creeds? Those I know backward and forward and I always will.

"As soldiers, we raise our right hand and swear an oath to defend the Constitution of the United States against all enemies foreign and domestic. That means everything to us. But the Scout Oath and Scout Law aren't far behind. They're about understanding a commitment to something bigger than yourself. They're about understanding that you are part of a team and you are part of someone else's mission to be better at whatever it is. It's that foundation that each of us has, and millions of other people who've gone through Scouting have that as a baseline. You see people from all walks of life who've succeeded and can trace that back to being Scouts or Eagle Scouts. Everything is based on the fact that I can do better and I can be better and there is more ahead if I keep on working hard."

"It took me more than five years to get my Eagle," Matchison added, not to be left out. "But by that time, you've accepted this foundation in your life. Eagle Scout is one of the foundations in your life and by the time you get Eagle, you know your character. I've never changed my ways since then and I like it that way. Those basic fundamentals: physical, mental, moral. They're always going to be there."

"It's service, too," said Dunlap. "And this is about the military as well as Scouting. I get so much more respect from my family because they know that I did my part. I stepped up to the call just like they did. I think that's something our generation needs. We've become such an individual society that I think people in our generation need to step up and, like JFK said, 'Ask not what your country can do for you; ask what you can do for your country.' I think that's what we need to do."

President John F. Kennedy's words live inside these Eagle Scouts, just as an eternal flame still burns at his tomb in Arlington National Cemetery. Shortly after leaving Walter Reed, I stood looking at the stones above President Kennedy's final resting place. I watched the small flame dance and flicker, but never die. Looking behind me, over Washington, D.C., I thought about how Eagles of my generation were living out the ideals on which the founders established our republic and its capital. I reflected on how far we'd carried these ideals beyond our shores. I thought about how we had answered President Kennedy's call, even though none of us was born when he issued his famous charge from the snow-covered Capitol steps in his 1961 inaugural address.

I read another line from the young president's 1961 address, etched forever at the gravesite: "The torch has been passed to a new generation of Americans . . ." He spoke of our parents' and grandparents' generations. Now that torch was passing to our generation. Now it was our turn to lead and to serve. Standing in Arlington, I found it easy to view President Kennedy's call with a military perspective. Then I remembered that it was this World War II veteran who had founded the Peace Corps, envisioning one hundred thousand American youth serving overseas, none carrying a weapon. His call for service and sacrifice clearly went out to everyone and, I think, has echoed into this new century and resonated with this rising generation. As I discovered in Benin and Washington, our generation stood ready to carry that light.

While many of our generation make great sacrifices, few offer sacrifices greater than those who, as Abraham Lincoln said, "gave the last full measure of devotion." Three men who gave that measure lay buried at Arlington Cemetery's Tomb of the Unknowns, a short walk from President Kennedy's gravesite. The unknown soldiers, one from World War I, one from World War II, and one from Korea, bear constant witness to the eternal and precise regimen of the Tomb Guard sentinels. Throughout the year, during all hours and all conditions, an elite honor guard paces twenty-one steps back and forth before the tomb. The soldiers dress impeccably in dark blue uniforms with white gloves. Their precisely honed walk and ceremonial drill mesmerize crowds. Several Eagle Scouts have served in their ranks.

Near the Tomb and sitting on a bench under towering oaks, leafless in winter, I met captains Paul de Leon and Matt Deurmeier, members of the Old Guard Regiment, the unit responsible for Arlington Cemetery. The captains graduated one year apart at the U.S. Military Academy, 2003 and 2004 respectively, and had each served a tour of duty in Iraq. One of Paul's classmates, Leonard Cowherd, never returned. "That's part of the reason I came here," Paul said. "I saw him buried here and saw the honors they gave him. I decided to come here and be part of that." Paul's eyes grew misty. He looked away.

Along with other members of the army's prestigious 3rd Infantry Old Guard Regiment, Paul and Matt help to honor the men and women laid to rest in Arlington. They participate in funerals and memorial services and render final honors to deceased soldiers. The army chose them carefully for this assignment and they take their mission seriously. Upon meeting them, I felt they were somehow part of Arlington and, in turn, this special place had become part of them. They had a quiet reverence about them. They seemed to belong here.

We stood together as the guard changed at the Tomb, a precisely executed pageant of salutes, turns, and synchronized steps remarkable in its perfection and solemnity. Each solider looked resplendent in his dress blue coat and lighter blue pants. Once a new sentinel had taken up his twenty-one-pace march, we followed the relieved guard below the Tomb to the quarters of the Tomb sentinels, a place very few outside the 3rd Regiment ever see. It was certainly a doorway I never imagined entering. In fact, part of me hesitated to enter, wanting to preserve for myself the unblemished image of the sentinels: stoic expressions, eyes hidden behind dark aviator sunglasses, a mysterious anonymity and aloofness. By this time in my journey, however, I'd realized that my trips seem to reveal personal sides of just about everyone, so enter I did.

Inside, I found several young men, hair exceptionally close-cropped, nearly shaved on the sides. I guessed they were all in their early twenties. Their winter uniforms, and in some cases their casual clothes, did not hide their obvious top physical condition. Every hour or half-hour, depending on the season, a fresh soldier would relieve the current watch. They marched in all weather and guarded the Tomb twenty-four hours a day. Two mirrors dominated the entrance area of their living quarters, and sentinels spend hours before them, perfecting their attire and routines. Photographs charting the Tomb's history covered the remaining wall space, and I soon leaned how well each sentinel knew the history of Arlington and the Tomb. These soldiers undergo an exhaustive application process, proving their military record, knowledge of American history, and devotion to the Unknowns. They must recite, verbatim, seven pages of Arlington history. If they dishonor their badge, whether on duty or years later, their name is expunged from the wall that lists each sentinel. During the hours they spend honoring our unknown soldiers—many at night with no audience—they develop emotional relationships with the Unknowns. The soldiers' respect for the deceased servicemen, and their genuine desire to honor them, impressed me deeply.

"I'm almost surprised *all* the sentinels aren't Eagle Scouts," Matt reflected when we left, only half joking. "They certainly share similar traits. Being an Eagle Scout sets the pace for how you conduct yourself in whatever job you have, wherever your life takes you, wherever you are in the world. Knowing that first and foremost you're an Eagle Scout, you know these are the values you started with and held. You may not know it at the time, but those are the values that make you the person you eventually become down the road."

Paul nodded in agreement, then said, "Service is one of those values, and that resonated throughout my career; a willingness to serve not just country, but people in general. That's an important lesson to carry on, especially in our generation."

"I think our generation has gone through a lot in the past ten years on the global stage," Matt said. "How we react to that and how we conduct ourselves during this time and how we come out in the end says a lot about who we are as a society or as a person. Eagle Scouts may come to the forefront to take charge. Others may see Eagle Scouts as a beacon: this is who we need to look to in order to get us through these times."

"I also feel like we have to be aware and informed," Paul added. "Know what's right to do and go with whatever your values are; but the key right now is being well-informed individuals. In Iraq, that was so important as we dealt with local citizens and leaders. You have to understand their perspective and know the facts."

By this time, we'd returned to the oaks near the gleaming marble columns and walkways of the Tomb. We listened to the resounding clicks of boot heels coming from the current sentinel on duty. I thought about the striking similarities between these polished sentinels and Eagle Scouts, and mentioned them to Matt.

"Being an Eagle Scout is like being a Tomb sentinel or in the Old Guard," he said. "People automatically hold you in a higher regard. You're also responsible for making sure you don't tarnish that view of what they hold the Eagle rank to be. You don't want to disappoint yourself or them or the people who've earned Eagle before you. That's part of our generation's responsibility."

The daylight had begun to fade and we left the hilltop to visit other members of our generation, other people who'd set high standards. Paul drove us down the hill from the Tomb of the Unknowns toward section sixty, on the southeast portion of Arlington's 612 hallowed acres. En route, we passed row after row of simple marble tombstones, marking graves of soldiers from wars past. Crosses were engraved on most, just above the name of the buried solider. Some were marked with Stars of David, others bore a Muslim crescent. We neared section sixty and the car slowed, the lines of tombstones flashing by slower and slower. The car stopped when we arrived at the last line. Outside, we looked south down the long corridor of white stones. Toward downtown Washington in the east, lay an open grass field, prepared for more servicemen who had made the ultimate sacrifice for their country.

"These rows," Paul said, indicating the last four rows of markers, "are soldiers killed in Iraq or Afghanistan since 2001."

I looked south down the aisles of marble slabs. I knew the numbers: more than four thousand killed in the Middle East. Everyone can read the tallies in the newspapers. Seeing the graves in Arlington and touching the smooth, cold headstones summoned very different emotions. Hearing Paul and Matt reminisce about lost friends brought a new perspective. Suddenly the magnitude of their death and sacrifice was real. I imagined hundreds of families, hundreds of mothers, wives, and children, weeping here as they buried a son or daughter, brother or sister, husband or wife. I watched Paul and Matt walk silently among their comrades.

I moved down a row behind Paul, noticing the birthdates on the headstones: 1975, 1979, 1981, 1984, 1985. My generation. So much potential buried here too early. Paul had come to visit Second Lieutenant

Leonard Cowherd III, his West Point classmate. I joined him at Leonard's gravesite, thirty yards down a line of simple white tombstones. The mist had returned to Paul's eyes. Standing above the grave, he told me that Leonard died on May 16, 2004, in Karbala, Iraq. At twenty-two years of age, he became the first war casualty of West Point's class of 2003. He had been married less than a year.

We lingered at his grave, then slowly left to join Matt, who stood at a more recent grave. "He was a classmate at West Point," Matt said, staring down at a headstone. "I didn't know he'd died until now."

Silently, we walked among these fallen servicemen, more than four hundred of whom died in Iraq and Afghanistan. They had all volunteered to serve. None wanted to die, but all were willing because they believed so strongly in the idea of America. I came upon one of the most recent graves: that of Eagle Scout Mark T. Carter of Fallbrook, California. Mark was the Navy SEAL I'd hoped to meet just months earlier. I thought about the SEAL candidates I met in San Diego—William Thomas, Eric Ramirez, and Jake Baker with his ever-present smile. By now, they had earned their Tridents and been deployed to active SEAL teams. I hoped that they were safe and I hoped Baker was still grinning.

It was late afternoon now; the cemetery had all but emptied. I turned east toward Washington, and looked over the undisturbed grass field that awaited the remains of soldiers yet to fall. A flock of Canada geese winged overhead, honking softly. The winter sun began to set behind us, splashing the Washington Monument and the Potomac River with a gentle red hue. The sky remained a clear blue. The dark shadows of evening began to stretch down the hill from the Tomb of the Unknowns, and a cold breeze picked up. Matt and Paul had joined me in gazing toward the Capitol dome, which rose above the city. We stood reverently in the peace that evening brings to Arlington, honoring the power of service, sacrifice, and memory.

SUDAN AND OMAHA

If you'd asked me to draft a list of places that had no connection to Africa whatsoever, Omaha, Nebraska, might have been at the top. Yet there in the center of America, I found myself carried back to Africa, a world I thought I'd left behind once my plane had lifted off in Cotonou, Benin. But then I found myself meeting Buey Ray Tut (first name pronounced *Boo-ee*) and Jacob Khol, two immigrants who never let boundaries or obstacles temper their aspirations or weigh down their spirits. In that way, they reminded me of the recovering warriors at Walter Reed. These two Sudanese cousins taught me several lessons, among them that you don't have to move to Africa to help or be touched by its people, and that you can still find a good meal of goat and pounded yams stateside.

Buey had driven Jacob and me several miles from downtown Omaha, toward their old haunt: the Wintergreen Apartments. We eventually reached a dead-end and Buey looked through the snow-dusted windshield of his Honda. His headlights shone on trees and a field of snow. "They closed the apartments a while back," he said, "but it's funny, I don't see them. Maybe it's just too dark." We drove down another street and parked the car near a cul-de-sac of newly built homes that Buey said had only mildly improved the notoriously dangerous neighborhood. I hopped out of Buey's two-door into the bitter chill of a Nebraska winter, and I pulled up a lever to release Jacob from the cramped backseat. He slid out, landing gingerly on an ankle he'd tweaked in a game of basketball earlier in the day. I jokingly reminded him that as a college senior, he was getting old. Buey left the hazard signals flashing and the three of us crunched into the nearby woods, which were carpeted in several inches of icy snow.

"This is what amazed me when I first came to Omaha," Jacob said, indicating the snow. "We never saw snow while I was growing up in Sudan."

Several minutes later, we all emerged from the woods onto a white field, dotted with trees. "It's gone," Buey and Jacob said in unison. They looked around at the spot where their old apartment building had once stood. The state had leveled the entire dilipadated, crime-infested complex.

"Man, I haven't been here in years," Buey added. "But there are so many memories."

"Good and bad, right?" Jacob said.

We stood there, Jacob warm in his stocking cap and down jacket, Buey shivering in his jeans and thin sweatshirt, and me somewhere in between. We began walking toward the back of the now empty field and we crossed an open patch that once saw football games and brawls alike. I heard about great footraces as we crossed the long, circular driveway, still distinct even in the heavy snow. Both guys clearly had athletic gifts, but I knew Buey ran track and cross-country at the University of Nebraska—Omaha, where he was finishing his senior year as vice president of the student government.

"Jake, did you ever beat Buey?"

"Not a chance," came the reply. "He's the fastest."

"Ahh, Jake's being modest," Buey said. "There were lots of good races here. I just wished we could have raced all the way out."

My companions and their families had arrived in the apartments in the late 1990s, refugees from Sudan. Buey's father had been taken as a political prisoner by the government and fled Sudan when his two-year prison sentence ended. Jacob's family faced similar circumstances. In many ways, however, life in Omaha proved worse. "Flat out, Wintergreen Apartments was a dangerous place to be," Buey said.

"The dark side was always there," agreed Jacob. "People pulled knives on us, guns on us, threw bricks through our window every single week."

"When you're here, you think, 'Man, is this what we're going to succumb to?' Our parents sure weren't having fun. They thought, 'We just got out of Africa and now we're back!' It didn't get any better."

"At least the people in Africa were nice about it," Jacob added. "Here, they just threaten you or trash your house for no reason. People used *African* as an insult: 'Hey, you African . . .' What, is that all I am?"

Everywhere the two boys looked, they could only see hurdles. Limits pressed on their aspirations from every quarter: violence, drugs, low probabilities of graduation, and few role models. The taunting only added to an already dire and very dangerous situation.

We stopped walking and Buey pointed to a copse of trees near the spot where his two-story apartment formerly stood. "My dad," he began, "one time, he was going to work, putting his keys in his car. This drug dealer is chasing some guy who runs by my dad and the drug dealer is shooting at the guy, misses the guy. The bullets go right by my dad's head and hit the car twice. Dad freaks out and runs back in the house and Mom's telling him he has to go to work. He says, 'We gotta move out!' Mom says, 'No.' Dad says, 'If you were shot at you'd move right now!' It was that bad."

The three of us continued crunching through the snow under the cold, clear sky until we reached a steep hill that Buey and Jacob remembered as a site for snowboarding and fights with local gangs. They laughed about learning to snowboard on sheets of old cardboard and pushing one another into the lone tree that awaited riders at the bottom. If any cardboard had been around that night, the three of us would have probably worn ourselves out on the snowy hillside.

Then Jacob pointed to a farm across the valley and started laughing. Buey smiled, and explained, "We ran through the farmer's field one day and he saw us, so we all took off running the other way. We all jumped over this fence, but one guy couldn't make it. The farmer had an electric wire for the cattle and the guy hit it and *boom*! He got up and got over, but we laughed about that forever when we got home."

"Laughing was so important," Jacob said. "It was a bad place, but when you have hope, everything lights up a little bit, so we had that. We were excited every morning to get up. We always had things to do. We had territories, my group versus Buey's group sometimes. There was always adventure going on. Sometimes fighting other groups, sometimes survival."

"We never succumbed to hopelessness," said Buey. "We knew we'd do what we had to do to get out of here. It was so bad that only three people were brave enough to come into our neighborhood: the police, Jehovah's Witnesses, and our Scoutmaster."

Dr. Lyn Graves served as Scoutmaster of Troop 33 in Omaha, a troop formed through the Boy Scouts of America's efforts to reach at-risk youth. Dr. Graves and Pastor Hart, the minister at the church sponsoring Troop 33, recruited boys from the Sudanese community into Scouting.

Dr. Graves asked if anyone was interested in going to summer camp; those interested, he said, should fill out a permission slip and bring ten dollars to the church on Friday. Jacob had begged his brother for ten dollars, but on Friday as the troop packed their vans, Dr. Graves wouldn't take the money.

"He was just trying to see how serious we were," Jacob explained. "We went camping at Camp Cedars and it was the best time ever. They had swimming pools, horseback riding, bike riding, canoes, archery, rifle and shotgun, Indian lore. The Platte River was right there, too, so you could fish—without the Scouts' permission! We were there for seven days and it was perfect." When Jacob returned home, he recruited Buey.

"We had a group of African friends in Wintergreen Apartments and we all wanted to escape that environment," Buey said. "We got involved with Dr. Graves, figuring that we could trust him if he was brave enough to come to Wintergreen. At the apartments, I was constantly made fun of because my clothes smelled like the African food Mom cooked. I looked forward to Scouts because they liked me and accepted me for who I am. After I started, I was hooked. I loved the things we did and Dr. Graves, you couldn't find a better leader. Dr. Graves didn't treat us differently, just as regular people. He trusted us, that was huge. Pastor Hart as well. They trusted us, respected us as human beings, and left room for us to make mistakes. I mean, I got to go to the World Scout Jamboree in Thailand—first time anyone had trusted me to go outside Nebraska by myself. Every time we camped, something bad happened weather-wise. It'd snow, rain, blow sixty mile-per-hour winds. It was great to see everyone come together and help each other. It made us bond so much going through those experiences. And Camp Cedars of course—a week by ourselves; no parents, no apartments. Jake and I still go back there with the troop."

"For me," Jacob said, his breath freezing in the cold air, "I enjoyed the fact that this was an opportunity for a bunch of guys to be close. Leadership was the best thing I got from that. It was like an internship. They teach you different ways to lead—and patience! Also the morality behind it—the Scout Law—it was what was needed at the time as teenagers to calm down and learn while having fun."

"Yeah, we found out early on that if you keep pushing your little guys around, they'll form a coalition and come back at you!" Buey added. "That's a life lesson learned in a humble way. You need to treat your people equally and tell them the truth at all times. That's part of leading.

Dr. Graves never told us what to do, but he always *implied* things. He said, 'This troop is going to be led by its leaders.' He stood back. We could be two hours late, and he'd say, 'You wasted everyone's time.' He'd add up everyone's time and say that you wasted fourteen hours! We were self-taught but supervised."

Jacob laughed. "I think those fourteen hours were lost because of Libby!" A female camp staffer named Libby had captivated Jacob and Buey, along with most other Scouts in camp. In a stroke of luck, she talked with the two cousins one day after lunch. Instead of going back to their camp, they stayed and put on their best charm offensive. When they finally returned to camp, an hour late, Dr. Graves didn't have to point out anything; they knew exactly what they'd done.

"We felt *so* bad," Buey said. "The way he almost ignored it made us feel so bad."

"It was a great lesson learned," Jacob concluded. "Nobody was there to take care of the Scouts."

"Let's talk about taking care of *us*," Buey suggested. He was dressed the lightest and I realized he was shivering as we stood there above the hill, our feet planted in the snow. We headed back to the car.

"Scouting really helped us endure our hard times at this place," Buey said, motioning to the surrounding fields and trees as we retraced our steps.

"And it gave us this positive light to live by," Jacob explained. "It gave us things to look forward to. You could endure those hard times because you knew a good time was ahead. The summertime? That's when everyone hangs outside. If we made a pie chart of the time we fought, in the summertime, sixty percent of our time was fighting. But we knew our summer camp was coming and we were going to escape for seven days, Sunday to Sunday."

"But maybe the biggest thing was that Scouting got me out of this environment," Buey added. "It showed me I was a worthy human being and not so different from anybody else. If you work hard, you succeed. If you don't, you fail. *That's* what makes you different from others; it's not necessarily what you're born with."

We reached the tree line, but before we crossed into the woods and returned to the car, Buey looked back at the site of his youth. "Our parents were so important," he said. "When bad things happened—windows broken and whatever else—they always kept us grounded, reminding us why we're doing what we're doing. My parents drove one car for two years just so I'd have a car when I turned sixteen. If you ever want to see parents put themselves second, look at my parents. My father bought one suit when I was in seventh grade and never bought another one. Thinking about it now, we never thanked them. They just went above and beyond. That place was a hellhole—excuse my language—but that's what it was. They made home a sanctuary, just like Scouting."

"Let's get some real African food and tea in us and get warm again," Jacob suggested with a sly grin. Despite his down jacket, he was ready to go. "Alvin, I know after three weeks away from Benin, you're starting to crave some goat and African spice!"

Shortly, Buey's Honda cruised into a strip mall, where one unit bore a hand-drawn sign labeling it the Sudanese Community Center. We parked and walked to the far end of the strip to a restaurant with boards over its windows. Whether as protection against the Nebraska cold or local vandals, I wasn't sure. Jacob opened the door to the International Café, and we walked down a ramp into the restaurant. Aside from the cold outside, I could have been back in Benin. Inside the simply furnished space, groups of African men sat engaged in lively discussion. Jacob joked that they only had two topics: politics in Sudan or how American politics affected Sudan. He identified the men by their tribes and noted that most still had refugee status, like both him and Buey. My white face drew several curious looks, but most people paid us little mind.

We reached the counter, where much of the day's fare had already been removed from the display shelf. It was growing late. Buey spoke in a native language to the proprietor, who left for the kitchen after pouring us three cups of traditional dark African tea. I made a move toward my wallet. Buey touched my arm and said, "You're on our turf. We got it."

The proprietor returned with a specially prepared dish of goat, lamb, and yellow rice with some variety of sauce. All I could think about were the countless live goats I'd seen strapped on the roofs of bush taxis, hurtling along rough roads in Benin. The cook motioned toward a nearby table. We sat down and began sharing the meal. Memories of Africa returned for all of us.

While Buey and Jacob clearly loved America, they maintained a loyalty to their fellow Africans. Africa remained their home, and they hated knowing how poverty, disease, and violence were perpetuating a vicious cycle from which few people could escape. Their parents and Scoutmaster always drove Buey and Jacob to make a difference and one day, while sitting on Dr. Graves's porch, they began talking about ways to bring positive change to Africa. They thought of ideas they could manage while still in America going to school. First, they hit upon a plan to provide badly needed shoes to people in Sudan.

"Then we wondered, is that really what they need?" recalled Jacob. "It'd be nice for them not to be stomping around barefoot on rocks . . ."

"No joke," added Buey.

"But when you think deeper, the basic is what everyone needs and water is *the* basic. We can't go without water. In Sudan, people have to walk for miles to get clean water—really, *miles*."

A mile in Africa doesn't equate to a mile in America. A mile in Africa ensures the walker receives a thick covering of dust from passing cars and gusting winds. Villagers walk along red-dirt roads, not sidewalks. They carry any belongings on their heads or backs. They walk barefooted or with sandals, not with Merrill boots. Little safety exists from vehicles, thieves, or the elements. Buey and Jacob saw how lack of accessible pure water cripples lives, economies, and potential.

"But with the wells we drill in this project," Jacob continued, offering me a glimpse of their vision, "we'll be saving them misery and also hours and hours of time."

"You've been there," Buey said to me. "What did you see as a real need? What we don't like about a lot of foreign aid is that they give bandage solutions. We wanted to start a project that could be self-sustaining. We don't want to do something to help people for a day. We wanted to have them work to help themselves; that's the biggest thing about what we want to do with Aqua-Africa."

Buey slid a packet across the table to me. I opened the cover. It was a detailed business plan, and I saw the work the two young men had invested in their project already. I saw the hope in their eyes and on the pages. I remembered the well-shopped business plan that became my first book. A large number of publishers reviewed my proposal and said, "No. Nobody cares enough about Scouting to read a book about it." I never ceased trying, however. After I ran out of money, and almost out of patience, Peter Joseph, a Massachusetts Eagle Scout and an editor at Thomas Dunne Books in New York, acquired *Legacy of Honor*. Together, we proved those naysayers wrong. I knew Buey and Jacob would face similar doubters; I also knew that they would find someone like Peter, someone who saw their potential. I was certain that they would complete this second Eagle Scout project.

In the spiral-bound proposal for Aqua-Africa, I found a page detailing the project's mission: to bring safe water to rural Africa by drilling wells and establishing continuing programs for maintenance. The Omaha pair had already contacted well-drilling companies in Sudan and neighboring Ethiopia to understand the costs, complexities, and ever-important local politics involved in such undertakings. Buey had himself visited Sudan several months before. There, he met the villagers, businessmen, officials, and other figures who held his project's fate in their hands. For him, the success of the wells came back to a universal ideal honed in Scouting: trust.

"People trust us," Buey explained. "We're African ourselves and we didn't disappear once we left. We came back to help. That makes all the difference."

The proposal outlined ambitious plans to drill a well in Maiwut, Sudan, that would serve nearly three thousand villagers. After that, the pair planned to enter other villages, gain their trust, and ultimately bring them safe water. The well in Maiwut would mark their journey's beginning. I don't believe they saw an end.

As I continued reading, I came to a page filled with numbers: cost of drilling, cost of transporting equipment into rural areas, cost of pumps, manpower needed. Changing Africa for the long term would not come cheaply. Another statistics-filled page caught my attention even more. It showed the numbers of wells drilled and number of people served. After a real start in 2009, the clean water from their wells would reach thousands, and thousands more each year.

"The biggest thing that's killing people is disease from unclean water," Jacob explained urgently. "We can't wait. Just as one example, I went into a clinic in Sudan, and asked them what their biggest problems were: parasites in unclean water. And we've done tons of research. It's not malaria or AIDS, not those big-name diseases people in the west know about. If you provide those people clean water, you improve every aspect of their life economically, socially, health-wise, every aspect of people's lives. They're much healthier, so they farm harder. They have more water, so they can irrigate crops and grow more. And then they have surpluses, and what do you do with surplus? Sell it to other people. We've created a microeconomic system. That's what we got from Scouts. Find the simple task and get it done. You don't have to find something extraordinary. Maybe Buey is, but I'm not smart enough to go after AIDS. Take the most simple things and make them effective. Make it everlasting and able to pay for itself."

First, however, they had to pay for the wells. With their business plan, the two had started to canvass the Omaha community to uncover a fellow Eagle Scout willing to invest in them and their mission. The search would undoubtedly prove difficult on occasion, but I believed the right person would surface. Truthfully, we can do very little by ourselves; those who believe in us have to step forward. Our generation, so full of ideas and optimism, yet so short of money and power, relies in a way on those older generations to believe in us and, often, invest in us. We want to change the world. At some point, we all recognize that we need help doing so.

As I digested the plan they had handed me, Jacob noticed me trying, apparently not very inconspicuously, to maneuver a piece of food from between my teeth. "You're such a rookie," he said, digging into his jacket. He produced a plastic-wrapped toothpick. "You can't eat goat without a toothpick! *Be prepared*, remember?"

I laughed and asked the guys another question about Scouting: What did it mean to them to be an Eagle Scout, especially once they'd left their Scout troops and entered adulthood? Buey responded first. "As an Eagle Scout, you're held to a standard the likes of which normal people don't experience," he explained. "If you found out an Eagle Scout did something wrong that's a shock, but it goes farther than that. You're surprised if they don't *actively* do something right. If you stay neutral, you're in the wrong as an Eagle Scout. In my vision, being an Eagle Scouts is *actively* trying to do good."

I agreed, but explained that I'd heard similar musings from Eagle Scouts of all generations; the high standard Buey mentioned stems directly from the collective reputation Eagles have established over the past century. I explained two of my main questions: How is our generation different and how are we creating a distinct legacy of our own?

Buey jumped in again. "Our generation is a little bit different because of the experience we had in comparison to older Scouts. Older Scouts were taught clean tie, clean shirt. Those Eagle Scouts from influential families are taught these things. Some of our generation is different because we don't necessarily have the same influence or money. At least in our experience, you're having lower-class people doing extraordinary things. We're breaking racial barriers, breaking socioeconomic barriers. You no longer have to be from a father named Edward who works at Northwestern Mutual. You could have a father named Juan or Khol who works in a factory making twelve dollars an hour. Our generation is also more culturally sensitive to every aspect of our society."

"Our responsibility is living in that culture," Jacob picked up, "realizing that you are an equal now. No matter what you do, there won't be a list of exceptions or list of certain requirements. You don't have an excuse not to *be* somebody. Our generation is expected to do something extraordinary every day as we're taught a Scout should do, with no excuses at all. There should be no reason why we're not going places. There should be no reason why Scouts' faces are not seen on the positive things in society. If we are taught those extraordinary things, we should share those extraordinary things instead of keeping them to ourselves."

"You can't put a face on Scouts anymore," Buey said. "In the past, a Scout was Timmy from the West Omaha suburbs. But now you can't put a face to a Scout. You can put *attributes*, but not a face. You can be Mexican, Japanese, African, everyone who calls themselves a human being can become a Scout."

Buey was right. Our generation of Eagles includes not only more Eagle Scouts per year than ever before—again, over fifty thousand annually—but a greater diversity of backgrounds and cultures than at any time in the past. Granted, Scouting has always helped working-class boys become successful—Wal-Mart founder Sam Walton, billionaire Ross Perot, Mayor Michael Bloomberg, and Verizon CEO Ivan Seidenberg all had humble roots. But Buey sees Scouting reaching into new communities, helping immigrants like himself have a chance at the American dream. Scouting provides hope and opportunity, he explained, and that's all that people need. He and Jacob know that sons of wealthy families and sons of poverty harbor the same ambitions. Scouting helped these two Eagle Scouts learn that their circumstances were not an excuse. "If someone is *willing* to do something, they're going to do it," Buey said. "Look at us. Two Africans from southern Sudan did it."

"All because we were offered the *opportunity* by the Scouts in Omaha," Jacob said. "If Dr. Graves didn't have the funding and he hadn't given us the opportunity, there was no way we'd have become Scouts. Reach out, I guess. Reach out. Somebody has to do something at some point to make things happen."

The founder of Scouting, Lord Robert Baden-Powell, on England's Brownsea Island at the first Scout encampment in 1907. In the coming century, more than 500 million young men and women would join the international movement he started.

Philmont Scout Ranch staffers Kelley Geiser and Travis Schreiber near Cimarron, New Mexico. More than 850,000 Scouts and leaders have hiked Philmont's backcountry since 1938.

AUTHOR'S COLLECTION

Left: Texas wrangler Lee Leatherwood, aiming to win a buckle at a Philmont rodeo
AUTHOR'S COLLECTION

Below: Eagle Scouts at the summit of Scouting, Philmont's Tooth of Time. Second from left is Chris Sawyer, fifth is Alvin Townley, sixth is Bryan Delaney. COURTESY OF JASON RZIHA

Left: Navy SEAL instructor Tom Campbell (left) with fellow Eagle Scouts and future SEALs Eric Ramirez, William Thomas, and Jake Baker in Coronado, California COURTESY OF BRIAN BARKER PHOTOGRAPHY

Below left: CBS *Survivor* contestant Burton Roberts in the Pearl Islands, Panama, during filming COURTESY OF GETTY IMAGES

Below: Ian Rosenberger, finalist on *Survivor: Palau*, watched by more than 20 million Americans per week COURTESY OF GETTY IMAGES

Twin surgeons Vince (left) and Vance Moss on a medical mission in Afghanistan
COURTESY OF VINCE MOSS

Vance Moss spends time with local Afghanis.
COURTESY OF VINCE MOSS

Vince Moss creates a bond with a young patient.
COURTESY OF VINCE MOSS

Marine biologist Eric Treml, Ph.D., at the Great Barrier Reef, northeast Australia. Eric has become a leader in global coral reef conservation research. AUTHOR'S COLLECTION

Above: At age sixteen, Matt Dalio started the China Care Foundation as his Eagle Scout service project. Nearly ten years later, the successful charity benefits orphans throughout China. COURTESY OF CHINA CARE FOUNDATION, PHOTOGRAPH BY LISA SLOW

Left: In Beijing, China, Matt Dalio shares photographs of home with an orphan. COURTESY OF CHINA CARE FOUNDATION

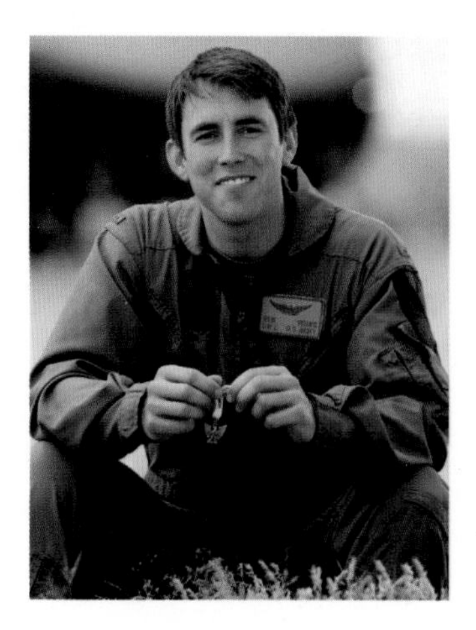

Apache helicopter pilot Ron Young, after returning home from his harrowing ordeal as a prisoner of war in Iraq COURTESY OF GEORGE FREY PHOTOGRAPHY

Peace Corps volunteers (left to right) Michael "Dutch" Portegies-Zwart, Collin Gerst, and Alex Litichevsky with Alvin Townley in Benin, West Africa. More than 10 percent of Benin's male Peace Corps volunteers were Eagle Scouts. AUTHOR'S COLLECTION

Alvin Townley with members of Scoutisme Béninois, the Boy Scouts of Benin. Today, nearly 30 million young men and women are Scouts in 156 countries.
AUTHOR'S COLLECTION

Iraq veterans and Purple Heart recipients (left to right) Brent Matchison, Bruce Dunlap, and Steve Gventer at Walter Reed Army Medical Center, Washington, D.C.
AUTHOR'S COLLECTION

United States Military Academy graduates and Iraq veterans Paul de Leon (left) and Matt Deurmeier of the 3rd U.S. Infantry Regiment, Arlington National Cemetery. Eagle Scouts compose nearly 16 percent of the USMA corps of cadets; other service academies log similar statistics. AUTHOR'S COLLECTION

Buey Ray Tut with young friends in East Africa. Earning the trust of locals is vital to Buey's plans for his native continent. COURTESY OF BUEY RAY TUT

Eagle Scouts Buey Ray Tut (left) and Jacob Khol in Omaha, Nebraska. The pair founded Aqua-Africa, a program to drill wells for villages in their home country of Sudan.
COURTESY OF BUEY RAY TUT AND JACOB D. KHOL

Climbing instructor Josh McNary scaling Red Rock Canyon outside Las Vegas, Nevada
AUTHOR'S COLLECTION

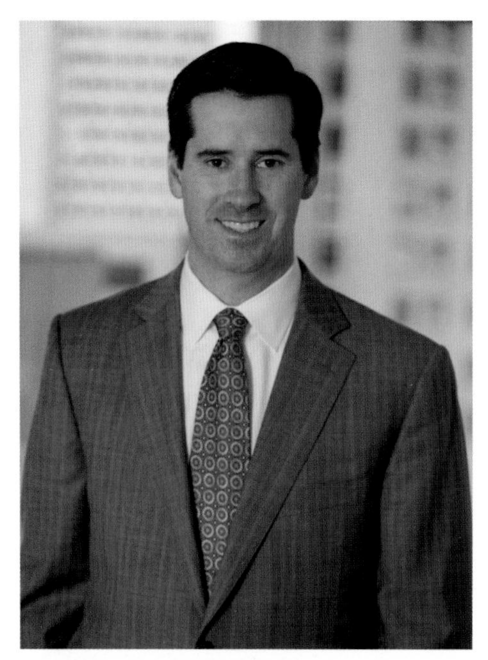

Tom Pigott, Seattle entrepreneur
COURTESY OF TOM PIGOTT

Lineman Deuce Lutui, Number 76 for the Arizona Cardinals, coaching NFL hopefuls at his youth football camp COURTESY OF THE ARIZONA CARDINALS, PHOTOGRAPH BY SHELDON CALDWELL-MEEKS

Miami Dolphins quarterback John Beck warms up before taking the field against the New York Jets in his rookie NFL season. COURTESY OF THE MIAMI DOLPHINS, LTD., PHOTOGRAPH BY NEAL GULKIS

Actor Jon Heder, one of five Eagle Scout brothers. Jon's film credits include lead roles in *Napoleon Dynamite* and *Blades of Glory*. COURTESY OF GETTY IMAGES

Jon Heder on his favorite back lot, the snowy woods of Oregon COURTESY OF JON HEDER

Second grade teacher and Scout leader Karl Brady with Cub Scouts from Pack 68 at Adamsville Elementary School AUTHOR'S COLLECTION

Teach for America corps member Craig McGowan fields questions from his ninth grade students at Banneker High School, Atlanta, Georgia. AUTHOR'S COLLECTION

Two generations: U.S. Supreme Court clerks Heath Tarbert (left) and Tom Saunders with mentor and fellow Eagle Scout Associate Justice Stephen G. Breyer COURTESY OF STEVE PETTEWAY, COLLECTION OF THE SUPREME COURT OF THE UNITED STATES

2012 Olympic hopeful Morgan House powers through a stroke. AUTHOR'S COLLECTION

Morgan House after winning the gold medal at the 2008 Pan American Canoe Championships in Montreal, Canada COURTESY OF MORGAN HOUSE

Top left: Olympic medalist Joe Pack flips during a freestyle skiing run in Utah.
COURTESY OF JONATHAN SELKOWITZ / SELKO PHOTO

Middle left: Travis and Lauren Amerine with their daughter, Ashlyn, in Meridian, Mississippi
AUTHOR'S COLLECTION

Bottom left: Pete Vincent emerges from the Hawaiian surf after paddling in the King Kamehameha Regatta.
COURTESY OF DALE VINCENT, PHOTOGRAPH BY JUDY VINCENT

Naval aviator Lieutenant Lee Amerine of the U.S. Navy's Squadron Fourteen—the "Tophatters" COURTESY OF MC3 JOHN PHILIP WAGNER, JR., U.S. NAVY; PHOTOGRAPH BY LIEUTENANT JARED BERGAMY, U.S. NAVY

Lee Amerine eases Number 212 onto Catapult Three aboard the aircraft carrier USS *Nimitz* while underway in the Pacific. The catapult takes just 2.5 seconds to launch a fully loaded F-18 off the deck. AUTHOR'S COLLECTION

Eagle Scouts from Squadron Fourteen and Carrier Air Wing Eleven aboard the USS *Nimitz*: (left to right) Rob Palmer, Trevor Estes, Carl Ellsworth, Lee Amerine, Chris Poole, and Jack Hathaway. COURTESY OF MC3 JOHN PHILIP WAGNER, JR., U.S. NAVY; PHOTOGRAPH BY LIEUTENANT JARED BERGAMY, U.S. NAVY

One of three brothers who earned Eagle in their father's troop, Dr. Lyn Graves followed family tradition and became a doctor and a Scoutmaster. Today he still runs Troop 33 in Omaha with its large complement of youth from disadvantaged backgrounds, many Sudanese. For his part, Lyn Graves always believed Buey and Jacob would succeed, with Aqua-Africa and in life. He recognized the passion both young men feel for their native Sudan. He saw them relate the skills they gained in Scouting and school to nation-building in their homeland. They always studied how to use their knowledge and assets to help their fellow Africans. "With them," their former Scoutmaster observed, "it never has been 'What's in it for me?' It's 'How can I use what I'm learning to serve southern Sudan?' They've always remembered where they came from. But they're clearly Americans now. Buey will get his U.S. citizenship soon."

The two young visionaries have passion, but also have discipline, which makes all the difference. "Buey and Jacob grew up in the most violent housing projects Omaha has," Dr. Graves continued. "Wintergreen had it all: the highest number of murders, highest number of rapes, highest number of assaults. I don't think they could tell you how many fights they were in growing up, but it was dozens and dozens and dozens. But they survived, even thrived, in the midst of that chaos. The fact that they chose well in that chaos speaks volumes. They chose to join our Scout troop; they had to bring themselves every week. They chose to graduate high school in a system where more black males drop out than graduate. Now, they're making the choice to graduate college and they have this core integrity. No doubt they'll make Aqua-Africa succeed."

In Buey and Jacob, I found two lives that Scouting changed, and possibly saved. I would encounter many more such stories before my journey ended, but my visit to Wintergreen Apartments showed me, for the first time, what was happening in thousands of communities around the country: Scout leaders were giving young people hope, opportunity, and a compass for a better life. They were studies in selflessness and their investment in time had an incredibly significant yield. These leaders reminded me what one person can do.

And, just as important, the Scout program was helping immigrants understand America and assimilate into our culture while retaining pride in their own. Troop 33 was an Omaha Scout troop with Sudanese roots. It was another reminder that our generation's world steadily grows closer, and that barriers to aspirations, information, and each other, are tumbling.

When I arrived home from Omaha, my family met me at my house in Atlanta's Morningside neighborhood. There in my living room, I shared stories about my most recent travels, but everyone seemed most fascinated by Buey and Jacob, particularly coming on the heels of my expedition to Benin. Over dinner, we talked about their lives in Omaha and their plans for Aqua-Africa. My father asked me how many wells they had drilled.

"None yet," I said. "But I know they'll do it."

I suddenly realized that *potential* is the great promise of this new generation. Nobody yet knows all that we will accomplish. We have aspirations as large as the sky over Philmont, and countless people have put their hope in us. For those of us who went through Scouting, selfless Scoutmasters gave us their time not because they knew what we'd become, but because they knew what we *could* become. For Scouts and others, of course, coaches, parents, and mentors have done the same. But that's why Dr. Graves helped Buey and Jacob lift themselves out of Wintergreen Apartments. And that's why Jacob and Buey have served as leaders at summer camp with Troop 33. They're already part of Scouting's cycle of giving. While following their dreams of helping Africa, they're shouldering responsibility for their community in Nebraska. In that, they reminded me how living the adventure of Scouting can take us across oceans or simply down the street.

PART II

Adventure at Home

Our generation's sense of adventure has led us to explore our potential and press our limits on every continent. We have left America's shores on missions of infinite variety, pursuing the thrill of the unknown. We haven't outgrown the idea of strapping on a backpack to discover new things in faraway places, and we still love the excitement of the road. But, more importantly, the Eagles I met also traveled with a greater purpose. They didn't just carry backpacks; they carried a genuine desire to help others and they brought change to places about which previous generations were only remotely aware. Our generation's sense of community has expanded far beyond Main Street and includes distant countries and continents as well as people we've never met. We seem called to meet those people and explore their lands, whether on brief excursions or tours of duty that last for years. But eventually, most of us come home.

I had circled the world and seen our generation creating a legacy in Africa, Australia, Europe, and a host of other places beyond our national borders. The lure of the boundless world seems to fade over time, however, and we begin to value things and people closer to home. Tom Campbell now spent most of his time in California instructing SEALs and being with his wife Tori in Del Mar, instead of deploying around the globe. Steve Gventer had returned to duty at home after two tours and two Purple Hearts in Iraq. And within two years, Alex Litichevsky and Collin Gerst would leave the Peace Corps and West Africa. Many Eagles have ventured far beyond America, but most return to build their lives here.

I wanted to learn how Eagle Scouts, those who've traveled abroad as well as those who haven't, plied their skills and shouldered responsibility in their home country, among their neighbors, and with their young families. How were they pursing their dreams and living the spirit of adventure? What was their mark on our nation? With yet more questions to answer, I began to seek out these Eagle Scouts.

OUTDOOR LEADERSHIP

Five hundred feet above the floor of Nevada's Red Rock Canyon, I leaned back from a sandstone ledge. I took a deep breath of the cool air that blew across the rocks from the north. Only occasional muffled sounds from below intruded on the otherwise pristine silence of the clifftop. My belay rope held me suspended, with my feet firmly against the rock face. I let my arms dangle, giving them their first break since I'd started the one hundred-foot vertical climb. I looked behind me, then down to the base of the cliff—two things I'd very deliberately avoided doing on the ascent. The desert spread out below, running unimpeded to the city of Las Vegas, Nevada, whose high-rises graced the far horizon thirty miles away. The cliff face extended to my right until it curved into another fold in the mountain. An outcropping of sandstone, striped with shades of red, orange, tan, and gray, bordered my left and only partially blocked two distant peaks, still dusted with white snow despite the warm spring temperatures we enjoyed nearer the valley floor. The blue sky suffered not a single cloud.

I thought about the last climb I'd done, back at Philmont. The forty-foot pebble near Dean Cow camp was simple compared to the face I'd just scaled. There, my motivation had simply been to uphold my dignity in front of Travis Schreiber. The present ascent however, was decidedly not easy and there was no dignity involved. Everyone in our group who attempted the climb faced a real challenge, and each of us needed the encouragement and skill of the other climbers. We each relied on the person who held the belay rope that would keep us from plummeting one hundred feet if we missed a handhold; a lot of responsibility to hand a relative stranger.

I savored my summit victory a moment longer and then called below to my belayer: "Rappelling!" Our instructor, Josh McNary, acknowledged my call and moments later I joined Josh and seven others at the bottom. I unclipped from the rope, looked up, and viewed the cliff from an entirely different perspective. It still towered above our group of climbers, but it no longer intimidated me. I was ready for a greater challenge. Josh McNary had seen that transformation happen hundreds of times.

Josh had met me at a nearby campsite the previous night, after I'd gotten only slightly lost on the thirty-minute drive west from downtown Las Vegas. Darkness had been settling fast, although when I stepped out of the car at our camp, I noticed the lights of Vegas kept the eastern sky nearly as well lit as the sun. To the west, stars had begun to shine, complementing the bright spotlight coming from the Luxor Casino in the east.

When I arrived, fifteen National Outdoor Leadership School (NOLS) students were making dinner at several picnic tables in the center of camp. Each wore a halogen headlamp, which made them look more like a swarm of fireflies than college-age students on a three-month wilderness expedition. Josh and I walked from my car to a table where he introduced me to his three fellow instructors. Then he resumed cooking the evening meal of pad thai. The only time we ate that well in Troop 103 was on the rare occasions John Kilpatrick, an adult volunteer, would offer us his Dutch oven meals. And I don't believe Mr. Kilpatrick ever ventured into Thai cooking. Then again, Troop 103 had never gone out for three months on the trail. Variety becomes necessity on long trips, Josh explained.

After an excellent meal, I added my tent to the ring of others that formed the border of our outpost. Thankfully, Josh had procured a good tent and cold-weather sleeping bag for me, since the warm day quickly gave way to a cold desert night. A stocking cap, sweater, and two shirts were adequate, but just barely. At least it wasn't snowing, I reminded myself.

The next morning began at 5:00 A.M. for me; my body was running on East Coast time—two hours ahead of Nevada. I unzipped the tent and poked my stocking-capped head into the darkness; the rest of my body remained warm inside the sleeping bag. The air carried a quite noticeable chill, and I ducked back inside. I finally emerged once the sun cleared the ridge behind us two hours later and brought some warmth to the camp. Soon, I watched instructors and students alike begin dragging their sleeping pads from their tents. They laid them out in front of Anna, one of the instructors, who was seated upright on her mat, legs crossed. I learned that morning yoga was a group ritual. I joined in and did my best not to tear anything.

With my body balanced and twisted into several shapes it hadn't previously known, I watched the early morning light turn the mountains a stunning red. I listened to the desert begin its day. Birds called and wind rustled the scrub brush surrounding us. Sounds from neighboring campsites soon followed, as did the distant noise of an occasional car driving along the main road. The sun began to warm the sandy ground as it rose higher in the eastern sky. For a few seconds at least, my overactive mind relaxed and I simply enjoyed being there.

A breakfast of egg sandwiches followed yoga and then everyone climbed into one of three white trucks with black lettering on the sides that read, "N.O.L.S., Lander, Wyoming." The crew had traveled a long way from the renowned program's headquarters and the expedition's mustering point. The fifteen students had come to NOLS so they could experience something no classroom or office offered. They had spent the preceding three weeks snow camping in igloos and tents in the mountains outside Lander. During those frigid weeks, they'd begun to change from a group of unfamiliar individuals into a team. Now, they had the distinct luxury of cooking on large stoves in temperatures that were well above freezing during the day. Temperatures still plummeted at night, but the lack of snow and ice was much appreciated. The group had arrived at Red Rock Canyon several days before I joined them, and would spend the next three weeks conquering a dizzying number of climbs. After that, they would spend two weeks hiking into, around, and out of canyons in southern Utah. Several weeks of paddling canoes, kayaks, and rafts awaited them after that.

A World War II veteran of the fabled 10th Mountain Division founded the National Outdoor Leadership School for many of the same reasons Baden-Powell developed Scouting. Like B-P, NOLS founder Paul Petzoldt believed no setting rivaled the outdoors as a school for leadership. NOLS instructors, many of whom are Eagle Scouts like Josh, lead expeditions to every kind of wilderness you can imagine worldwide: the Canadian Arctic, Brazil's Amazon Basin, the Himalayan Mountains of India, and a host of other locales in America and around the globe. Many students use the trek as a break from typical college education, but the program offers adventure for students and adults, age fourteen and up. Some treks last an entire semester; others several days. The expeditions aren't unlike a Philmont Rayado Trek, particularly when Eagle Scouts are in charge, as was the case here.

I rode shotgun with Josh, and as our small caravan of white trucks drove to a trailhead in nearby Red Rock Canyon National Conservation Area, he offered his reflections on what students—and instructors—experience. "The wilderness is its own teacher," Josh said, one hand on the wheel of the Ford F-350. "I can highlight things and coach them, but the experience is really the teacher. The joy for me is that after thirty days, I may not necessarily see the impacts in my students, but it's safe to say that several years down the road, students have to reconcile themselves to what they experienced. It's so intense, living with strangers, cooking your own meals, putting on wet socks every morning—it's so real, we have to reconcile ourselves. There's nowhere to run or hide your weaknesses. For many, it's the first time they've had to experience something so real. Some come from homes with no money, some have too much—and both can be a real crutch."

Presently, we arrived at the trail and began a mile-long hike through stunning desert to a rough ridge that we ascended as a nineteen-person train of hikers. Once on top, Josh ushered everyone into the shade of a large boulder—typically hot desert weather had returned by this time—and began the day's lesson on gear placement. He explained the intricacies of placing steel cams, metal stoppers, and hands into tight rock crevices as a climber ascended a rock face. The following week, Josh explained, they would be placing gear themselves, relying on those often tiny metal devices to protect them from falling off a cliff. If they fell, and had placed their gear correctly, they would be suspended, almost incredibly, by a rope running through a metal nut jammed into a crack.

Josh proved a fine teacher. He knew his topic and brought a lighthearted passion to his instruction that, in no small feat, captured the attention of his students. Once everyone had observed the examples he'd set in a nearby rock, the group split in two and I accompanied Josh and Scott, our two instructors, and seven others to our first climb. We hiked around the base of an enormous rock face, until we finally found the route we aimed to tackle. We scrambled up the rocky slope past a herd of mountain goats, then pulled ourselves up a narrow passage to an outcropping several hundred feet above the valley floor. A good forty-foot drop fell away from the edges, so we didn't need Josh's encouragement to stay away from the precipice and get our ropes in place against the cliff.

Josh and Scott lead-climbed the face, each trailing a rope behind them. Unlike us, they didn't have the luxury of a rope safely anchored to the cliff's summit, but they moved freely and easily up the cliff, reaching for handholds and pushing themselves ever-upward with their legs. They'd climb ten feet, then place a cam or stopper into a crack. After anchoring the gear, they'd run their rope through an attached carabiner. Then they continued their ascent, reasonably sure their anchor would hold if they slipped in the climb ahead. They reached the summit and secured anchors for the safety ropes that the rest of us wouldn't risk climbing without.

Each of us climbed the routes our instructors had opened, and the mood grew lighter as the afternoon progressed. Good-natured heckles from below became as common as words of encouragement. As climbers grew more comfortable at height, the taunts coming from above increased as well. The group stayed on the rocks until the mountains' shadows began to stretch east toward the city. Josh and Scott made a final ascent and untied the ropes from their cliff-top anchors. Those of us at the base stuffed helmets, ropes, and gear into our backpacks.

We trekked back down the mountainside, past the herd of mountain goats that had been observing us all afternoon. The trail had disappeared, or rather, we couldn't find it, so we took a bearing and set off toward the parking lot through fields of boulders, prairie grass, and cactus. Soon enough we rediscovered the trail and I fell in line behind Josh. We talked about the day's lessons and climbs. Josh patiently listened as I shared how much I'd learned. At some point, I realized he'd heard this countless times: people sharing how much his program had affected them. I realized that Josh McNary was very fortunate, and perhaps, like Eric Treml in Australia, a true Mexican fisherman. He lived in boots and shorts, sunglasses, and a well-worn ballcap. He spent his days outside with young people who shared his passion and were always eager for him to teach them. Clearly, Josh was living an adventure and fulfilling an obligation to younger generations. But it didn't come without trade-offs, he admitted as we continued the hike back to the trucks.

"The rewards of this job won't show up in my bank account," Josh said. "But I've learned that being wealthy goes beyond money." He smiled. "Or at least I've convinced myself of that!"

When it comes to types of wealth and what you should value, you're the only person whose opinion matters, he explained. He'd seen hundreds of students go through treks only concerned about traits that *others* valued. They almost seemed afraid or ashamed of the talents they had to offer. From Scouting, Josh and I both knew a successful troop or trek needs people of every type, and a well-run expedition encourages everyone to contribute what they're able.

"People tell you to value different things as you go through life," he continued, as we neared the trail's end. "*They* probably value different things in life. Being an Eagle Scout, you've decided on what *you* think is important and that makes all the difference.

"Being an Eagle Scout gave me something *I* could place value in. It stood for a set of beliefs to which I could anchor myself and know those were of value. When you carry those beliefs beyond Scouts, their value shouldn't change."

Josh traced that self-valuation and self-confidence to his Scoutmaster, John Wolly, who he considers the first figure in his life to accept who he was as an individual—fully and entirely. It's difficult to imagine the confident, flashy Josh McNary I met in Nevada as a quiet, sensitive kid, but he was. That proved difficult for him in schools and circles that didn't seem to value qualities like being reflective or considerate. He found a different reception in Troop 340 and Scoutmaster John Wolly. "With him, I didn't have to try to be anything other than who I was," Josh explained. "And not only was that okay, it was something of value."

At this current point in his life, he'd found his purpose in helping students find their voices as individuals. That, he felt reasonably sure, was of significant worth. "Once they learn what they value and embrace that, they're in a much better place to see the truth that exists in our world," he explained. "I hope they develop their own sense of leadership and it becomes something they can apply. I don't care so much *what* my students value—well, to an extent—but I do want to see them actualize it. If they're going to have integrity, if their values and actions are in line, they not only need to understand *what* they value, but have the skills to actualize those values. If a student values prayer in school, I hope they work to make that happen. If a student values taking 'In God We Trust' off the dollar bill, I hope they work to make that happen. I love to teach and love watching my students wrestle with our world."

Sometimes, those lessons don't set in right away, however. I personally began to understand Josh's point years after college and even after I'd written my first book. Likewise, Josh had jumped from college into graduate school for international development with a specialty in environmental sustainability at George Washington University, more concerned with what people told him to value than what he himself valued. Between his years in grad school, he spent a summer on a NOLS expedition and found himself remembering his days in Scouting. As a Scout, he had worked at Camp Kia Kima, earning thirty-five bucks a week as he learned to put pride into his work and view himself as part of a larger group. Kia Kima got him hooked on spending his summers outside, and he went on to spend four summers on the conservation staff at Philmont.

"At summer's end, you've been in a rhythm, you've been outside, you have stories to tell, you're tan, you're strong, and you'd done something few others had done," he said. "You were outside and you sensed you were doing something good." Completing the NOLS trek reminded him what he enjoyed, where his passion lay, and what he should value.

"After that time outdoors with NOLS, I realized I was in grad school to fulfill what I *thought* I should be doing," he said. "Not what I *wanted* to be doing."

Like many people, Josh had signed up for graduate school due to the common dilemma of wanting to change the world and yet not being quite sure how. His devoutly Catholic parents had encouraged him to travel overseas as a young man. Like surgeons Vince and Vance Moss and Benin's Peace Corps volunteers, he realized the world needed help. But serving a tour of duty overseas didn't suit him and he eventually realized that he could help bring about change globally by helping young people at home develop a more informed perspective on life and the world around them. He figured that the people who would drive the scientific advances that would aid the developing world already had food in their mouths and money in their pockets. They were the rising leaders in the developed world, and he stood convinced that the experience he had in Scouting could also benefit them. He found the NOLS program strikingly similar to Scouting, and he leapt from his fast-moving academic train to join NOLS as an instructor. Now he challenges others to look beyond traditional limits on rocks and in life. He teaches them to overcome obstacles and lead others toward worthwhile goals. It's his way of making a mark.

"I realized you can change the world on a day-to-day basis," Josh explained. "It doesn't take curing cancer or negotiating world peace. Daily interactions are the foundation for tomorrow being better than today."

He summarized the other component to his philosophy with a quote from writer Joseph Campbell: "Follow your bliss." He realized that if he were to be of any use to anyone, he needed to put his energy into something he believed in and something he loved. In his words, he needed to find something that "fed his soul, that would make the world a better place." After seeing him at work, I'd say he found it.

Josh seemed refreshingly comfortable in his own skin. I pegged him as one of those individuals who seems to revel in the moment and be content with life, knowing he was pursuing a worthwhile purpose. Whether cooking, teaching, or climbing, he always carried a certain confidence; not arrogance, just a comfortable self-assuredness that attracted his students. Being able to lead a three-week-long wilderness backpacking expedition or practically run up a vertical rock face does that for you, I suppose. On my next climb, Josh gave me a glimpse of that confidence and ability.

Like a Scout leader, Josh had me push boundaries on my first ascent. And like a Scout leader, he pushed me even farther on my second day. The first day had lent me some base of confidence: okay, I remembered that I could climb a rock without falling. The next day, he equipped me with more technical skills and put me on a rock that made the previous day's crag look easy. On that second day, Josh led a smaller group of four students and one writer to Ragged Edges, a vertical rock face in the eastern section of the park. The rock wall rose straight up. Again, Josh climbed toward an anchor, placing gear as he went, pushing himself upward with his legs, and trailing the safety rope he'd set up for those of us below.

My hands never sweat, except when I think about climbing. Even when I sat down to write about the day's climb, I found my fingers getting slippery. At the base of the cliff, I tossed a chalk ball between my hands, which helped dry them out and gave me a fair shot at gripping the tiny handholds that I'd need to keep my body close to the rock as my legs did the real work of climbing. Josh had found me a pair of climbing shoes, rubber-soled booties that were more uncomfortable than any shoes I'd ever worn. Climbers typically order them at least a half size too small. I'd worn a pair the previous day, but Josh had saved the lessons on toeholds until my second day. He explained how having my toes forced into an almost agonizing curl would help me. I was skeptical, but as I began climbing, I discovered the shoes acted like glue and I could grab a firm foothold on the tiniest of nubs basically by using my big toe. I finally understood how climbers scamper up ninety-degree inclines. I didn't so much scamper, but I definitely moved more quickly.

Forty feet up, the handholds disappeared. I was stuck. "Get into the crack," Josh called. He referred to a narrow fissure that ran the entire height of the wall and that was just inches to my left. It offered no more handholds than the rock where I was stuck. "Jam your hand in there," he called again. I remembered the lesson on gear placement from the day before and turned my left hand vertically and shoved it into the crack. Then I brought my thumb inward behind a small ledge, locking my hand in place at a narrow spot inside the crack. I leaned back. My locked hand held my entire weight. I moved my legs up. I wedged my right hand into the crack, slightly higher. I rotated my thumb and my hand locked into the crack a second time. I moved my legs up again. I repeated the sequence, faster and faster, with more and more confidence until I reached the anchor point and heard applause from my fellow students. My hands were slightly bruised and scraped, but my confidence was very much buoyed. Suddenly, rocks and heights, as well as the untried and unfamiliar, didn't seem so challenging.

On my last evening in camp, another instructor drew cooking duties, so Josh and I spent the time before dinner talking about Scouting's future. The similarities between NOLS and Scouting had struck me, but I wondered if programs like NOLS were supplanting Scouting, or if modern times were doing that on their own. No need to worry, Josh assured me, as we sat on a truck's dusty tailgate in the waning afternoon sunlight.

"Scouting is absolutely relevant," he said. "It teaches certain intangibles that are life skills. It teaches personal valuation of efforts. It teaches pride in one's work. It teaches pride in being part of something larger than yourself. It gave me a sense of purpose and meaning. It put me in proximity to people who were exceptional role models. It told me it was okay to be a kid with my personality and interests. It requires you to come to terms with uncomfortable things, be they people, a cold sleeping bag, or poorly cooked food. In a Scout troop, there will be one kid you can't stand and he's not going anywhere. He'll be there at summer camp with you all week long and you've got to come to terms with him."

While Josh believes firmly in the NOLS program, he still believes in

Scouting. Shortly after we had first planned our Red Rocks expedition on the phone, he'd volunteered to lead a local Scout unit in Lander. When he became involved, he watched his Scouts' knowledge grow and their awareness of life outside Wyoming expand. That led him to another observation. The program opens eyes. It first opened his eyes to the world outside Greencrest Lane in Memphis, Tennessee. Now, he hoped he could help Scouting do the same for his Scouts in rural Wyoming. And he hoped his Scouts would open his eyes to their world as well. That was all part of being an Eagle Scout, he explained.

"For some," Josh lamented, "Eagle has been glorified as a pinnacle or wreath to rest on. For me, I see it as a starting point. It was a stepping stone. It's a lifelong achievement. I've committed myself to a number of things, service, living intentionally, evaluating the implications of my actions. I think that if we, as Eagle Scouts do that, we can continue to give value to what it means to be an Eagle."

That's increasingly important since our generation faces new challenges brought on by the ever increasing demands placed on our small planet and its resources. Josh observed that our generation is slightly angry at what was left for us. "I think we're the first generation to look back at our parents and say, 'Thanks for putting a roof over my head, but why'd you have to screw up the world doing it?' The students who leave this course will have their own share of that burden to carry. Our generation has to come to terms with overpopulation, climate change, food supply, switching our energy sources to renewable ones. Americans cannot use as many resources as we do and expect that not to have consequences. We have to deal with that."

Josh hoped that programs like NOLS and Scouting will help our generation and the generations to follow deal with new realities and responsibilities. In essence, he'd returned to stewardship, the idea that defined Waite Phillips, the founder of Philmont Scout Ranch. Phillips knew that those original 127,395 Rocky Mountain acres were not truly his; they were only in his care for a short time. He could have permanently changed the land's character, but instead of constructing oil rigs or developments, he decided to preserve the land forever. To Josh's point, we are all stewards of the earth. What gifts or problems will we leave our children, and how will they view us as a consequence? That will define our generation's legacy.

Neither Josh nor I had two acres to our names, let alone more than one hundred thousand like Mr. Phillips, but that didn't matter. As Scouts, we still had a duty to serve as stewards of nature, principles, values, and institutions such as Scouting. Stewardship requires action, and I saw Josh passing on his appreciation for the natural world and Scouting's values by teaching students at NOLS and leading his Scouts in Wyoming. He was a great reminder that we are all just transient caretakers; how we shoulder our duty and what we leave for others will forever define us.

As we finished our conversation, Miles, one of my new climbing companions, approached us and offered me a ragged spiral notebook. "Our crew keeps a journal and we wanted you to write today's entry, if you wouldn't mind," he said. Feeling very much part of the team, I sat down after dinner to write under the silver light of my headlamp. After making several observations about the just concluded day, I wrote,

> For me, this ends my stay with the group. I'm leaving with some interesting thoughts, however. I started this long journey to find out how other people were pushing their limits—I hadn't thought much about my own. Then on the rocks I found people who encouraged me to climb higher, literally. Let me tell you—I'm not comfortable one hundred feet above the ground, but I climbed through that limit. I know I can do it. I saw a real team encouraging each other and certainly felt part of the team's mission for these past days. I'm just wishing I could stay longer and see how the coming weeks will end up shaping the lives of everyone. Cheers, guys—and good luck . . .

Had I held on to the journal longer, I might have added my thoughts while I lay wide awake at 6:00 A.M. the next morning—which was at least an improvement over 5:00 A.M. My conversation about values with Josh had reminded me of a conversation I'd had two nights before I left Atlanta for Nevada. I'd joined Randy and James Rizor for dinner at their Atlanta home. Major Randy Rizor, MD, had just returned home from a tour of duty as an anesthesiologist in Iraq and his son James was enjoying his last weekend of spring break from Rollins College in Florida. We met in Randy's wood-paneled study, surrounded by years of memorabilia he'd collected as a Scoutmaster and as an instructor for the Boy Scouts' prestigious Wood Badge adult leadership course. Behind the chair where I sat was a kudu horn, a musical instrument fashioned from the gray, twisting horn of an African kudu antelope. It was exactly like the one blown by Lord Baden-Powell on the plains of Africa and on the shores of Brownsea Island. Randy believes fervently in the Scouting ideal, and he'd passed the tradition on to James and his brother Crawford, who both earned Eagle with nearby Troop 74.

We moved into the dining room where I got to enjoy a home-cooked meal and the philosophical conversation that's never in short supply around Randy. The discussion drifted from James's spring break to the more serious subject of what American society values, a question that had particular relevance for James as he faced decisions about his life's path in his upcoming last year of college. He was grappling with how to follow his passions for teaching and people when the incentive structure of society pushed him toward higher-paying pursuits, which weren't his passions.

"America seems to be on such a monetarily based system when it comes to life aspirations," James observed. "How successful we're considered is often contingent on the money we make in a job. We don't look to see if a person is happy; we just assume once people have money or things, they'll be happy.

"Then you have Scouting," he said.

By comparison, Scouting is an organization of volunteers, giving their time, asking nothing in return. Everyone works as a unit. Older Scouts tutor younger Scouts, making sure they're okay on their first campout. Did they pitch their tent correctly? Did they cook their meal? Success can be whether you learned (or taught) a lesson or made it through a camping trip. It fosters a family mentality that helps build a sense of collective citizenship. As Baden-Powell had envisioned, the Scout uniform hides differences in background and class, which allows deep bonds to grow among everyone in a troop. "The sort of brotherhood that exists in Scouting," James said, "inspired me to look for other pathways in my life."

James planned to pursue his major in anthropology during his senior year then move into a teaching field or perhaps continue anthropological studies in China. Being the son of a physician, medicine also appealed to James, even as the healthcare system creates uncertainty for doctors. Regardless of the route he would eventually take, he explained that his parents and Troop 74 taught him to look for rewards beyond finances. Those lessons encouraged him to pursue his dreams and place value in what mattered most to him, not others. "Boy Scouts taught me that it's okay not to be in a position of wealth or power," he explained, "and that it's great to be helping others and just be happy being a good citizen."

During his tour in Iraq, James's father Randy had thoroughly enjoyed living the minimalist lifestyle at Camp Speicher near Tikrit, Iraq. He explained that in some ways, life seemed much easier and less stressful when he had several uniforms, a small box of belongings, and little else. That reminded me of Scouting. While society often focuses on accumulating possessions, possessions become very literal burdens on backpacking trips. In the woods, Scouts learn to live with the minimum, to live on exactly what we need. James and I both remember breaking down the packs of Scouts who brought too much gear on hikes and lagged behind as a result. At Philmont, I remember tossing out a fellow Scout's electric razor, police-size Maglite, and replacement batteries—all luxuries that slowed him down.

Scouting taught us to get along with less and be happy doing it. In those environments, we learned to value others for who they were, not what they had. We learned to take care of others in our troop, not worry about ourselves. The more I considered the point, the more I realized that is perhaps one of the greatest gifts Scouting has given our generation. Learning how to focus on others had prepared many Eagles I met to make sacrifices later in life to fulfill their duty to the people, institutions, and places around them. It's much easier to concern ourselves with our neighbors when we're not burdened with ourselves.

As the hour moved toward 7:00 A.M., I emerged from my tent to watch the desert sunrise. Wandering through the sagebrush at dawn, I continued thinking about the separate conversations I'd shared with Josh McNary and James Rizor. Josh had already chosen to place his own value on his life and career. The path James would pursue remained unclear—he was only twenty-one—but he had begun to confront the issue.

Valuing paths according to their income potential would suggest that our society attaches little worth to teachers, artists, and firefighters. Clearly, that's not the case. Those occupations are of exceptionally high importance, even though salaries and accompanying perks might not indicate it. I had resolved to set my own value on my life and not worry about what others thought. I wasn't entirely sure where my trail would lead, but I felt confident that it was taking me in a good direction. I was continuing an adventure that started in Scouting and I felt satisfied that my experiences were of value. The less I worried about money or the next big choice, the happier I seemed. Other Eagle Scouts of my age have discovered that same freedom and, I think, that's why they so readily and passionately step into such lower-salaried but rewarding fields as teaching, the military, public service, and outdoor leadership.

After my last session of morning yoga, Josh and I talked together as his students loaded the trucks with gear for another day on the rocks. I wasn't ready to leave. I'd enjoyed spending time with someone as reflective as Josh, who'd helped me consider the larger questions of this journey. It wasn't just how Scouting had shaped us; it was the question of what we would become. Each of us faces that question about our future and we each reply with our own answer. We measure our answers against the guiding values that we first adopted in Scouting: Are we acting as leaders, stewards, servants, and—still—good Scouts? Then we must make choices about what we value and what we need. No answers are wrong; they're just uniquely personal and meaningful. What *does* matter is that we make choices that reflect our obligations and responsibilities to Scouting and to others. Are we pushing our limits and following our passions and dreams? Are we improving the lives of others? Millions of us will hopefully consider our decisions in that light and make choices of which we'll be proud years into the future. What is alternately exciting and daunting, and important to remember, is that the sum total of all these choices and actions will ultimately shape the future. As I had been reminded, each of us has a special role to play in defining that future and shaping the legacy of our generation.

ROLLING THE DICE

By the next evening, I had arrived in Seattle, Washington, wearing my now weathered Peace Corps ball cap and several days' worth of desert dirt and stubble. The bellman at the hotel eyed me warily as I hauled my battered backpack into the ornate lobby. Several years ago, I would have felt terribly inappropriate and out of place, but I was becoming more comfortable in my own skin—and I was on a mission.

At the front desk, Amelia, the hotel's receptionist and, as it happened, the daughter of an Eagle Scout, didn't seem to mind the scruff or dust and warmly welcomed me to Seattle. Minutes later, I walked into one of the most sorely needed—and greatly appreciated—showers in recent memory. My next stop was a soft bed with real pillows. I'd definitely swung from one type of adventure—camping in Nevada—to another. The Eagle Scout I'd come to see in Seattle was a very different type of person than Josh McNary. Josh was all about roughing it. Tom Pigott's business depended on people not roughing anything.

The next morning arrived with the infamous Seattle rain, which settled over downtown. I immediately missed the expansive vista that awaited me outside my tent near Red Rock Canyon. Another hot shower and clean clothes were adequate consolation, however.

Scrubbed and shaven, I walked downstairs to find Tom Pigott. One year had passed since I'd last seen the Seattle native, but I had no trouble spotting him amid the morning crowd. He was dressed in an immaculate dark suit, his hair perfectly combed. The difference between Josh and Tom, at least in appearance, struck me and I thought for a moment about the very different trails Eagles follow. Then Tom's easy smile and welcoming handshake ended that train of thought. It was good to see him again.

Like me, Tom was the son of an Eagle Scout and had seemed predestined to reach the rank himself. For Tom, Scouting became an important element in a life as adventurous as any other I'd encountered. He just lived it in a suit and tie.

We found one umbrella remaining at the hotel's bell stand, so we stepped into the cold rain outside sharing the cover, each only partially sheltered. We navigated the crowds on Pike Street, Seattle's main thoroughfare, and walked toward the Puget Sound waterfront. As the famous Pike Place Market neared, Tom stopped at a parking lot at the corner of Second Avenue and Pike.

"Here it is," he said.

Here was what? I saw cracked asphalt, faded parking lines, and a smattering of wet cars. A slightly dilapidated nail salon occupied the opposite corner, and an aged parking deck loomed to the south. Tom saw none of that. He saw potential. He pointed down Second Avenue to the city's newly opened art museum. Then he directed my attention to a towering crane completing a new Four Seasons hotel nearby. A gleaming new office tower stood one block away and condominiums were rising to our north, quickly replacing rough storefronts. Tom saw what would be, not what was. He saw the vibrancy of downtown Seattle growing from the elegant shopping district several blocks behind us to the gritty heart of the city, the Pike Place Market, which lay one block ahead of us. Soon, his own new flagship luxury hotel would replace the bleak parking lot and add a new profile to the city's skyline.

From beneath the umbrella, he gestured to the parking lot and explained that next year, a six-story hole would replace the lot and shortly thereafter, a steel superstructure would begin rising to a height of thirty-six stories. His arm traced the upward progress. His eyes shone. The building would add its own signature to the city and its own flavor to the downtown market district. He pointed out the future entrance, now just a junction of concrete sidewalk and worn asphalt. Guests, he explained, would cross that seam and enter a hotel that would cater to their whims and needs. Most of his waking moments—save those reserved for family and Scouting—were given to building his vision. He joined every meeting. He helped design guest rooms as well as negotiate with city regulators. Menus, parking, advertising, staffing, finance: Tom's hand guided it all.

Candela Hotels, as he'd christened the venture, wasn't just entertainment or speculation for the young but accomplished entrepreneur.

It was the latest venture to which he'd dedicated his heart and considerable intellect. He also hoped it'd be the last.

The son of a successful businessman, Tom could have easily joined the family company upon graduating from Stanford University. That route didn't suit the spirit of the youngest Pigott, however. He never saw a reason business shouldn't be an adventure, so he made it just that. Tom had taken an interest in international affairs as a student at Stanford, studying abroad in Switzerland and Japan. Like many others, he discovered the vast and varied perspectives that exist beyond our shores. He also realized he could choose to follow a different path, one not quite so common or easy to navigate. When Tom graduated, he left the familiarity of the West Coast and began working for the Caterpillar corporation in Japan. He loved it, and after two years, he passed up the opportunity to return to America and signed on for another position in Asia, this time in China. He studied business and Chinese culture in Beijing then rejoined Caterpillar in Shanghai where the American company was launching new dealerships and developing its Chinese operations.

"Compared to Tokyo, Shanghai was the wild, wild East," Tom reflected. "After forty years of communism, there's an explosion of capitalism and people have a real entrepreneurial spirit. They think anything is possible—the biggest buildings, the best new businesses. It's a country in the remaking and being in Shangahi, I was at the epicenter."

That spirit took hold of Tom and eventually he wanted to try his hand at starting a company of his own. In the late 1990s, at the age of twenty-six, he returned to Seattle. Home to Internet revolutionaries like Microsoft and Amazon.com, Seattle had become the epicenter of America's own remaking. Tom dived into the nearly out-of-control technology sector. He joined Nextel, which appreciated his international experience, and without having much say in the matter, he soon found himself in Brazil. He spent six months watching the Internet revolution take place in his hometown without him, and finally, he could no longer stand it. He returned to Seattle to roll his own dice.

The phrase *well-studied* suits Tom perfectly, and he carefully researched different markets once he returned home. Before long, he noticed a boom in mail-order pharmaceuticals. He investigated the sector further and discovered a tremendous opportunity: none of the dominant drugstore companies focused on customer service and people were turning to mail-order prescriptions in response. Additionally, the major stores had not yet adopted the Internet as a sales channel. Tom realized that the efficiency of online ordering far outstripped that of mail orders, and with little hesitation, he jumped at the chance.

"I wrote a business plan and then got some people with great industry experience," Tom explained. "I'm not a pharmacist and almost nobody had started Internet companies at this point—this is 1999. If you could move quickly and execute well, it could be viable."

He started Soma.com, an online pharmacy, and the new company found a hungry market. Tom doubled his staff each month. The growth surpassed his expectations and, at the age of twenty-nine, he saw an idea grow to become a successful business. Others noticed, and soon, he received a phone call out of the blue. It was CVS, the nation's largest pharmacy and drugstore chain. CVS had yet to build a full online presence and rather than building CVS.com from scratch, they wanted to buy Soma.com. It was the call nearly every entrepreneur dreams about.

When Tom sold his company to CVS, he had just turned thirty and got married shortly after the deal. It was a big year. He stayed on to run the online pharmacy with his existing staff in Seattle and joined the executive team at CVS. His was the youngest face in the boardroom.

As part of CVS, Tom now had access to a customer base of seventy million CVS shoppers. Consequently, CVS.com grew rapidly. "It was absolutely fascinating," Tom recalled. "I went from pure entrepreneurship to joining a Fortune 100 company. But they left me independent in Seattle to run the Internet segment. Talk about the best of both worlds."

Tom stayed with CVS until the company decided to move Internet operations to their East Coast home office. Tom wasn't about to leave his native Northwest, so he began searching for a new opportunity. He looked in one area after another; common threads among them were few, except that all were fledgling businesses. Tom finally realized he'd become a serial entrepreneur. He relished the challenge of starting something from scratch and craved the thrill of taking risks, putting everything into an untested idea, then making it happen.

One of the many people who have a streak of green remaining from their Scouting days, Tom explored opportunities in clean energy. He soon joined a local venture capital firm led by fellow Eagle Scout Andy Dale. The VC firm looked for opportunities to invest in new businesses and help them grow. Tom soon helped broker a deal with a fuel cell start-up, but he found himself missing something.

"If you're in this business, you're either more excited about being an entrepreneur or being a venture capitalist," he explained. "VC is fascinating, but there are lots of different investments and little day-to-day work. As an entrepreneur, it's blood, sweat, tears, and risk. I found out I'm an entrepreneur."

He enjoyed building one company at a time, dedicating everything to a single focus. But he wanted to focus longer than two years. "I said I'm going to start one more company and I did research like I did for Soma.com. I found an industry where there was opportunity for me to start a company and build a true long term career. I didn't want to flip it or get bought out. Building Candela Hotels into a global, high-end hotel brand is what I want to do."

That brought us to the corner of Second Avenue and Pike, where Tom and I stood imagining the future beneath an umbrella in the Seattle rain. By this time, Tom's enthusiasm had me envisioning what was to come. He let me imagine the Candela tower a bit longer and then suggested we walk to the market, one block west. On the way, he was clearly feeling buoyant about his new venture.

"What's not to like?" he reflected. "Luxury travel, luxury hospitality, an exciting field where you meet people from all over. Honestly, I've lost the itch to start another company. Now it's building a long-term company that continually does exciting things. It takes some people longer than others to find the field they want to stay the course with—like you and me. I've tried plenty, but I'm ready to put heart and soul and passion into building Candela into a world-class company and global brand—that's ambitious and won't happen overnight."

When Tom began talking about the long term, I realized how the idea of adventure seems to change depending upon your stage in life. For many of us, particularly when we are teenagers, adventure consists of anything that can result in serious injury. It's about thrills and excitement. As we begin to mature and move into life as adults, the concept of adventure seems to evolve naturally into something with long-term satisfaction and significance. I had begun noticing that adventure for thrills alone eventually becomes unfulfilling. To be sustainable, adventure needs an element of duty. Otherwise adventurers of every sort begin struggling to find meaning in life. As he matured as a businessman, Tom found less adventure in flipping companies; he sought something more lasting, more significant, and more fulfilling.

We crossed a cobblestone walkway and snaked through a flock of tourists listening to their guide at the entrance to the Pike Place Market. Ten steps later, the largest display of fresh seafood I'd ever seen confronted us. The day's deliveries glistened under the lights, half-buried in ice and only hours off a Puget Sound fishing boat. The shopkeepers wore rubber aprons and boots and thought nothing of tossing whole fish onto the counters to prepare them for customers and to entertain tourists.

The men in the boots, some aged twenty-five, some fifty, alternately joked and pitched their catch to customers. They seemed supremely happy doing a job I'd never considered, and probably would never consider for the simple reason that neither my skills nor comfort zone extend to commercial fishing. I'd seen the show *Deadliest Catch*, narrated by Eagle Scout Mike Rowe. Fishing off the Alaska coast worked for some, but it just wouldn't for Tom or me. In all of the miles I'd traveled, I had seen the thousands of occupations and callings on which people spend their days. Some are beyond my ability and others are entirely unsuited to me for a host of additional reasons. Amazingly, everyone seemed to find a calling in something, sooner or later. That makes the world work, and Scouting had given us an opportunity to sample the field.

Tom had far surpassed many fifty-year-olds in experience, so I pressed him for a little extra wisdom on the matter of careers. "Regardless of what you do, you have to understand your own makeup and personality and your bands of comfort," he told me. "By way of example, many people a heck of a lot smarter than I am don't want to start a company from scratch and hire that first person! You don't have to choose your career right out of college, but you should get different experiences and truly understand what you love to do best. That's what it's about."

Our fathers, Eagle Scouts Chuck Pigott and Alvin Townley, Jr., both spent their entire careers with their own companies. Tom and I both sidestepped the family businesses, leaving them in the hands of our brothers. We both remembered our fathers' skepticism and concern as we switched careers. We had to help them understand how our generation differed from theirs. The stigma tagged to changing jobs had faded, but Tom observed, "There's still that phrase, 'A jack of all trades . . . and master of none.' You want to set some boundaries in your mid- or late-twenties and think about how you're going to build some expertise and contribute to society. What's your purpose going to be? Isn't that what we learned is important in Scouts?"

We left the hustle of the market and Tom led me across a street and into a coffee shop. "While we're talking about entrepreneurship," he said, "I thought you'd like to see where Starbucks started."

We entered the shop that three friends had started in 1971, but it wasn't until Howard Schultz became involved that the Starbucks brand began its not-so-long march to ubiquity. Tom clearly admired what Schultz accomplished, particularly in the company's first twenty-five years. He took a staple product like coffee, turned it into a gourmet experience, and realized astounding results. I think Tom sees some of Schultz in himself. He wants to transform a common service and product—lodging—into a unique experience.

I ordered our drinks—interestingly, neither of us wanted coffee—and we lingered inside before returning to the light rain still falling outside. "What Scouting does," Tom continued, picking up his earlier train of thought, "is provide this fantastic opportunity to build moral values and leadership within young men. Once those things are instilled in you, you have an obligation to be a leader in whatever your chosen profession may be or in whatever endeavors you have in life. That's in your field *and* in your community. You understand the importance of volunteerism and philanthropy. It's not enough to be a leader in a financial sense. Eagle Scouts in particular need to give back to the community."

Tom still holds on to memories of Troop 430, which met across the street from his childhood home in Bellevue, Washington. Working toward Eagle, he learned about spirited competition as he raced his best friend to the rank. Tom won by six months. While he led in the race for Eagle, he didn't always lead the troop and learned how to follow others, something he holds equally important. Really, everyone has a boss in some regard; even a CEO reports to a board of directors. Everyone needs both to lead well and follow well. Tom learned how on campouts during the winters where Scouts slept beneath eighteen-inch-thick roofs of igloos they'd built in the snow. During the summers, he learned to lead on backpacking trips through the rainforests of the Olympic Mountains and along the rocky slopes of the Cascades.

"On those trips," Tom recalled, "when you're twelve or thirteen, you're looking up to kids who are sixteen or seventeen. Those guys really influence you. Then in a few years, you'll be sixteen and a new twelve-year-old will be looking up to you, so you have to have high standards. It's a virtuous cycle."

When he joined the Caterpillar corporation in Japan shortly after graduating college, Tom worked with an all-Japanese team that placed a premium on teamwork. "The nail that sticks out gets hammered down, they say," Tom joked. His years being led by others taught him how to lead and how to share credit for success. As an American, he also gained insight into a system where superstar individualism did not run amok. In the end, the experience prepared him, even encouraged him, to pursue entrepreneurship and the leadership that comes with it. When he started Soma.com, he was reminded that just as leadership accompanies entrepreneurship, responsibility accompanies leadership.

"You do have a great responsibility as a leader, regardless of your sector: professional, nonprofit, or a household," he noted. "You have to hold yourself to a little higher standard. Getting tired can be part of the requirement. There can be great benefits of being in this position, but part of the challenge of being leader is that you can't get sick or skip a day or sleep in or not show up. Everyone else is always there and you have to lead from the front. That's a responsibility you need to accept if you want to become a truly respected leader. Get ready to work harder than anyone."

We left Starbucks and walked back past the future site of the Candela tower. We paused again on the corner, both imagining what would be. Tom sighed with some satisfaction. "I think all of the experiences I've had have led to this opportunity, including Scouting," he said. "To do this, you have to have perseverance and a certain disposition to risk—calculated risk. Then it's the excitement of trying to build a great company and team. It's the opportunity to have a vision and see it realized through a tremendous amount of hard work—and mistakes! Someone once said never underestimate the power of sheer determination. If you have that mind-set from a business perspective there's not much you can't accomplish. If you never give up, you're never going to fail. Scouting teaches that. Perseverance is so important in everything, the path to Eagle, backpacking trips, merit badge work, everything. Scouting also taught me to keep that moral compass through it all. I'm not going to sacrifice everything for success—my family, my integrity, I don't compromise there. Lots of things make you successful; hopefully I'm a more successful husband and father than I am a business person. Scouting formed the basis for that and is still very much part of who I am."

Tom lives in a world of wealth and luxury—it's his business—but he doesn't make his life about wealth and luxury. He stays oriented to his sense of purpose and measures his success as a husband and father. Some Eagle Scouts stand out because of what they do; others stand out because of how they do it. Either way, you cannot separate Scouting from the life of an Eagle Scout. Tom or I can certainly identify particular lessons we learned on campouts, but really, the way we learned to live during our ten years as Scouts just became part of us. We don't necessarily act with the Scout Oath actively in mind, but it's there. Its values are so deeply seated that they influence our decisions and even more fundamentally, who we are. I saw that apply to Eagles camping in the Nevada desert, dwelling amid urban sophistication, and living everywhere in between. I also found it in what I once thought was an unlikely place: professional football. I never thought I'd see an NFL lineman raise his right hand and repeat the Scout Law. Then I met Deuce.

BEYOND THE SPOTLIGHT

When I arrived in Tempe, Arizona, bright sunshine covered the expansive green fields of the Arizona Cardinals' training facility. Given its desert location, the field experienced little *but* sunshine. The air smelled of freshly mowed grass, and the field seemed hushed. It reminded me of a high school field just before school ends at three o'clock: quiet with anticipation. Coaches and volunteers gradually materialized and began setting up orange cones and an assortment of obstacles between the chalked yard lines. They weren't making the arrangements for the muscled professionals of the National Football League's southwestern franchise, however. This day, everything was dedicated to a group of boys and girls from a nearby middle school. The students buzzed with excitement. Soon, they would meet the Cardinals players who would serve as their coaches and mentors for the day. One would be offensive lineman Tautusi "Deuce" Lutui, Number 76.

I made my way onto the field and met with various others gathering for the afternoon: staff members, media, and players. They all asked whom I'd come to meet. From their instant reactions to his name, I discovered that Deuce Lutui ranks among everyone's favorite Cardinals. The common response was, "Deuce is the best with kids. He's a big kid himself." I also heard, "He makes it the best, every single event he does. His mentality is 'I'm going to have a good time and everybody who's with me is going to have a good time.' " Everyone I met agreed that few players love children more than Deuce.

"Sometimes, I have more fun than the kids do!" Deuce would tell me later that day. "I also have a big family and my older siblings and cousins were a big influence on how I acted. I feel it's important for me to be a positive role model to kids in my community."

But Deuce doesn't just appear, shake hands, and then disappear at charity events. He told me about one young man he met at Phoenix Children's Hospital. "Two years ago I met a boy named Andrew who had undergone a double lung transplant and was fighting cystic fibrosis," he said. "I kept in touch with Andrew over the past two years because of the amazing person he was. He passed away about three weeks ago and I was crushed. Doing this kind of work in the community really puts perspective on life and gives you an appreciation for what God has done in your life."

Continuing to mentor the youth of Phoenix, Deuce always meets the local high school player of the week, who joins the Cardinals for practice each Friday during the fall. Shortly thereafter, Deuce hauls his teammates to nearby Mesa High School, where he once played. Together, they yell for the Jackrabbits and relive countless Friday night games of their own high school days. During the off season, the lineman runs the Deuce Lutui Kids Camp at Mesa's Lindbergh Elementary School, which he attended years ago. Apparently unfulfilled by just serving his old neighborhood, Deuce also stages camps for special needs children and for young people from Mexico through the Hands Across the Border Foundation. Several months after I met him, I recognized a certain lineman playing flag football with children at the Super Bowl's NFL Experience: Deuce, of course. He seems never to want to grow up—although as a father of two, he can't always be the kid.

On the particular day I'd come to Tempe, he had to be an adult. Just before the Cardinals event began, his father was rushed to the hospital. Deuce went there immediately to be with him. For Deuce, duty to family has always come first.

By the day's end, his father's condition had thankfully stabilized and Deuce joined me near the Cardinals' training facility, where children and players alike had long since left the fields. The six-foot-four, 330-pound lineman and I sat down together and his thoughts drifted back to Scouting in Mesa, Arizona, a Phoenix suburb just ten miles from where we sat. He regretted missing a day in the sun with students, but he understood his responsibilities.

"I always tell the kids to 'be prepared!' " He let out a deep laugh. "I guess I had to be prepared today. But that's the Scout Motto and it goes a long way. Be prepared in everything; that sums it all up. Preparation prevents poor performance.

"I'm lucky I can help teach that to kids," he reflected. "Being able to outreach to communities where I grew up and to really be involved in that has been a blessing. When I was younger, seeing professional athletes come into our communities was a big thing. Even if you didn't know the guy, or know his name, but knew he was tagged NFL or NBA, the influence that has on a little kid, to see an athlete come into the community and visit with the kids is huge. It reminds me to pay it forward. And knowing these kids look up to me, I always play a little harder on Sunday."

Giving back is something he learned in Scouting as well. "More than anything, Scouts taught me service—to serve my troop, my country, to really serve others all around us," he observed. "That's what we did in Scouting and it taught me a lot. . . . It's service to fellow beings, and being in the service of God. I get satisfaction from serving other people for free and not getting reimbursed. Being an athlete in the professional business, some people get some big-time cash to make an appearance. I think it's important to do charity work out of your heart. I think I get paid by seeing smiles on faces and getting thank-yous. And it's just a good time.

"But, even being a father and husband today," he continued, "Scouting prepared me to be in the service of people. It also taught us to help our fellow countrymen and that's the main idea when I involve myself with Cardinals charities."

Nobody who knew him was surprised that Deuce found his way into professional football. After all, he arrived in the world already weighing a whopping twelve pounds. "As you can imagine, I love Mama very much," he said with a trademark grin. His given name, Taitusi Latui, soon became "Deuce," though not as a reference to his size and weight, he jokes. Taitusi is pronounced *Dai-Dusi*, thus "Deuce." The football-player-to-be watched his two older brothers join Scouting in their native Pacific island nation of Tonga. The barefoot island adventures of the older Latuis had already fascinated their younger brother before the family immigrated to Arizona, where both promise and tragedy awaited them.

Deuce was six years old when his family's van flipped over in a terrible accident. The crash killed his younger sister, put his father and one brother into comas, and severely injured his mother. Recovery was slow, particularly as his father and brother had to relearn basic skills after awakening from their comas. They even had to learn how to speak again. With both parents impaired, the young Latui children were suddenly responsible for the family's well-being. Deuce remembered maturing quickly to meet the challenges of having disabled parents. "Scouting taught me a lot of discipline and patience to prepare me as a young man to face those challenges and the challenges I have now," he said. "I think that all ties together, what I learned at a young age. It prepared me to be where I am now."

After earning his Eagle Scout rank in 1999 at age sixteen, the rapidly growing Deuce focused on football. He eventually went to the University of Southern California, joining coach Pete Carroll's offensive line. There, Deuce was the only married player. The day of the 2005 Orange Bowl, he spoke with his wife Pua shortly before taking the field to play for the National Championship. She told him he would be a father when he returned home; she was in labor with their son Inoke. That knowledge apparently didn't detract from Deuce's ability to protect the Trojan backfield during the game. While Deuce held the Oklahoma defense at bay, running back Reggie Bush and quarterback Matt Leinart led the Trojans to 525 yards of offense and fifty-five points, clinching the national title. The following season, Deuce earned first team All-American honors and Coach Carroll named him the Most Valuable Lineman. Through it all, he upheld his family duties. His 2006 draft selection by the Arizona Cardinals was particularly meaningful; he would be returning to his family's home in Arizona.

As a Cardinal, he found himself challenged more than ever as he competed against the best players in the world. NFL linemen hit harder, weighed more, and knew more tricks than anyone he'd faced at USC. The dedication he acquired in Scouting led him to study playbooks and watch game films for hours, devote himself to practice and weight training, and keep his weight down to 330—a difficult assignment for someone with Deuce's size and love for good cooking.

"You have to be disciplined in those areas where if you procrastinate or fail in your job, it can mean losing it. It's a competitive business," he elaborated. "Being able to compete with the best of the best at the highest level of football every week: that's a challenge I have for myself. Especially as a new guy, I try to rise to the occasion of these athletes week in and week out."

I always have trouble understanding, really, the work that goes along with the bright lights of professional football, and the diligence that accompanies any well-paying, high-profile, and seemingly glamorous occupation. C'mon, is it really that tough to be Tiger Woods? Miss a few days of practice and maybe you finish in the top five instead of at number one, but you still walk home with endorsements, prizes, and fame. But Tiger Woods and Deuce Lutui view competition and achievement in a different way. Their natural gifts and competitive spirit started them on great journeys, but their passion made them succeed. When that passion and accompanying work ethic truly become part of you, they never leave. Every match and every practice matters. Seeing how ardently Deuce prepares for each game and understanding how hard he works reminded me that his fame and success are not something to envy, but something to celebrate and aspire to myself. Though probably not on the football field.

Hard work aside, Deuce simply loves the sport of football. Competing against players he admired on television as a teenager thrills him every Sunday. He loves being face-to-face with the best. His greatest joy as a football player doesn't come on those Sunday afternoons, however. The true happiness the game gives him is being able to provide for his family and represent his hometown Cardinals. "I grew up with this team," he said. "And I was a big-time fan. Now I'm a member of this organization. And I'm providing for my family. Those things are what I enjoy most." And his family had grown by one more with the arrival of daughter Melenani in 2006.

That evening, when the football fields were empty and silent, Deuce and I found ourselves standing at attention as a Scout color guard posted the colors for the weekly meeting of a Tempe troop. The audience of Scouts and parents eyed the two visiting Eagle Scouts, an author and an NFL lineman, standing against the wall with our hands over our hearts, reciting the Pledge of Allegiance. I'm sure the 330-pound NFL star attracted much more attention than I did.

Deuce hadn't been at a Scout meeting since he reached Eagle himself, and tonight, he would be speaking to the troop. "What am I going to say?" he asked me, only slightly serious.

"What was all that talk about 'being prepared'?" I asked with a smile.

He laughed. "Hey, you may hear some familiar quotes," he joked, referring to our conversations earlier in the day. He flashed his grin as the Scoutmaster introduced him and he walked to the stage. He did just fine.

Deuce and I slipped out of the meeting early, and talked under the lights in the parking lot before we parted. The Scout meeting had rekindled memories and he reminisced some more about cooking for himself and surviving off the land. Then he remembered enduring winter in northern Arizona. "One of my most memorable experiences was the Polar Bear award. We had to sit in cold, cold, water for a certain amount of time. It was up in northern Arizona and it was crazy. It was a freezing experience just to get that badge!"

The most valuable lesson of Scouting for Deuce? "The Scout Law," he answered immediately. I then watched a 330-pound NFL lineman recite it, all with his irrepressible grin.

"Just being that, having those characteristics speaks for itself. That's what a Scout is, and I'm proud to say I'm a true Scout. I'm proud to say I'm an Eagle. I'm sure there are a lot of Scouts out there, but probably only a few in the NFL."

I wondered and decided to find out. Deuce would probably have been as surprised as I was to find a collection of NFL Eagle Scouts that included the Packers' Brady Poppinga, Baltimore's Pro Bowl tight end Todd Heap, and Chris Hoke of the Pittsburgh Steelers, who would soon line up against Deuce and the Cardinals in Super Bowl XLIII.

On February 1, 2009, the Steelers and Cardinals met in Tampa to battle for the NFL Championship. Deuce continued his outstanding postseason play, protecting quarterback Kurt Warner as he passed for nearly 400 yards. Unfortunately for Deuce, the Steelers scored the winning touchdown with seconds to go. He took it in stride, thankful for a great season. There would be other shots at the championship.

Back at the Scout meeting in Tempe, Super Bowl XLIII was still a season away, and Deuce began quizzing me: Scout slogan, Scout motto, Scout Oath, Scout Law? After a day of fielding questions, he apparently wanted to do the interrogating. He good-naturedly assessed each of my responses. When he was finally satisfied, we shook hands and wished each other well on our respective adventures. Deuce left for home in his oversize black pickup. I left for the airport with Sheldon Caldwell-Meeks, who worked with the Arizona Cardinals. Sheldon had plenty to say about Deuce as we drove along Interstate 10 to catch the night's last flight out of Phoenix.

"Deuce, *where* do I begin?" Sheldon laughed as he accelerated into the far left lane. "You probably got that reaction from a lot of people you spoke to today, right?"

I laughed and nodded.

"From the beginning," Sheldon said, "Deuce was just extraordinary. He wanted to be out in the community more than the norm, especially since he's from Mesa. As soon as he was drafted by the Cardinals, he approached us and wanted us to put him out in the community every single Tuesday."

Sheldon explained why that was particularly significant. National Football League players have one day off per week: Tuesday. Meetings and practices fill Monday, Wednesday, Thursday, and Friday. Travel, meetings, and more practice fill Saturdays, and the players take to the field on Sunday for games. The team schedules community projects and youth programs on Tuesday, the players' one day to spend with family. Most players don't volunteer often.

"But Deuce," Sheldon said with a chuckle, "he approached us and said, 'I want to do something every single Tuesday.' That just speaks about what being out in the community means to him. He's a huge family guy, we know that, but he's so passionate about being a role model to young kids and doing something good for others."

Sheldon laughed, thinking about what he was going to say next. "Let me tell you something else," he said. "We have a special appearance jersey for every player on the team, one they wear to events. We have to make five or six jerseys for Deuce on a regular basis because he's known to pull the jersey off his back and give it to somebody! It's happened so many times I can't even count. There aren't really many guys like him."

Deuce is, without argument, one-of-a-kind, but after I left Phoenix, I discovered others who shared his fame and talent, as well as his dedication to family and Scouting.

Several years ago, only three people believed John Beck would ever wear an NFL jersey: John and his parents. As a five-foot-six high school freshman tipping the scales at 115 pounds, naysayers and realists had an easy case. John did not look like a football player, and certainly not like someone who could ever survive a hit from a truck like Deuce Lutui. Other players John's age towered over him, as he noticed when they'd help him to his feet after they'd sacked him. Again and again, people told him that he wasn't meant for football at the high school level, let alone the NFL. But he doggedly stuck with the game, and resolved that he'd ride the sport all the way to the professional leagues.

"People were quick to tell me I wouldn't make it," he said, "but I can honestly say there wasn't a day in my life when I thought I wouldn't play in the NFL. My mom always told my brother and me, 'My two boys will earn Eagle Scout.' We never questioned if we'd get it. We'd just have to do the things to make it happen. I applied the same idea to football."

That wasn't too hard since football has always been John's passion. "I love every aspect of the game," he reflected. "Working extra, practice, weights, throwing balls to receivers. All of it.

"I'm also very competitive with myself and others," he explained. "I feel like I've always known the things I could achieve and I've committed to reaching that. I don't want to fall short of what I could be. On the field against another team, you have adversity. Trying to earn Eagle, you have adversity. I've had adversity all my life. Being small but playing with the big kids, it's just another case of adversity. I'm used to adversity. I push through it."

After battling two more years of adversity, John began his senior year of high school standing only one inch above six feet; he weighed 170. He wasn't small, but college football programs wanted six-foot-four quarterbacks who carried over two hundred pounds. Size aside, John made a strong argument to Pacific-10 Conference recruiters. The Mountain View High School football team won twenty-five games and lost only two while John played quarterback. He led the Toros to the Arizona state championship his senior year. That same year, several organizations selected him as Arizona player or quarterback of the year, and he earned scholar-athlete honors while setting a state record by tossing forty-two touchdown completions.

Big schools also wanted someone who'd stick with their program for four solid years, and John complicated his case by deciding to spend two years serving a mission in Portugal for the Mormon Church. The mission was a choice, but John had always planned on doing it. Someone his size stubborn enough to stick with football wasn't going to change his mind for college recruiters. Interest from Pac-10 teams consequently evaporated. Only two teams kept his career aspirations alive, but even they'd have to wait.

At age nineteen, John landed in Lisbon, Portugal, not speaking a lick of Portuguese. For the next two years, he'd speak with his parents just four times and play football only eight times. He spent his time serving others and sharing his faith, which had to be strong considering the sacrifices—including the possibility of never being in the NFL, his lifelong goal. The odds were already against him; few people would have recommended compounding them with a two-year hiatus.

He felt a spiritual call to serve abroad, and once he arrived in Portugal, he discovered that he loved his work. Deciding to answer the call in the first place proved more difficult than carrying out the mission itself. In Portugal, he soon replaced football with soccer and found himself doing something for his church he believed important. Initially, he couldn't speak the language, but he wouldn't let his own shortcomings interfere with his purpose. He explained that the message he was sharing was too important for that. John worked well into the night, often missing dinner, as he shared his faith and served the community. On those too frequent occasions, the evening meal was peanut butter and jelly sandwiches scarfed down at a bus stop. "As a missionary you feel urgency," he said in explanation. "During the first year, you think you'll be there forever, then the second half, you realize how short a year is, how important the work is, and you really want to make the most of it. We were sharing our faith and helping out in the community where we could, and you realize how much there is to do, so it's really a calling."

His fellow missionaries felt the same, and many served for their two years at the cost of losing girlfriends back home. Missions aren't easy on relationships or on the missionaries themselves. They require mountains of self-motivation, as young men and women devote time to prayer and planning at their home before setting out each day into the surrounding area. There, they share their faith with everyone they meet, sometimes walking up to strangers and just starting a conversation. They also undertake community service projects, activities often familiar to former Scouts. In Portugal, John and his companions faced early mornings and long days of work, walking, and some hostility, which helped the group bond even tighter in their isolation thousands of miles away from America. They supported each other closely throughout their two years. Many were Eagle Scouts, John noted. And as often happened at Scout camp, when John had trouble waking up, one of his fellow missionaries would drag him out of bed. Since he'd been losing weight, this proved a much more manageable task for his friends. Other days, he'd return the favor. He didn't often need his friends' help, however. Despite not playing football, he didn't stop training for it. He rose regularly at 5:15 A.M. and went running to keep his legs in shape.

"I knew I would come back and play," he explained. "If I didn't want to lose my legs, I had to train. But the mission was the most important thing and we were supposed to start at 6:00 A.M., so I didn't want to take away time from being a missionary. I was up early for running, then pull-ups, push-ups, and sit-ups."

In 2003, John arrived at Brigham Young University in Provo, Utah, underweight and under-practiced but in passable shape. He started four games as a twenty-two-year-old freshman, passing 279 yards in one game. By the end of his sophomore season, the six-foot-one John had put the size issue to bed. He started most games and clearly commanded the attention of the NCAA's Mountain West Conference. He passed for more than three thousand yards and showed everyone his deadly long-field arm, completing passes of over fifty yards in six games. The next season, he broke 3,700 yards in one season and set conference records by hammering Boston College with forty-one completions and steamrolling Texas Christian University with 517 yards and five touchdowns. His reputation grew in his senior season as ESPN named John one of the nation's top quarterbacks and Heisman Trophy rumors circulated. He backed up the accolades by completing 69 percent of his passes and throwing for nearly four thousand yards. The chance at an NFL career was his, just as he always knew it would be.

He remembered working hard for team scouts in the NFL Combine, essentially a week-long tryout, and leaving pleased with his performance and confident the draft would include him. Several teams flew scouts to Arizona to watch John work out, but on draft day, he still sat watching the television, wondering if, when, and who. When the fortieth pick came, John and his wife, Barb, learned they were going to Miami. "What wasn't to like?" John asked. "I really love fishing and you can't complain about the sunny weather!"

When he arrived, he also found a real challenge. His new team occupied the low berth in the NFL rankings. The offensive line had trouble holding opposing defenses at bay and Miami quarterbacks were often hurried or sacked; the Dolphins could have used a Deuce Lutui. John started several games during the difficult season, hoping to turn the team's season around. After each start, however, he left the field frustrated after he gave 100 percent and his team continued losing. His spirits remained undaunted, however, and he was looking forward to his next season. Besides, he'd long since learned to handle a little adversity.

During those first NFL games, John also suffered some pain as opposing teams' linebackers and tackles found their way through Miami's offensive line. "I've been playing the game since I was age eight, so I've been getting hit my entire life," John explained. "I've always been a smaller kid, but always felt tough and could take the hits. It's just part of the game, but the hits are hard in the NFL, no doubt. But when you're out there, it doesn't enter your mind. It's not until that next day that you feel like you've been hit by a car!"

Since John and Deuce Lutui both played offense, John would never have a run-in with the 330-pound Cardinal. And while they are different people and different players, they share something important.

When I spoke with John, he and his wife Barb were in the middle of remodeling their suburban Miami home, with all the attendant clutter and stress. Their eleven-month-old son Ty had been sick, adding to the busyness around the house. Talking with John about his life at home, I realized how both John and Deuce grounded themselves in their families. On the field and in the community, they carried larger-than-life status. People wanted their autographs. People asked for pictures with them. They were NFL players and something special. They both realized fame's fleeting nature, however. Living only for that fame would ensure an unhappy life of ups and downs dictated by whimsical public opinion. When their careers ended, as each inevitably would, they'd fall out of the public eye and its accompanying validation. They knew they had to control their own lives and make their own happiness.

"Family has to be the most important thing," John told me. "Football is only one part of my life. Family will be forever. For me, I know family will always have to be the top priority. Family and faith always keep me grounded. I'm blessed with an awesome wife who understands the passion and that I want to be a champion. I know I've gotta do things in return and be the dad I need to be for Ty."

Like Deuce, John recognizes a duty to Ty's generation, and younger generations in general. As a Scout in Arizona, he first began to recognize the cycle of giving that is such a part of a significant and meaningful life. He saw the leadership role his Scoutmaster filled. He observed how boys learned to respect their leader because he was in charge, but also because he was there to help them. John found the same care and leadership in his coaches later in his life. "The coaches want me to be successful," he explained. "Everything that a coach does is to help make me successful. He's not there for his own personal gain, just like a Scoutmaster. Scoutmasters aren't earning merit badges. They're there to help Scouts be the best they can be."

John honestly surprised me when he said he was already involved in Scouting in Miami. He'd been in south Florida less than a year and much of that year had been spent on the Dolphins' training fields and in their weight room. That left precious little time to spend with his wife and son. Regardless, every week the Cub Scouts sponsored by John's church could look forward to going to their meetings and seeing their leader, the quarterback for the Miami Dolphins.

"I was a Scout myself and now I'm helping younger Scouts as a leader," John said. "In my role, I only try to help the kids. It's all about helping the Scout be the best he can be. When the Scouts understand that, they can achieve all they want."

I knew another missionary who understood the same thing.

Several years before John Beck ventured to Portugal, Oregon native Jon Heder served his church mission in Japan. Jon Heder didn't return to play football like John Beck, but he enthusiastically took up a slightly less known sport that has propelled him from being a relatively anonymous college student to a well-known persona in Hollywood and in homes across the nation.

America first met Jon with the release of the film *Napoleon Dynamite*, in which he reintroduced America to tetherball. Jon played the title role of a curly-haired, socially awkward high school student who lives with his grandmother and misfit brother in rural Idaho. The film became a national sensation and Napoleon Dynamite, with his thick glasses and moon boots, became an icon. But the phenomenon first started as a nine-minute black-and-white short film, reminiscent of a Cinematography merit badge project. Created by *Napoleon* director Jared Hess and starring Jon Heder, *Peluca* introduced the characters that would become Napoleon and his sidekick Pedro. Infamous scenes involving the school bus, Tater Tots, and a wig for Pedro all appear in the short. Like his fellow Eagle Scout Steven Spielberg, Jon started with simple films, but chased dreams of something bigger.

Since *Napoleon Dynamite*'s release in 2004, Heder has starred alongside Diane Keaton, Jeff Daniels, David Spade, Mila Kunis, and Will Arnett in films like *When in Rome*, *Moving McAllister*, *The Benchwarmers*, and *Mama's Boy*. He also appeared in NBC's *My Name Is Earl* and provided voices for the animated features *Surf's Up* and *Monster House*, nods to his early love for animation.

Jon always makes sure his films keep both him and audiences entertained, and his fun continued in 2007, as he costarred with Will Ferrell in *Blades of Glory*, another cult success. He played the role of naïve, but good-hearted ice skating champion Jimmy MacElroy. Reflecting on Jimmy's character, Jon said, "Jimmy was very different from me, but there's that innocence there. I have a little of that and it goes back to Scouts in a way. Jimmy always expects the best of people. Hopefully as Scouts, we're not only trustworthy, but also trusting in a nice way. Just maybe not as much as Jimmy."

He paused, enjoying the rare silence that had come to his Los Angeles home while his young daughter Evan napped. His wife, Kirsten, had left Jon in charge for the afternoon. "This is what I want to do: be in film," he continued. "But I want to hold on to the standards I've been brought up with. I want to uphold them, not preach them. That goes right along with what I learned in Scouts. I want who I was growing up to be in my movies. Yes, acting is stepping outside your self, but I want some of my characteristics in my roles. And alongside acting, I love storytelling. Bringing a character to life is telling a story. Who is this person, why are they the way they are?"

Jon doesn't claim to know where Napoleon Dynamite got all of the aspects of his eccentric personality, but Jon will forever be known for playing him. "Napoleon was much closer to me than Jimmy MacElroy," the actor explained. "He was unlike any other character I ever have played or will play. He was so close to me but very, very different at the same time. There are parts of Napoleon's character that are straight from Scout camp or straight from [writer-director] Jared Hess's life as a Scout, or my life, seeing my younger brothers in Scouts and life. I was a little more well rounded than Napoleon, but Napoleon is the type who would love Scouts. He'd have some tough times because he's so awkward, but in the end, he'd love it because of the skills he'd learn."

Growing up as sons of a Scoutmaster, all five Heder brothers earned Eagle in Troop 147, West Salem, Oregon. Doug, Jon's twin Dan, and Adam all earned the rank quickly, but their youngest brother Matt took longer. He eventually got it, with the brothers' collective "nurturing," Jon said with a laugh. "But really," he added, "I don't see how it would've been possible for any of us *not* to get it because of Dad."

Dr. James Heder earned Eagle at the young age of thirteen, which, Jon joked, he never let his sons forget. Dr. Heder had been raised by his mother and Scouting had helped him cope with not having a father present at home. He's been paying back Scouting ever since and served as Scoutmaster for all his boys.

"Dad was a doctor and doctors are very cool with pain, accidents, and fixing things," Jon said, then laughed. "When a Scout got hurt, a log could be sticking thru the kid's arm, blood gushing, and Dad—all calm, cool, and collected—would just say, 'Okay, Jim. What should you do about that?'

"But he took time for the Scouts who needed the most help. He really was a great Scoutmaster. He was always prepared, but he didn't prepare everyone else. He'd let them learn. I remember trips when nobody brought the right food or right anything, and that's just a mild example of the mistakes we made. Scouting helped me learn. You don't get upset and down on yourself. Realize there'll be another time. You gotta remember, 'Next time I'll do this or won't do that.' You'll feel like you're prepared the next time. It really does teach humility in a good way. You're humble and teachable, you're not full of pride."

In Scouts, Jon learned to be prepared and how to learn from—and teach by—example. Now, being prepared often means having a jacket ready for Kirsten at a chilly movie theater. He confessed that was a remnant of many weekends spent snow-camping, a favorite family activity. The Heder boys routinely trekked into snowy Oregon woods during the dead of winter for weekend camping trips. He remembered skiing cross-country to wilderness campsites, carrying packs filled with food and clothes. They'd find a good spot where the snow was wet, but not too wet, and build snow caves. They still do it today whenever they're together.

"From Scouts, we have so many stories of kids building caves wrong," Jon said. "They'd wake up with their sleeping bags floating! They'd end up in Dad's dry cave and somehow he'd always turn the weekend into a good experience and they'd come back. Usually."

One trip, the snow proved too wet for safe caves, so some Scouts used their skis to support a plastic tarp, which served as their shelter, for a while. They had supported the tarp in various locations with skis, Jon explained. As snow fell throughout the night, the plastic began weighing and straining against the points of the skis and eventually ripped wide open, covering the sleeping Scouts below with fresh powder. Jon blissfully slept through it all, but discovered the mistake the next day.

"I remember getting out of my sleeping bag that morning," Jon said. "I looked around me at this white winter wonderland—all white. I see a few mounds where our patrol was sleeping under piles of snow. They were still warm because their sleeping bags were wrapped in plastic, but all their gear was covered in snow and you had to get out of your bag at some point! One kid never did another trip with us again!"

Jon still loves snow camping and he tried to share his passion with a Scout troop in notoriously well-heeled Malibu where he served a stint as a Scout leader. "But it was Malibu," he explained. "All they wanted to do was surf! Well, I knew snow-camping. Then when I finally got them to the snow, they all just wanted to go snowboarding!

"But all those experiences in Scouts and with Scouts make you want to do more outside and more with Scouting," he concluded. "Right now I have a daughter. Am I going to keep having girls? I need a Scout! But it doesn't matter. Whoever I have, I'm taking them camping. That's how I want to raise my kids. And wherever I end up living and raising my family, I want to be involved, be a Scoutmaster, take kids out and show them how good—or not—I am outdoors.

"That's our responsibility as Eagles," he continued. "To teach the next generation. Lots of us are starting families. We need to understand fathers' obligations, husbands' obligations, and teach kids how to be good humans. In my opinion and in my experience, the Scout Law, everything that makes a Scout good, is what works. It's universal and unchanging."

Jon Heder, John Beck, and Deuce Lutui all live by those values they learned while growing up—perseverance, service, duty to family—and they had passed them to other young people through Scouting and their service work. They are also beginning to instill those ideals and habits in their own children as new fathers, and that seemed important. I noticed the satisfaction they derived from their families. They had all achieved celebrity status—their names and faces were known to people across the country. Yet, they still placed family first and, if necessary, would put their careers aside entirely for the sake of those for whom they cared most. And as I'd soon find out they weren't alone in making that choice.

TEACHING FOR AMERICA

Not far from Jon Heder's home exists a very different Los Angeles. In contrast to the sunny palm trees and affluence often associated with Hollywood, South Central L.A. has broken sidewalks with dilapidated stores, empty parking lots, crime, and poverty. Gang violence has earned the neighborhood a notorious reputation, and although local politicians have recently begun to call the area "South Los Angeles" instead of "South Central," little more than the name had changed. The Hispanic population now exceeds African-Americans, but otherwise, the neighborhood's past isn't really past. Ethnicities and names may shift, but poverty's symptoms remain the same. Forty-three percent of families here live at or below the poverty level and crime hasn't subsided.

Hannibol Sullivan, an Eagle Scout who worked with the local Boy Scout council, drove me through the neighborhood's streets, offering me a glimpse of another world. I saw iron bars guarding windows and doors on many of the small, pastel stucco houses. Laundry hung drying outside apartments in dated housing projects. Even though school was in session, groups of young people congregated on corners and near gas stations that also had barred windows. I saw how easily gangs could prey upon teenagers trapped by circumstance, crime, and lack of opportunity. Hope seemed a scarce commodity, except in the places Hannibol would show me.

I felt quite safe riding through South L.A. with Hannibol, who looks a bit like his name would suggest. His former lineman's body fit snugly into his Ford Expedition, and the big SUV, windows appropriately tinted, seemed to lend us a respectable presence as we cruised through the area. With his size and sunglasses, Hannibol looked tough enough to have come from these streets himself. In fact, he grew up on the equally rough streets of the Bronx in New York.

He had come to this very neighborhood years ago to attend the University of Southern California, a lush, academic oasis amid the surrounding urban decay. Several years after he graduated, Hannibol began working with principals and teachers in local elementary schools to start, grow, and maintain Scout troops and Cub Scout packs. Neighborhood children face an array of bad influences when they leave the walls—literally, security walls—of their elementary school each day. For them, Scouting provides opportunity and a path out of poverty's vicious cycle.

"Without hope, South L.A. would look a lot different and a lot worse," Hannibol said as we pulled into the fenced parking lot adjacent to South Park Elementary School. He turned off the engine and laughter from the adjacent playground filtered through his tinted windows. "Hope is opportunity. Hope is Scouting. Hope is youth football. It's anything that takes kids out of their immediate surroundings and gives them a path and something positive to do.

"Scouting gave that hope to me," he said, stepping down from the driver's seat and closing the car door. "It kept my friends and me off the streets in New York, kept us focused, gave us a sense of direction that other kids didn't have. We got to interact with kids from different ethnicities and different communities. Heck, I was in an Islamic Scout troop and went to Catholic school.

"It also taught me to be independent. My Scout friends and I had been working at Scout camps so much that when we went to college or the military, we knew how to function without parents. Open a bank account? No problem. We'd learned about banks and finance in Scouting. As for college, I had an extended family through Scouting, so I had people tell me about different colleges, whereas other kids didn't have those resources. That's how I came to USC here in L.A."

Hannibol never left Scouting. During his college summers, he returned to New York and worked construction jobs during the week and at Alpine Scout Camp on the weekends. He and his leaders knew those jobs would keep him off the streets and on a path that would lead somewhere positive. Ultimately, they did, and in the late 1990s, Hannibol began working for the the Boy Scouts of America in Los Angeles, serving urban youth in places like South L.A. and South Park Elementary. He oversees the Los Angeles version of the same program that helped rescue Buey Ray Tut and Jacob Khol from Omaha's housing projects. His role, he explained, involved starting troops and packs, developing new after-school and weekend programs, recruiting and training leaders—and *keeping* leaders, he wanted me to note. Engaging leaders like Dr. Graves in Omaha is the key to the program's success. And typically the more trying the circumstances, the more dedicated a leader that is required.

Many children in South Los Angeles are surrounded by a chilling set of pressures: unemployment, violence, and neglect. They regularly witness drug deals and shootings, and live in a neighborhood with a violent crime index that is about 490 percent higher than the Los Angeles County average. Last year, the South Park community alone reported more than eight hundred incidents of aggravated assault and nearly one thousand burglaries. Hannibol explained how ethnic gang violence dominates the area. "Black, Asian, Guatemalan, Mexican, El Salvadorian, Colombian, you name it and they have gangs," Hannibol said as we walked toward the school's office. "And you can't just say 'Hispanic' anymore. People from each country in Latin America are unique and proud of their background. But regardless, the bad element, the ones in gangs, will prey on these young people."

Inside the school, we met Karen Rose, a principal who offered her children a haven from the surrounding dangers. She explained how Hannibol's efforts for the students, whether they were in Scouts or not, made an important difference. Eighty-nine percent of her students receive free or reduced-price lunches; they face the challenges of poverty each day. She seemed genuinely thankful that her students had Scouts as an option, a path other than trouble.

"I'm trying to work with teachers and principals, like Karen and others here, and give the kids an opportunity to get *out* of their community," Hannibol explained, as we continued our tour of the schoolyard where students were playing after class. "We want them to have the opportunity to see people in a positive light. On the streets, these kids are taught to look down on police, teachers, probation officers, and other people who are really trying to help. The gangs see them as enemies and that becomes the culture these kids fall into because, like I said earlier, gangs dominate the culture. Scouting brings people in from different careers to bridge that gap and try and explain to kids that this is how you need to behave and act—in a positive manner. It's not beating them over the head. It's 'Hey, you're facing some challenges but we want to go on a camping trip so let's see how we can work around these challenges out there.' Scouting is effective here. If you have one hundred kids in Scouts, you'll lose twenty to gangs, dropping out of school, or some other bad element of this place. If that one hundred weren't involved in Scouting, you'd only have twenty who'd make it out of here. The other eighty? Lord knows where they'd end up."

After meeting with teachers and students, we returned to Hannibol's Expedition. He looked at the children in the schoolyard as we walked back to the parking lot. Statistics told him that more than one in four would drop out before graduating high school. "I recognize a few of them as Scouts," Hannibol said, "but a lot of them aren't, and that's okay. We're just doing our best to get them all on a good path or in some good program so they can get the skills and motivation to get out of here and never have to come back."

"How do you do that?" I asked. "How do we—America, our generation—do that?"

In just a short time, South Los Angeles had overwhelmed me. Politicians talk about equal opportunity and level playing fields. The children I saw within the security fences of South Park Elementary often can't even see the playing field. And most people can't see these children. They appear in the background on local newscasts of shootings in neighborhoods most of us avoid. We switch the channel and forget them. Well, they can't change the channel. They must survive every day in South Los Angeles and hope they find people who believe in them, like Hannibol or Karen Rose. If they can't find figures like that, they'll be lost. In that sense, these adults embody their hope.

We pulled out of the parking lot and drove back toward infamous Crenshaw Boulevard, Hannibol still thinking about my last question. "There's no one answer because it takes more than one person or group," he finally said. "Thousands—probably millions—of children grow up like this. We need thousands of people doing what they can to bring a little hope to places like this and to their kids. We each do it a little differently but we have to do something, one by one. That's how our generation will change it."

Although she lived in Atlanta, I expect Chevai Andrews would have been familiar with the realities facing the children of South Los Angeles. I met her when I visited the classroom of Eagle Scout Karl Brady, who taught Chevai's second-grade class at Adamsville Elementary School in southwest Atlanta, another area where hope was sometimes scarce.

Nearly 90 percent of the school's students are eligible for Georgia's free lunch program, reflecting the poverty of the surrounding neighborhood.

In Karl's classroom, Chevai and I stretched out on a blue rug, bearing the seal of the United States. Chevai lived in the housing projects nearby, and her mother had worked at the local McDonald's until it closed. She now worked at Burger King. To use a computer, Chevai walked to the public library nearby; her family couldn't afford one.

But she had a spark of enthusiasm and a goal. Why was she here? "To get an education," she said emphatically. When she was older, she explained, she wanted to help people who had breathing problems. I wondered who in her family had similar health issues; I wondered how they paid for treatment. I filed those thoughts away so I could focus on Chevai.

She read *Arthur's Lost Puppy* to me as we sat together on the rug, and I saw how earnestly she tried. Most words she read well; at some, her bright eyes would narrow, she'd pause, and I'd help her. Sitting there with this child, I wondered how her family had dealt with the challenges of poverty. Were there figures in Atlanta, like those in Los Angeles, who could encourage her? At least in the classroom, she found inspiration in her teacher, Karl Brady.

When I walked into Karl's classroom earlier that day, fourteen pairs of curious eyes watched me try unsuccessfully not to draw attention to myself. Their teacher, a 2006 Wake Forest University graduate, regained their attention when I sat down, and he concluded his lesson. As the class prepared to leave for their homeroom, a boy named Terrell walked over to me with a book the class had been reading. The story centered on a genie in a bottle who protected the girl who'd liberated him from a gang of unruly boys. Terrell explained that his favorite part came "when the genie says he'll beat them up if they mess with the girl." Maybe those weren't the author's exact words, but the idea certainly caught Terrell's interest.

As the classes changed, and Terrell left, I thought about what this second-grader had said, and it seemed there was something deeper there. I mentioned it to Karl.

"The violence is definitely a part of their everyday existence," he said. "They relate to it. A student in second grade was on the news because she got shot and killed during a botched home invasion at her apartment complex. That really shook the school up. And then last year I had a student whose dad got shot in a gang-related shootout and he was really shaken up and acted out against everybody. Another day, I brought a black Maglite to class for a demonstration, and when I pulled it out, the class said basically in unison, 'That's like what the police have!' That's unfortunately their world. It's what they know. We try to give them something different here."

Growing up in Asheville, North Carolina, Karl had experienced a very different world during his childhood. "In my area, you were poor if you were parking a three-year-old SUV in the student lot," he said. "It was just a warped perspective I had." Then as a student at Wake Forest, he saw Teach for America posters and for the first time learned about the realities of educational inequality. He had never heard of the term, but became intrigued as he studied it. He realized how teaching fit within the university's motto of *pro humanita*—for the good of humanity—and remembered thinking, "This could really be my generation's calling, to fix something that's wrong with America."

The Teach for America program recruits top college graduates like Karl from across the country, offering them training and an opportunity—or a challenge—to bring hope into the lives of students in underserved schools. More than four thousand students join the corps each year for a two-year tour of duty. Karl, now in his second year with the program, confessed that his first year had been as much a test for him as it was for his students. Like Paul Oxborrow found in Lokossa, Benin, the inaugural year of teaching rarely proves easy, and four students with chronic behavior problems made Karl's particularly memorable. Every time he attempted to involve their parents, he hit a wall.

"It's not like when I grew up," he explained. "If the teacher had a problem with me, she'd call my mom. If she didn't reach my mom, she'd call my dad, and that was big stuff 'cause I knew that there was something bad gonna go down that night!

"But with these kids, the phone numbers change so much, because when you're making so little money, you've got to make the choice: in the winter, do you pay the phone bill or do you pay the heating bill? And these kids already know about rent. When I was eight, I thought *Rent* was a musical on Broadway. That's what I knew about the word *rent*. But they know that Mom's gotta pay the rent, but then she's got to make the choice to pay the heating bill or the water bill. I've got kids whose water gets shut off all the time. Sometimes, to reach them, I have to call a friend's house where they're staying. I had a girl who was homeless last year and her mom kept her going to school, which was good, but she still missed forty-two days. Those are some of the challenges with these kids, and so many things are not really their fault."

Those challenges became very personal to Karl, as with other young teachers. Before entering a competitive program like Teach for America, most of these college graduates have only known success, but urban schools can change that quite rapidly. "You're used to being a hard charger, trying something and making it work," explained Karl. "You're used to leading an organization with people that are into it and want to accomplish something. Then you come into teaching, and through Teach for America, you teach in inner city schools. It's the first thing you've ever tried so hard at and failed. But through failure, you become not only a better teacher, but the person you are on the other side of your two years, even of the first year, is completely different. It's a sobering world. I'm not in my bubble anymore. I can't surround myself with people that are just like me. I've had my bubble burst in every way imaginable, because there were a lot of stereotypes that came with me. People think, 'Oh, the problem has to be the parents in these inner-city schools; the parents aren't doing anything.' Well, most of my parents were involved last year. But it's the different pressures that are on the parents. Those pressures wouldn't normally be associated with parents in the suburbs or high-income areas. It's a different set of pressures for them entirely."

Karl thought that what worked for him as a suburban student years ago might benefit his current students. During the long trial that was his first year of teaching, Karl stumbled across a group recruiting students for the Boy Scouts in his school. Karl introduced himself as an Eagle Scout and offered to help. "They brought me on board," he remembered, "but I really only wanted to be a consultant, if you can think of it like that. I just wanted to show up and supervise the kids."

Soon, and perhaps inevitably, Karl was leading a Cub Scout pack at Adamsville Elementary School. At year's end, Pack 68 received Pack of the Year honors for the district. Only ten boys attended regularly—the size of a single "den" in many large, suburban packs—but everyone considered Karl's pack a great success. He considers it a success himself, but for different reasons.

"I had a kid in my room that was, I won't call him a troublemaker, because I don't like to label kids, but he constantly found himself in trouble," he explained. "I got him into Scouts and we developed a really good bond, and through the year, he would obey more and more if I told him to do something. And then, the secretary at school asked him one day, 'Juan, why are you being so good?' He said because he's in the Boy Scouts. So that was really when it all hit home for me that I was doing my job not only as Scout, but as a good member of society."

Weeks after I'd read with Chevai, I returned to Adamsville Elementary for a five o'clock Scout meeting. I found Karl in his uniform, Eagle knot sewn over his left pocket and well-worn Philmont belt around his waist. His Scouts didn't wear uniforms yet; most would receive free Scout shirts when they reached their next rank. I remembered several boys from my earlier visit and I soon found myself shedding years and cutting up with the Scouts and, along with them, receiving looks of reprimand from Mr. Brady. I found their innocent energy quite contagious, but I was very glad I was not responsible for convincing them to pay attention.

In the library, the pack sat around a table—one of those you can scarcely fit your knees under if you're over five feet tall. I sat on top of an adjacent table. Karl had each Scout conduct part of the opening ceremony. Karl led the Pledge of Allegiance, while Asad held the flag. Eddie led the Cub Scout Law, Greg led the Promise. The Scouts, second- and third-graders, practiced folding the American flag following a demonstration put on by Karl and me. After that, the pack split into small groups to work on requirements, and I helped a particularly bright third-grader research a famous American. Todd picked Bessie Coleman, and he taught me about one of the first female African-American pilots. In turn, I taught him about writing. With my occasional help, Todd pieced together a fine paragraph on the famous aviator and happily turned in his paper. At the meeting's end, he proudly told his mother that he was one step closer to his Bear rank and one step closer to being an Eagle Scout.

The theory of natural selection would likely have eluded Karl Brady's second-graders, but Craig McGowan's ninth graders dug right in. Looking less like a high school teacher and more like a Philmont ranger with a tie, Craig assembled his fourteen seventh-period students in the hallway just inside the doors to southwest Atlanta's Banneker High School, a school of fifteen hundred where half of the students receive free or reduced lunches and only 43 percent of economically disadvantaged students graduate. Every day, Craig and his students faced a statistical struggle. But there he stood, doing his best, wearing hiking boots, Carthartt pants, a full but nicely trimmed beard, a blue fleece over his shirt, and a loosely knotted necktie. Craig distributed handouts explaining the day's lab assignment and corralled his students against one wall of the hallway, where he made sure each read the full two pages. I followed the students' example and read over the lab, which would demonstrate natural selection. Once the class had satisfied their teacher that they understood the plan, Craig led them outside toward a grassy median in the parking lot. The bright sun had warmed the air to a pleasantly endurable temperature, although the students kept their coats pulled tight. Jets from Atlanta's airport rumbled overhead.

The students gathered around their teacher as he scattered dry black beans around the median. The seeds bounced on the cold earth and spotty grass before coming to rest. They represented prey, teacher explained to class. Craig then distributed tools to the students—plastic knives, forks, spoons, and forceps. Some would use their hands. With their given tools, each student assumed the role of predator. At their teacher's call, the students dropped to their knees and raced to capture their share of prey—that is, place beans in their cup with their various tools. If they couldn't collect the minimum number in time, they "starved and died." Upon reincarnation, they would adopt a different tool. Sixty seconds later, Craig called time. Predators with particularly inefficient knives perished in round one, victims of natural selection. In succeeding rounds, those with forks and spoons also perished. The ranks of predators using their hands or forceps grew and soon eclipsed users of all other tools. Nature had selected the best predators. The students understood the lesson, while I think Craig and I also understood a different, deeper lesson.

We both watched students learn how creatures with poor tools eventually perish, pushed out of the evolutionary race. We silently wondered how many of these students might find themselves edged out of a similar contest. Would they have the right tools to compete? Fate had dealt them a difficult hand. Other children their age, many of whom lived only a few miles away, already had a head start: well-educated parents, supportive neighborhoods, a safe home. Through the blind lottery of birth, few students at Banneker had those advantages and accompanying tools.

Some people pontificate on the problems of inequality and others do something about it. Craig had joined Teach for America and now spent nearly ten hours a day at Banneker High School. He helped Atlanta's forgotten students develop skills and knowledge so they wouldn't fall prey themselves to a too familiar cycle of poverty and neglect.

Craig led the students back to the building while being assailed from all sides by questions, most pertinent, a few not. One particularly bright student, Annie, walked back to the classroom with me and I used the chance to ask her what she thought of her teacher.

"He's fun," she said without hesitation. "He makes it interesting. Some people think he's too hard though. I just think he's trying to make us smarter."

An Eagle Scout and Brown University graduate, Craig held high standards for himself and his students. After the three o'clock bell sounded, releasing waves of students into the hallways, Craig and I sat down together in his concrete-walled classroom to discuss his first year as a teacher. Results from the natural selection experiment still remained on the whiteboard.

"The kids really respond well to someone who will both push them and show them that they care about whether they achieve those expectations," Craig explained, loosening his tie further. "I have very high standards for them, but I'm constantly working with them to help them get there and show them that they *can* get there. You can't just assign this big assignment so when they don't turn it in, you can say, 'Well you should've done that. You failed.' They don't respond to that."

Craig hopes to help his students become more independent, which goes along with meeting his expectations. At the ages of fourteen or fifteen, it's time for them to take responsibility, something their teacher first learned in Troop 75 of Ridgefield, Connecticut. Craig remembered falling homesick on this first trip to summer camp. He had never been away from his family for an entire week. But, he explained, he went ahead doing things without his parents—he had no choice, of course. He had to go to meals, go to merit badge classes, and get himself ready each morning without his parents' guidance—or the direct guidance of any other adults, for that matter.

"At camp, you're forced to figure things out on your own," he explained. "You realize, 'I can do this. I can go away from my family for a week and not die. Yes, I can cook for myself for a week and I won't starve. I might not eat *well*, but I won't starve.' "

He tries to instill the same lesson in his students, and for some, he might be the only source of that direction. For students unaccustomed to being pushed academically, Craig's teaching methods offer a shock.

Those proficient at working the system and completing a series of multiple-choice exercises must suddenly begin to think critically when they face Mr. McGowan's science lessons.

"They look at me like, 'What the heck is this? Where are the normal work sheets? What's with all this thinking?'

"I'd give a question and they'd look at me for the answer. I'd say, 'You tell me—what do *you* think?' I really want to focus on developing their critical thinking skills across the board, in all subjects.

"You'll always have some kids who are more naturally talented than others. Some are very good in science and math, but are weak in literature. I see my job as trying to get kids away from the crutch of 'I'm not good at science, therefore I'll never be good in science, therefore I don't have to try.' Kids use that as a crutch, as an excuse. I see my job as, 'Okay, you've never understood it, but why does that mean you can't understand it now? Maybe you're really good at art. I'm terrible at art. It takes a lot of effort for me to draw something that's not hideous. Doesn't mean I can't do it, it just takes a lot of effort and that doesn't mean it's not worthwhile.'

"Some of these students—certainly not all—have so much in their lives pushing down on them: lack of stable home life, lack of stable community, negative economic pressures. My job is to mitigate that. I was lucky. My parents and community would've made sure I graduated and went to college, whether I had great teachers or not. But for some of these kids, if they don't have great teachers they won't go to college because nothing else is pushing them. All it can take is one great teacher who says, 'I believe in you. You can do this. No, it's not easy, but you can do this. Come after school and I'll help you. I'll help you with your other classes, too. I'm here to show you what *you* can do.' It's not going to happen with every kid you teach, but if you can reach one or two or three, you've gotten somewhere."

That reminded me of how this generation is changing our future: one or two lives at a time. Individually, our acts of principle may seem futile, and I found many people overwhelmed by the endless needs we face. Collectively, however, our actions will shape the world's future.

This fact is particularly apparent for those who've gone through Scouting, Craig observed. As a Scout, he recognizes an obligation to live—or at least try to live—by the basic guidelines of the Scout Oath and Law. He repeated both for good measure, then commented, "As a teacher, I try to instill some of that in my students. We should always take advantage of situations where we can influence other people in a positive way. The skills we've learned as Scouts put us in positions of leadership. We end up there. Maybe not right away but eventually in life we'll probably end up in some position of leadership where we'll have influence on other people. It's our obligation to take advantage of that in a positive way and try to positively impact not only the lives of people we're directly leading, but also the people they impact."

When I think of America's greatness, I often discount—unintentionally—the poverty surrounding Adamsville Elementary School, Banneker High School, and the hundreds of schools like them. I tend to forget about these students and their families. I had rarely been to their neighborhoods. I didn't know their streets, hopes, and trials. I had walked into their classrooms fairly certain we had nothing in common; I wondered if we ever would. But I found the students eager and bright, and most important, motivated by their teachers. I shared a book with Chevai. We read together and I watched her discover language. I joined the boys of Pack 68 and saw them look to Karl and me as brother Scouts. I watched Craig inspire his students to think critically. They had hope, and particularly in Karl and Craig, they had teachers who cared.

One evening after I visited their schools, Karl and Craig met me at one of my favorite neighborhood restaurants. Craig brought along Evan Sterling, another Teach for America teacher and Eagle Scout. We four Eagles talked about Scouting then predictably the conversation moved to their most recent weeks at school. Karl's had involved pack meetings and standardized tests, and Craig's had culminated with the natural selection lab. Evan, however, had treated a gunshot victim.

The twenty-two-year-old teacher had gone to the McNair–South Atlanta high school basketball game on a recent Friday night. As the crowd left the gym after McNair lost the game, a gunshot sounded on the nearby street. Students rushed back into the gym; Evan went straight for the sound. He used his training as an EMT to treat the nineteen-year-old victim until the ambulance arrived. Aside from a lot of modesty, his dominant emotion as he recounted the story was sadness and perhaps hurt. He was so disappointed that gun violence found its way to an Atlanta high school.

But that sadness took hold *after* he'd rendered aid. He'd reacted quickly and stepped up in a situation where doing nothing might have been less complicated. His actions reminded me of two other Eagle Scouts who faced danger at their schools in two incidents that had forever scarred our generation. In April 1999, two teenaged gunmen entered Columbine High School in Littleton, Colorado. They carried sawed-off shotguns, a semiautomatic carbine, a handgun, an assortment of knives, and a collection of homemade bombs. With their arsenal, they launched a shooting rampage that ended a long era in which schools were considered safe havens. Fifty-two students immediately felt that change when the two armed teens burst into the school's quiet library at 11:29 A.M. and opened fire. Their shotguns quickly found Evan Todd, a fifteen-year-old defensive lineman on the football team. Evan fell, injured. For the next twelve minutes, the two killers stalked the library, taunting and shooting students who had huddled futilely beneath tables and desks. The attackers killed or wounded twenty before returning to Evan, who suffered wounds in his face, neck, and back from their first blasts. They asked this Eagle Scout for a reason to spare his life. Apparently, he gave them one and soon thereafter, the gunmen left the library.

Fortunately, the shotgun blast had only inflicted minor wounds and Evan escaped from the library. Once outside, he found a wounded handicapped student and carried him to the safety of a sheriff's car. He then returned and came upon another student, bleeding profusely from a severed artery. Evan dropped to his knees and rendered first aid until paramedics arrived. They soon carried the wounded student to the hospital where he would ultimately survive. Evan's fellow students remembered him keeping himself and others calm, and helping the police outside assess the situation inside Columbine High School.

Eight years later, another Eagle Scout kept his wits when a student began an even deadlier rampage on the campus of Virginia Tech in 2007. Thirty-two people died in a morning of attacks by a single student armed with a pair of semiautomatic handguns. After opening the attack in a dormitory, the gunman entered the Norris Hall classroom building and chained the doors, locking everyone inside. He then stalked the halls, continuing his assault unhurriedly. When one class heard the shooter walking down their second-floor hallway, a sizable six-foot-two senior named Kevin Sterne, an Eagle Scout, and two others pressed themselves against the door. The shooter tried to force open the door, but the students' barricade held. The action Kevin and his two fellow students took likely saved the class.

There was a price, although Kevin would say it was small. Frustrated by the barricade, the gunman fired several rounds through the door. Two bullets found Kevin's right leg and sliced open an artery. Blood began gushing from his thigh and Kevin instantly knew he wouldn't survive unless he stopped the hemorrhaging. As miraculous as anything else, he managed to remain calm and clear-headed. He found a spare electrical cord and bound it tightly around his leg, stemming the blood flow. The photograph of four police officers carrying Kevin from the building became one of the most famous images of the shooting.

It's unfortunate that these young men had to use their skills in schools, the places where teachers like Karl, Craig, and their students should be safe. But when things do go wrong, Scout training often takes over. Sometimes, the idea of a person using his Scouting-learned skills may seem trite. In fact, it's often made into a joke. But Evan Sterling, Evan Todd, and Kevin Sterne reminded me that those abilities and the presence of mind to use them truly matter in the most vital moments.

Millions of young men receive the same training as did these three Eagles. While I hope those millions never need to use their lifesaving skills in a similar emergency, I realized they could, and every year, Scouts and Eagle Scouts regularly take action to save the lives of others. What could have greater impact on the future than saving a life? That is a gift Scouting has indirectly given many people who have been rescued, in ways literal and figurative, by Scouts who were doing their duty. It could be a Kevin Sterne protecting his classmates from a killer, or it might be a Craig McGowan helping students rise above poverty. Either way, I found Scouts throughout the world clearly giving of themselves to create a better future for others.

ON LAW AND CITIZENSHIP

Back in the nation's capital, I rumbled beneath the National Mall on the Metro, stopping at the Capitol South station. I rode a familiar escalator toward the street, the same one I had used when I interned in Congress, and emerged into a cool D.C. night and walked north along First Street. Instead of entering one of the three House office buildings or the beautifully lighted Capitol, however, I continued past the Library of Congress to the U.S. Supreme Court. Floodlights illuminated the white marble of what I still consider the most impressive building in Washington. The lights chased the shadows from the massive portico of the classical building and its sixteen Corinthian columns. I slipped around to a side entrance and walked through an empty marble hallway, where portraits of justices of the past watched me as I walked toward the central bronze statue of John Marshall, the storied chief justice who first defined the Court's role.

The last time I'd arrived in this building, I'd come to meet Justice Stephen Breyer, an Eagle Scout from San Francisco's renowned Troop 14. I had called the justice's office several days before this trip, hoping I could find an Eagle Scout among the thirty-six law clerks who thoroughly research each case that comes before the Court, preparing detailed briefs that help the nine justices decide important issues of Constitutional law. Now, I again found myself in the Court, this time to meet two of the three Eagle Scouts who served as clerks, one of the most prestigious positions a lawyer can ever hold.

Tom Saunders met me at the statue of Justice Marshall. Tall and thin, Tom clerked for Justice Ruth Bader Ginsburg and had an impressive legal résumé already: Harvard undergrad, Yale law. He carried not a trace of the ego that might easily accompany such a pedigree and in that sense, he remained very much a Scout from Troop 35 in Towson, Maryland. The Court had closed several hours earlier; now the security personnel, clerks, and I had the building to ourselves. Tom and I walked down the corridors, musing about the Court's history until we heard Heath Tarbert's wingtips clicking down the hallway to meet us. Heath had attended Mount Saint Mary College in New York and had planned to join the FBI. After graduating from law school at the University of Pennsylvania, however, he won a scholarship to study in England. He returned to private practice in the United States until Justice Clarence Thomas picked him as a law clerk.

"So, does the justice himself select you?" I asked after we'd exchanged introductions.

"Actually, yes," Heath answered. "I interviewed for an hour with the current clerks, then an hour with the justice himself! The fact that I could go in and have a sit-down conversation with a Supreme Court justice for an hour? It's an honor. Even if I hadn't gotten the job, I could tell my grandchildren that I sat down with Justice Thomas for an hour!

"But I'd have been honored to sit with any justice, and whatever the justice's views are, they want clerks to give it to them as straight as possible and they can decide the points of law. Justices don't want ideologues."

Justices and clerks are united by their common respect for the Constitution and the American legal system, as Scouts are connected by the Scout Oath. For me, Scouting served as a great leveler. I could talk as easily with a sixteen-year-old Scout as I could New York City Mayor Michael Bloomberg. I remember meeting Justice Breyer for the first time, much as Heath had met Justice Thomas. A brief scheduled interview became a relaxed two-hour conversation about law and Scouting. Heath found the same with Justice Thomas, and the two attorneys began building a relationship of mutual respect and common interest during that first interview.

"In the interviews, they mainly engage you analytically," Tom added as we continued to walk the empty corridors. "Do you think on your feet or do you give canned answers? When you reach a certain level, everyone has similar credentials. The question is, can this person work in this chamber, work long hours for a year, and serve the justice?"

"Or," I joked, "can this guy work like a dog?"

"Right," Tom replied with a laugh that bounced from the ornate ceilings above us. "We do, but like Heath said, it's an honor and it's amazing work to be doing."

"They always use the phrase *lightning strikes*," said Heath. "There are so many people you went to law school with who you think would make a much better Supreme Court clerk than you, but at the end of the day, you got it for some reason and you march forward."

For both young attorneys—thirty and thirty-one years of age—receiving the call changed their lives and left them with grins on their faces for months thereafter. Tom had spent the past several years working for an appellate law group in Washington where he shared a hallway with eleven former clerks. That helped him keep the new position in perspective. He wasn't the only one to receive such an honor. Among the former clerks, however, he noticed a tinge of sadness that he hoped he would avoid.

"Four or five years later," Tom observed, "they'll say they're not sure if they'll ever have a better job. What you're doing is so important and so rewarding that even though you're exhausted and you just went to bed a few hours before, you'll wake up and say, 'Okay, this is going to be another great day.' "

Tom added that clerks also risk becoming overconfident. "They forget that they got the job because lightning struck three times," he said. "They think they want to be on the bench one day. Being a justice or judge is a powerful and fantastic job, but there's no track for that, especially because people get tapped late in their careers. They leave as a thirty-year-old clerk and they're already thinking about their confirmation hearing when they're fifty-five. That seems like a crazy way to live your life. From my perspective, you just have to say, 'I've had this fantastic experience but now I'm going to live a full well-rounded life. I'm going to be part of my community. I'm going to stand up for causes I believe in and not worry that the Senate Judiciary Committee might be scrutinizing me years down the road.' "

"My goal, I think, is to be something like people in the early republic," Heath added. "They were great citizens. They had a private life and were in private business or law, but they also contributed in the public sphere as citizens. Whether it be a stint in government, serving in government positions, or helping out in other ways. You never know what opportunities will present themselves. It's an adventure so you stand ready."

By this time, Tom had led us into a large conference room off a main hallway. We found moldings and ornate oil paintings adorning the walls, consistent with the rest of the elegant building. We sat together in three leather chairs next to a painting of nineteenth-century statesman Henry Clay and turned the conversation to Scouting and citizenship.

Continuing his theme from the hallway, Heath observed that Scouting represents one of Alexis de Tocqueville's schools of democracy, the places where the nineteenth-century French observer found Americans learning and practicing civic duty. Specifically, three merit badges required for Eagle—Citizenship in the Community, Citizenship in the Nation, and Citizenship in the World—taught Heath about citizenship on all levels and guided his path in life. He served his college community by involving himself with student government, and he viewed going to law school and working with the federal government as a continuation of Citizenship in the Nation. Then after law school, he decided to explore citizenship on its broadest level. When we met, he planned to continue his adventure in law at the War Crimes Tribunal in The Hague.

"That's citizenship in the world," Heath observed. "You're dealing with legal issues that cross borders and terrible things like genocide and war crimes. You have the opportunity to contribute on those fronts. The people working there for the United Nations are from all different countries, but I'd expect some of them are Scouts."

"At heart," he elaborated, "I think Scouts worldwide have the same standards as we do and share the ideas in our Scout Oath and Law. Those creeds embody Scouting and the Aristotelian virtues—Aristotle wrote about being a good citizen—so I would think some of the world's best citizens would be attracted to those kinds of endeavors. I wouldn't be surprised if Scouts were well represented there in The Hague."

"I completely agree with Heath," Tom chimed in. "One of the most important things about Scouting is that it turns your attention outward toward the world around you. It helps you start thinking big right from the beginning. I find for us, we can get bogged down in the minutiae of legal doctrines and what the law is, but Scouting helps you remember the broader picture and that law's about how communities get along and how conflicts get resolved.

"And while there's the Scout Oath and Scout Law," he added, "we have the Constitution, something that embodies the principles by which we stand. Every clerk and every justice takes an oath to defend that."

"It's in many ways the adventure that started with the founders of our country," Heath said. "They handed down the Constitution and the court has the job to defend the Constitution, to apply the Constitution, and to interpret the Constitution. As a clerk, you're part of that process—a process that began at the very founding of the republic."

Tom and his fellow clerks relish their year-long opportunity to research issues that will affect the lives of other citizens. But I found that Tom and Heath seemed to appreciate another aspect of their job just as much. Daily, they worked directly with Justice Ginsburg, Justice Thomas, and other justices. As young attorneys, they could not find more accomplished mentors. It reminded Tom of Scouting.

"The Court mirrors the intergenerational aspect of Scouting," Tom reflected. "A lot of Scouting is adult leaders passing down knowledge and values from one generation to the next. What's so interesting about *this* particular job is that people who have years and years of their careers behind them and are the wise elders of the community are working with people who are very young, just at the outset of their careers. I feel there is some of the same dynamic that there was in Scouts. Justices are showing you the ropes and trying to pass along not only technical legal knowledge, but also the sense of respect for the rule of law and all that embodies.

"Take our fellow Eagle Scout Justice Breyer," Tom continued. "One of the great privileges of working at the Court has been the opportunity to see how tirelessly he works to forge connections with students and attorneys just starting their careers. He takes time to meet all the clerks and to share with them the wisdom he has accumulated through years of public service."

"Right," said Heath, "Justice Breyer understands, as Scouting teaches, that we all have a duty to pass the mantle of leadership from one generation to the next."

I thought of President Kennedy's quote: "The torch has passed to a new generation of Americans." Then Heath brought me back to the conversation as he moved to another point. The breadth of experiences clerks receive from their work and from the justices themselves replicates the education he received in Baltimore, Maryland's Troop 740. Badges as diverse as Wilderness Survival and Atomic Energy had filled his merit badge sash by the time he turned eighteen. Both badges offered extremely different lessons and challenges. Very different merit badge counselors taught each.

"As a result," Heath said, "Scouting gives you a well-rounded quality that other people who just did one thing for fifteen years didn't get. Here in the Court, we see cases every day, all types of matters under the law. You get that breadth of legal knowledge so it's a wide ranging adventure."

Both clerks understand the pleasure that accompanies learning new things each day, and they appreciate the attitude needed to tackle those unknowns. In Scouting, they learned to face any challenge. Tom made the point that, in Scouts, nobody ever shirked a merit badge because they didn't know something about the subject. He and others in his troop willingly accepted, if not sought out, new areas to explore. The exploration became part of the excitement. Had I not been a Scout myself, I can't imagine where I would have learned about subjects as varied as aviation, survival, oceanography, and first aid. I doubt I would have ever learned to sail, rock climb, or kayak. For many teenagers, Scouting offers the only chance for these experiences.

"Being an Eagle Scout translates easily to law as well," Tom told me. "Law is a profession where unfortunately some people have lost sight of the nobleness of the pursuit and end up chasing money and doing ethically questionable things. I would hope that people who are coming from Scouting, and who are Eagle Scouts in particular, will have a sense that that's just not the way you behave in the community. Hopefully the sense of fulfillment you get from all the honest work and public service you do to reach Eagle shows you how rewarding that can be. I think that lessens the temptation to chase the material prizes; you have more of a sense going in that you'll look back in thirty years and not be fulfilled by chasing cash." Like rock climbing instructor Josh McNary, they, too, had learned to value more than financial rewards.

I asked them how those lessons affect our generation. Heath responded first and told me that we need to consider the future more than preceding generations, and he regretted that too many people think only about the present. Their wants and appetites can consume them, and he saw concerns for tomorrow slip away or put off until it's often too late. He knew he had to resist that trap. "If we're going to plan for the future, that's what we need to do," Heath said. "Leave the world better for the next generation."

Considering the years ahead, Tom believes Scouts have a particular responsibility to be stewards for the environment. So many of our experiences took place outdoors, in natural places, and he wants us to consider whether we'll preserve those spaces and the accompanying experiences for the next generation. He lamented the fast-rising communities that are spreading outward from cities with no consideration for natural space. He remembered spending hours each week exploring neighborhood woodlands with his friends when he was younger. They had adventures away from their parents. They made mistakes and learned. As he put it, the woods allowed him a few more feet on the parental leash. Despite the mistakes and misadventures that occasionally took place, Tom ranks that time in the wilderness with friends among his best memories and best experiences growing up. Ruefully, he noted that his small woodland fell to a developer's bulldozer just last year.

"Scouting serves as a reminder to modern society that we need to not be so structured and fearful of the unstructured," he said. "That's an important part of learning the leadership and self-reliance we got through Scouting. People like us who've had the opportunity to have that experience need to carry it forward and remind people who haven't had that experience that this is something we need to preserve and advocate for."

Tom paused and looked at me guiltily. "I don't want to talk your ear off," he said. Then his phone rang. Mountains of work for tomorrow still remained for him at 8:00 P.M.

"And I don't want to get *you* in trouble," I replied.

Tom said his good-byes and left for another long evening with his fellow clerks in Justice Ginsburg's chambers.

After Tom left, Heath and I walked down the hallway toward the chambers of Chief Justice John Roberts. Heath led me to a door just past the Chief Justice's main office. "This is the Oval Office of the Supreme Court," he said, opening the heavy wooden door. It revealed a small anteroom that led to another heavy door. The door was cracked and Heath pushed it open to reveal a long, stately conference room. A series of tall windows formed one wall. A ceremonial desk sat in the room's center. To my left were nine high-back, black leather chairs arranged around a beautifully polished wooden table that gleamed under the lights. Notepads and pencils were neatly arranged like place settings. The back of each chair bore a brass plate with its occupant's name. A stack of split firewood lay perfectly stacked on the nearby hearth.

Since the building opened in 1935, the Justices' Conference Room has witnessed deliberations on each case that has passed before the Court. In the room where I stood, justices of different eras decided *Brown v. Board of Education*, *Roe v. Wade*, *Gideon v. Wainwright*, *Miranda v.*

Arizona, *U.S. v. Nixon*, and countless other landmark cases. The history of the room seemed palpable. As with so many places in Washington, here, the pure ideals of government shone. You sense and remember the greatness and uniqueness of America's institutions. You love the country just a little more.

I felt encouraged knowing that five of the nine justices who currently had seats at this table had taken the Scout Oath as young men. When Justice Breyer took his place at the table, he became the second Eagle Scout to join deliberations in that room; former Justice Thomas C. Clark had preceded him. The two Eagle Scouts presently in the room looked around, perhaps not entirely sure if they should be there. We mused about the Court's history and future; we imagined the debates that took place around the table.

I stood there with Heath, neither knowing nor caring about his political views. Likewise, I neither knew nor cared where Tom stood on issues of the day. Their justices, Mr. Thomas and Mrs. Ginsburg, certainly differed on many legal and political philosophies, but then, only relative to the narrow divisions that have surfaced in the American polity. Much like the common ground created by the values of the Scout Oath and Law, the common values of our liberal democratic republic's constitution unite these justices, their clerks, and hopefully everyone in America. While people may hold varying opinions of verdicts, they believe our institutions and processes work. Likewise, while some will disagree with opinions issued by Justice Breyer, or any justice for that matter, they hopefully understand that his values are based in the Scout Oath; his decisions made in the spirit of duty and honor.

Heath and I slipped out of the Court through the loading dock, making way for an escorted black Suburban that was carrying one of the justices back to the office for a late night of work. We shook hands at the driveway's end on Second Street and I walked down the pebbled sidewalk to East Capitol. The dark trees of the Court and the Capitol hushed the sounds of the surrounding city. I crossed Independence Avenue and walked the block to the Capitol South Metro stop on First Street. On the walk, I felt oddly relieved.

Far from reminding me of the partisanship that often polarizes America's politics, my visits in Washington with clerks, soldiers, Capitol Hill staff, and others had reminded me how vital shared values and common understandings are to our nation. The people I met there reminded me how much we have in common. That makes it all the more disappointing that some dwell on our differences to no end, or rather, to their own selfish ends.

Most public servants in America don't live in Washington, however. Refreshingly, many have little interest in ever *going* to Washington. Most work at local and state levels in cities and communities across the country. Thirty-year-old Rodney Glassman serves as one example of how the spirit of public service starts far from Capitol Hill.

My day had started at 5:30 A.M., well before the sunlight hit Tucson, Arizona, and I'd finished a television interview by seven. I left the hot lamps of the studio and soon landed at a local radio station where city council candidate Rodney Glassman had just completed what I'm sure was his second or third interview of the day. He and I met in the station's narrow hallway.

"I'm just asking for twenty dollars," he said, eyes bright and grin wide. An optimistic air surrounded him, up to his tightly curled hair. The toothy, yet sincere smile on his tanned face almost made me hand over the campaign donation. But not quite.

"Okay," Rodney conceded. "So you're next, eh?" The big grin did not dissipate. He sidestepped so I could make my way down the hallway to the radio studio where he'd just completed his interview. The Tucson election was several weeks away and the Rodney Glassman campaign was in full swing. With Rodney, however, things are always in full swing.

Rodney bested me by fifty-two merit badges, earning seventy-four in Fresno, California, as the only Jewish boy in a Scout troop chartered by the Mormon church. When he served as chaplain, the prayers were in Hebrew. When he ran for city council twenty years later, he leaned back on those diverse relationships. For his campaign treasurer, he picked the very Republican president of the Mormon Church in Tucson, though Rodney is a Democrat. He absolutely relishes the opportunity to surprise people and bring together different perspectives.

"Real early on," he told me after he'd won the election, "I learned about transcending political divides, and I've always been able to accomplish that. As councilman, quality of life issues aren't subjective. I'm building parks and improving public safety. Everyone is interested in those things so my job is to bring people together.

"At the local level, I work with all types of people. Heck, I had a meeting yesterday with a nine-year-old, an eleven-year-old, and their dad, who is a police officer. They have some open acreage behind their home and they want to put in a soccer field and baseball field. And we're going to help them get it done. They're going to raise fifty thousand dollars of funds or in-kind services, but we're going to help them get it done—and we might make some Eagle Scout projects part of it."

Scouting gave Rodney a deep sense of volunteerism and at age twenty-three he started the Glassman Foundation in Tucson. At first I assumed he had family wealth. Wrong. He opened the foundation with $2,000. Seven years later, the foundation annually raised and contributed $200,000 to Tucson's young people.

"I always enjoy helping people," he said when we met the day after our radio interviews at the Glassman Foundation Youth Expo, which brings together Tucson groups like the Boy Scouts, Girl Scouts, Boys & Girls Clubs of America, and 4-H. Rodney explained that the expo provides a buffet of opportunities for young people to choose from. "We do have to raise a lot of money for the event, but I don't have a problem asking people for money! That is, asking for good causes. That's the key. In Scouts I learned to pick up the phone and call merit badge counselors, so now I can pick up the phone and call anybody, whether to raise money or to deal with an issue. And like I said, I don't mind asking when it's for other people!

"To me, being a Scout made me who I am," Rodney reflected. Then he related how his experience taught him to help other people and make the community better. It taught him to treat everyone with kindness, understanding, and value.

I left Tucson the next day feeling positive about the members of our generation who were entering the political realm. From staff members in Washington, to state university board members in California, to politicos in Georgia, I found many who held beliefs like Rodney. They may not have all gained those lessons in Scouting, but their dedication to their community impressed me. Most seemed content to do their part, whatever that might be, and make a difference in the life of their community.

Sometime before I met Tom and Heath at the Supreme Court, I heard a radio interview with a former presidential cabinet secretary—name and party are unimportant. "We don't really know what to do as citizens," the former secretary said flatly, speaking about our fellow Americans. "Our sense of efficacy as citizens and the practice of citizenship is almost completely gone."

I was driving at the time and almost wrecked. The statement utterly shocked me. Where had the former secretary been? With whom had he been speaking? Obviously not with the same people I had. Please don't tell the Peace Corps volunteers in Benin or the soldiers at Walter Reed that citizenship is gone. Let's also not share that with the teachers, doctors, and the endless list of others who, each in their own ways, are being good neighbors.

Just weeks after I'd heard the radio interview, I traveled to the U.S. Military Academy at West Point, where one thousand of our most talented young men and women volunteer to serve America each year. I visited West Point in the fall, when the brilliant hues of the Hudson Valley foliage know no equal. After spending two days with cadets and professors alike, I tossed my backpack into the bed of Eagle Scout Mike Jones's pickup truck and we headed to the train station on the opposite side of the Hudson.

I had already been reflecting on the sense of citizenship and sacrifice so tangible on the 207-year-old campus, and Colonel Jones encouraged my thoughts as we drove. "There's a great deal of talk these days about freedom and sacrifice," said the father of three Eagle Scouts, who also served as the academy's director of admissions. "The humble families of West Point and here in Orange County, New York, really feel that sacrifice. They also really believe in the idea of freedom and the duty required to preserve it. They're the ones bearing the burdens. September eleventh hit us hard—lots of NYPD and FDNY families live here. The conflicts in the Middle East hit us hard. It's difficult seeing your classmates, the classmates of your sons and daughters, and the sons and daughters of West Point lose their lives or come back injured. But serving others is something we've chosen to do because it's our duty."

The cadets and families of West Point know something about sacrifice, as do the families of police and firefighters everywhere. Their goals are not related to perks and possessions. Their aims honestly relate to family and serving others. They simply hope to be the citizens our country needs. They bear the sacrifices too many others simply talk about and don't truly understand. Civil servants and soldiers will rarely experience great monetary wealth, but they accept that willingly and live with a peaceful sense of purpose and contentment. They enjoy a wealth of a different kind. They appreciate their families and derive satisfaction from others. These are the people who hold our country together. They, along with Tom Saunders, Heath Tarbert, Rodney Glassman, and the many millions who share their spirit of service, are the reason citizenship is not dead.

ADVENTURES TOGETHER

Years ago, I stood next to my long-time friend Sean O'Brien as we took the Scout Oath for the first time in Troop 103. On our honor, we promised to do our best to fulfill our duty to God and country. We would help other people at all times. We would always keep ourselves strong in mind and body. We would lead our lives according to virtues shared by Scouts throughout the world.

We were eleven years old when we first made that promise. Before that, we'd probably made the Cub Scout Promise together in Pack 577, but neither of us can quite remember that far back. But I definitely remember standing next to Sean when our Scoutmaster Paul Lee gave us the Eagle charge on the night we received our Eagle medals. Paul told us we would forever be "marked men." People would always expect more of us. Sean and I had both turned eighteen by then—neither of us had much time to spare before the deadline that was our eighteenth birthday—and the ceremony marked the end of Scouting for us.

At least, we both thought that at the time, and for several years thereafter, Scouting was in the past. As I began the journey that led to my first book, however, Scouting returned and our friendship rekindled as I shared what I found with Sean. It made us both remember the spirit of Scouting and how it remains part of us both. It forms the root of our friendship and has nourished that friendship throughout the years since we left Troop 103. So it came that I stood next to my old friend once again when he made another promise before another gathered audience.

I stood next to Sean at the front of a South Bend, Indiana, church, wearing a tuxedo instead of a uniform, watching his bride Lenore walk down a flower-lined aisle escorted by her father. After several readings and hymns, Sean and Lenore exchanged marriage vows. As I listened to him say his vows, I remembered the countless times we'd said the Scout Oath and Law together. What eventually occurred to me was this: Scouting had marked one phase of life for Sean. This was another phase, and he had vowed to live both in the same way.

In Scouts you develop as an individual and as a troop. In marriage you develop as a pair, a partnership, and ultimately as a family. I hadn't personally begun that journey yet, and probably won't understand it fully until I stand at an altar myself. Traveling to South Bend, however, offered me a glimpse of this next phase of life that so many of our generation are now entering.

The night before Sean's wedding, a local restaurant hosted the rehearsal dinner. After dinner and a video montage of Sean and Lenore's younger days and years together as a couple, Sean's brother Kevin stood. With the exception of his glasses and tie, Kevin looked much as he had when we trekked together across Mount Phillips at Philmont years ago. He still had a youngish face, unlike his older brother Sean, whose broad face, with its ever-changing goatees and beards, gave him an older, professorial air.

"When I think of my brother," Kevin began, "I think about loyalty. It's always been there. At Oak Grove Elementary, Sean always watched out for me, and I was one of the best football players in Troop 103 because Sean made it clear that anyone who laid a finger on me would have to deal with him." Kevin smiled at me, then looked at Sean.

"Don't," Sean said. "I hate that story."

Kevin just grinned. "I remember playing flag football and Alvin"—he gestured toward me—"decided to tackle me. Alvin stood up and Sean blindsided him and pinned him. Then—"

"Really," Sean implored from his seat, only half serious.

"Then Sean stood up and said, 'Anyone who messes with my brother answers to me. And I wrestle for Lakeside!' " The room erupted. Sean and I both turned red.

"Loyalty has always been a characteristic of Sean's," Kevin continued. "He'll be standing next to Lenore tomorrow, making some serious promises, so there's no question of his loyalty to her. Beyond that, I really think loyalty brought them together. They're so committed to issues of justice, so loyal to people who don't get a say or who never receive due attention in our world. So I see their commitment to each other growing out of the commitment they both have to social justice, to the marginalized, to the least favored. But it's not just commitment, it's a genuine care for other people. That's what I really respect about them and what will make their marriage stronger. Their marriage won't be about the two of them, or even about the two of them and their children. It will be about their family and the world."

I had not had time to visit with Kevin since arriving in South Bend, nor had I seen him since he got married himself and moved to Tacoma, Washington, so we talked after the toast. We recounted stories about our trek to Philmont and other Troop 103 expeditions, then Kevin expanded on his earlier words. He reflected on the loyal relationships Scouting builds between people, ones surprisingly deep for teenagers. He also recalled that Troop 103 reflected the diversity of high school. Scouts hailed from every stereotypical group—athletes, nerds, skaters, average guys, the wealthy, the not-so-wealthy, troublemakers, and many others. "In a place with common structure and purpose, different types of people get along," Kevin said. "In Scouts, you're all in it for the troop, so there's a common loyalty there.

"One other thing," he added. "The loyalty I'm talking about in Scouts and with Sean and Lenore is a *generative* loyalty. It doesn't draw down all your time and energy; it makes you able to be more loyal and more giving to others."

For Sean and Lenore, that loyalty creates an ever stronger relationship that becomes a study in selflessness. They always consider the other in their choices and give freely to one another, enriching their lives immeasurably. In the case of a Scout troop, that common basis in loyalty creates a rare and special community of trust. Scouts and leaders take each other at their word, and trust each other to do what they promise. They don't worry about dishonesty, so they can focus wholly on the important aspects of their mission.

Kevin's words also reminded me of the Honor System at my alma mater, Washington and Lee University in Lexington, Virginia. While it stresses that students cannot lie, cheat, or steal, the Honor System isn't a restrictive set of rules; it's more of a spirit. The system frees the community from the stress and burdens of dishonesty: classrooms and labs are open around the clock, students leave backpacks and books unattended, they can schedule their own final exams, and relationships between students and faculty are based on mutual trust from the beginning. When I served on the committee entrusted with overseeing the Honor

System, nearly one-quarter of our elected members were Eagle Scouts. As Scouts, we become accustomed to living in a community based on loyalty and trust. We tend to seek out and create similar communities later in life, whether at college, in our places of work, or in our personal relationships.

The next day, the groomsmen met for lunch while wives and girlfriends got ready for the late-afternoon wedding. Sean arrived in downtown South Bend at the unassuming CJ's Pub. The groom was relaxed, calm, and reflective. Over the din of college football streaming from televisions hung around the room, we talked about the afternoon's ceremony. Then perhaps inevitably, our talk drifted back to Scouting.

"Certainly, reciting the Scout Law once a week for several years teaches you the value of saying what you live and living what you say," Sean told me. "I definitely think Order of the Arrow ceremonies and courts of honor teach you to take promises seriously that you make in public in front of people who are committed to you. A marriage ceremony is very different from that, but part of the premise has common roots.

"I knew very early on that I wanted to make a very serious commitment to Lenore," he explained. "I knew that within weeks. So from very early on, it was simply a matter of getting things together along the way, figuring out the larger questions of how we would live our lives as a couple, how we would pursue our dreams both independently and together."

I saw the deeply felt loyalty Sean had developed to Lenore, but also to friends like his brother Kevin and me. Scouting fostered that for him, although he certainly learned loyalty to his family and church long before he put a Cub Scout hat on his head. "Scouting," he went on, "and I'm talking about the troop and the Scouting Movement, earned my loyalty by being well organized and conceived. You learn about loyalty to a patrol, loyalty to the people in that patrol. As a senior patrol leader, you develop a loyalty to all Scouts in the troop. You move up the ranks and feel loyalty to Scouts younger than you. Loyalty runs from higher to lower and the other way as well. I always felt younger Scouts needed to be treated fairly and taught well. In Scouts and after Scouts, it's really important to maintain connections to people and good relationships with people. I think when people earn loyalty, it should be something that's lasting."

Sean believes that being an Eagle Scout entails a lifelong devotion to the ideals of Scouting and he hoped people would always remember the obligations of their rank. "When people call me an Eagle Scout it's always accurate," he observed, "although sometimes they'll say it in a joking, or even pejorative way. But it's something I'm proud of so anything negative they may say about it is unimportant to me. I hope others would feel the same way. The behaviors that get labeled with 'Eagle Scout' are generally upholding high ideals. I would hope that anybody who had gone through Scouting to its highest rank would still live up to those ideals. I don't think they should necessarily be waking up every day saying, 'I'm an Eagle Scout, so . . . ,' but I hope that they'll have those twelve points of the Scout Law as part of who they are, and that they would do their best to live accordingly. Life gets compromised and life can be hypocrisy and falling short and making mistakes. But as ideals, what we learn in Scouting holds up. It's worth having those kinds of ideals. Those are how we should relate to each other as a community.

"Stay with me," he cautioned, "I'm not getting too leftist. But we do live in a capitalist system and capitalism at its very core is driven by greed and selfishness. Now, it has a lot of great aspects to it; it just depends on people who *aren't* selfish and *aren't* greedy. Our personal virtues and our civic interest have to correct the system's shortcomings."

While at Washington and Lee, I took a number of classes from politics professor Bill Connelly. Most of those classes incorporated Alexis de Tocqueville's observations about American society. The Frenchman noted that our country's true virtue lies in being driven by industrious, free individuals. The potential defect of this virtue, however, lies in forgetting everyone but ourselves. As a liberal democratic republic operating under capitalism, America is rightly fueled by self-interest, but there is always the risk that individuals can focus on themselves at the expense of others.

Professor Connelly explained, and Tocqueville understood, that American life depended on civic virtue mitigating this defect. As true citizens, we need to respect and contribute to the common good. From that idea stems philanthropy, community, and public service. What's important, and what Scouting seems to teach, is that each of us has a duty to something larger than ourselves.

Tocqueville used the phrase "self-interest properly understood." His point: We need to understand that our self-interest relates directly to others in our community. We need "schools of democracy," programs like Scouting, youth groups, or high school service clubs, that let us practice citizenship and help us realize that our interests interrelate. We need to exercise loyalty to each other, as youth and adults. It's all an academic way of saying we need to be good neighbors.

The Scouts I was meeting had learned that lesson in their patrols and in their troops. They were part of a greater entity, just as Sean and I were part of Troop 103, with all of its different, and sometimes ragtag elements. Eagle Scouts had—and still have—a duty to their brother Scouts and to Scouting's enduring spirit.

The following weekend, I stood alongside another Eagle Scout on his wedding day. In fact, I stood next to four Eagle Scouts and one Philmont conservationist. My cousin John Wiggins and his groomsmen, James Burnham, Robert Coleman, and Jeremy Uchitel, all earned Eagle together in Decatur, Georgia's Troop 175; John's sister Mary Ellen worked as a Philmont staffer. We had gathered in the courtyard of Chicago's Notebaert Nature Museum for the marriage ceremony, which marked a new step in John's five-year relationship with Nicki D'Onofrio. Once the bride-to-be had walked down the aisle with her father, we watched two individuals become a couple.

Their relationship began in San Diego, California, after John, a dual U.S. Naval Academy and Georgia Tech graduate, returned from deployment on the fast attack submarine *Salt Lake City.* Shortly thereafter, Nicki had moved to San Diego from Connecticut. The two spent several months playing on an Ultimate Frisbee team together before John decided to press his luck. Sticking to what he knew best, he invited Nicki on a hike, and they shared an afternoon on the Pacific Crest Trail, just north of San Diego.

"During that time we spent hiking," John told me after their wedding, "we really bonded and realized it was going to have more potential than going on a few dates. Sharing an activity like that was very important to me—hiking was where I'd learned to build relationships. In Scouts, it was all about having nothing to do but talk and look around and enjoy where you are, and so being a bit more grown-up now, it still gives you the opportunity to share things about your lives that you might not otherwise—and in this case, share things that you wouldn't on a typical first date.

"We knew each other before we went hiking, and while I wasn't going out with a stranger, I didn't have a great idea of who she really was.

But I was surprised by the things we talked about. She was very open and friendly. I had thought of her as one of the cool kids, thought that she wouldn't be interested in the kind of things that I'd be interested in. So I didn't have a high expectation for a relationship. But she surprised me on that hike. She opened up to me and told me things I didn't consider standard first-date conversation. In a period of one day, I got to know her on a tremendously deep level. Hiking and spending time outside really changes dynamics in relationships, and that's what I really got from Scouts; it makes you build great relationships, although I never thought of James, Bob, or Jeremy in the same way I think about Nicki!"

As a member of Troop 175, John and his friends learned to enjoy and value backpacking and other outdoor adventures. They had plenty of opportunities since their troop often ventured out twice a month. Those trips into the mountains of the Southeast introduced John to hiking, and then got him hooked. The adults allowed the boys to lead the weekend trips, which John did as senior patrol leader until his best friend and groomsman James unseated him in an election.

"But the adults," John continued. "I can't imagine how the adults managed to devote that much time to us." Many of Troop 175's leaders had sons who long before had earned Eagle and left the troop, but they remained, giving three hours a week, at least one weekend a month, and one week during the summer—not unlike a peacetime Army Reserve job. John and his fellow groomsmen all appreciated the environment of support and learning the leaders created. They showed the Scouts how to lead a life. In them, John found examples to emulate.

John and his friends had always served as youth leaders in Scouts and one day, they'll be those adult leaders; in fact, Jeremy is already leading a Venturing crew. The friends remained part of each other's lives after leaving Troop 175, and all came to Chicago for John's wedding. Shortly before the ceremony, the wedding party stopped at the Buckingham Fountain, one of the world's largest and most striking. Sunlight covered the landmark fountain and streams of water gushed from its 134 jets and cascaded into the broad pool at its base. A queue of wedding trolleys lined the nearby curb and we jockeyed with several other parties to secure prime photo spots. Our photographer arranged our group in every conceivable way and snapped pictures. One arrangement placed the wedding party's five Eagle Scouts together and it made John think. Before that moment, he hadn't truly considered how Scouting had shaped his friendships.

"Those are just the people I'm closest with," he said as we walked back to the trolley. "That says as much as anything about my Scouting experience."

Attending Decatur High School near Atlanta, John had many friends among his classmates, but he rarely spent much time with them outside of school unless they were in Scouts. He had a much deeper relationship with the Scouts from Troop 175 and thus spent most of his after-school hours with them, but not necessarily in Scout activities; they'd become close friends through Scouts and those friendships grew well beyond troop meetings and campouts. I clearly saw the connection. Within school's rigid structure, little chance exists for real, deep human interaction between tightly scheduled classes. And how much more difficult is it to connect meaningfully with a school of a thousand versus a troop of forty? When you're on a three-day backpacking trip with a small group, you have little to do *but* connect. That time together proved critical in developing lasting friendships. In marriage, John also drew on the commitment that Scouting taught him. At first, he didn't know his ultimate goal for his relationship with Nicki, although a second and third date were clearly on his short-term list. John has never dated often or casually, so just by asking her out, he committed to being with her for some time. Whether Nicki realized that at the time, I'm not certain. As their excellent first-date experience repeated itself on successive excursions around San Diego, John saw more potential.

"By the end of that first year, I really had a positive outlook," John said.

"Hey, it's not a weather report!" I joked. John has always had a serious edge.

"You know what I mean," he said, smiling. "It felt like it was heading somewhere. Then I left for a second six-month deployment on the *Salt Lake City*. Six more months beneath the Pacific Ocean. We both found that when you don't have someone, you miss them even more, and that let me know how valuable the relationship was. Six weeks after I left, Nicki flew to Singapore to meet up with the boat."

When that news reached our family in Atlanta, we knew John was serious. We all began concocting ways to visit San Diego and meet Nicki. When his cruise ended and he returned to California, the couple discussed him leaving the navy and moving to a new city. They spent a reflective weekend hiking in nearby Idyllwild and decided on Chicago—for both of them.

"There wasn't any thought of me going somewhere and her not going," John remembered. "The commitment was really finalized then. We may not have been engaged for another year after that, but both of us knew we were heading down that path with certainty. I'm a very impulsive and intuitive decision-maker, so there wasn't much real thought. I like to think about things after the fact. I think I make pretty good decisions, they just happen to be based on gut. I felt good about this one.

"But," John said with a self-deprecating laugh, "look at the length of time it took! I guess I gave myself a lot of time to correct any errors! But really, there were none. Nicki's perfect for me.

"Nicki and I decided to take that adventure and live our lives together. If you want to call it marriage, you can. But I think our adventure together really started when we left San Diego for Chicago."

They put the Pacific Ocean behind them in 2005, bound for Chicago in John's tightly packed Audi. They had carefully planned a week-long expedition, but their plans changed in Nevada. The one hotel in the small border town where they'd planned to stay had no space available. They drove to Las Vegas and still couldn't find a place to stay. It was past midnight and John was incredulous at the lack of hotel space and delirious with sleep. Nicki took the wheel and drove to Zion National Park, where they pitched their tent at 6:00 A.M. and slept for two hours before the ranger woke them up, wanting camping fees.

"It was a pretty adventuresome start to our life together," John said with a warm smile. "And there have been lots of adventures since: changing jobs, buying a home, making new friends. Maybe at some point we'll move on to other adventures like having kids.

"You know, I've always gotten a little lonely on the trail by myself. At Philmont, I'd hike by myself sometimes, but it always made me lonely and introspective—not in a sad way, but just reflective. It's interesting how that translates into marriage because there are ways in which you're never alone after that. You have this person you're married to always there supporting you and being with you on the trail."

By this time on my journey, I was realizing that all adventures don't entail combat boots or a climbing rope. I had started this second journey thinking just that. Adventure, I had felt sure, could be found only on a peak, river, or trail, doing something dangerous or exhausting. Some lessons from Scouting needed longer than others to take root, I suppose.

Clearly, Scouting taught me that adventure concerned discovery and overcoming challenges, but I hadn't considered the spirit of adventure in a broader way. In San Francisco, California, I found an Eagle who learned that lesson before I did. Talking with him helped me realize that Sean and John were still living an adventure; I just needed to view the idea in a different light.

Growing up in the Rocky Mountain town of Golden, Colorado, Jay Tankersley quickly grew to love the outdoors. In Colorado, you have little choice. His troop ventured into the Rockies, to Philmont, and as far away as Ely, Minnesota, where he shared my experience of canoeing through wilderness lakes at the Northern Tier Canoe Base. We both remembered the pristine lakes, expansive forest, and ubiquitous mosquitoes.

"When the sun went down, you *had* to be in your tent," Jay remembered, laughing. "Outside there were enough mosquitoes to make as much noise as a four-lane highway. Some guys—much to our enjoyment—would get eaten alive if they had to get out of their tent to go to the bathroom!"

By spending time at the canoe base and in the Rockies, Jay knew a type of adventure that was easy to spot. Boots and paddles generally equated to high adventure, no question. His understanding of the concept broadened after he left Scouting and began pursuing a career. He found adventure working with fellow students on projects at the Tuck School of Business at Dartmouth. Like Tom Pigott in Seattle, he found it researching new companies as a young venture capitalist. He also found it when his company was going under and he volunteered to stay on without pay. He believed the firm could make it and after twenty days, he was doing the work of twelve other people. As the company recovered, Jay became the center of the entire sales organization. The complacency of former colleagues who sat by passively like victims shocked him. "You have to take charge of your own destiny," he said. "I knew from experience and Scouting that I had to do something and that eventually I'd be able to right the ship."

"For me, adventure has changed," the thirty-one-year-old observed. "I used to have to scare myself to death. Now it's different. Adventure doesn't have to be associated with great scenery; it can be camaraderie, tasks you set your mind to, and the goals that you accomplish. Adventure can be associated with the people you're with and whatever your goals may be."

Jay didn't offer his thoughts on romance or marriage, but he started me thinking. And shortly thereafter, my friend Townsend Bailey brought adventure and marriage all together.

Throughout my journey for this book, Townsend had provided me with perspective whenever we met at neighborhood haunts or each other's nearby homes. Showing our Scouting roots, we always walked. Living in Atlanta's most walkable neighborhood made that all the easier. One evening, we cooked dinner with his wife, Christina. Like Eric Treml, Townsend had married an artist and very talented chef. Gourmet burgers were the fare and we ate dinner in their eclectically decorated dining room.

"You know, adventure really is an attitude," Townsend said during the meal. "*What* you do may change over time. What's important is that you keep the perspective—finding out more about yourself or a question or maybe your friend or girlfriend.

"I love adventure and have always climbed mountains and gotten outside. And I still do that. But for me now, going on an adventure—of any sort really—with Christina makes it so much better. That's one of the ways you know it's right between you. It's an adventure itself to find the right person, then once you find her, leading a life together becomes the adventure."

Many of our generation had already embarked on the adventure Townsend described, and that John and Sean were living. Until I spoke with Sean and John, however, I hadn't considered Scouting as an experience that would have anything to do with romantic relationships later in life. That was, of course, my oversight. Friendship seems to create the foundation for marriage much more than flaring passion, and Scouting truly teaches friendship, although leaders would rarely use that phrase; *leadership* and *teamwork* often substitute. During weeks at summer camp, along Rocky Mountain trails, or in canoes on Minnesota lakes, Scouts practice the qualities that make good friends and sustain those friendships for weeks, years, and lifetimes. The boys already recite the traits of good friendship at weekly meetings when they say the Scout Law, which includes the points of trustworthiness, loyalty, and helpfulness among others. Being in the wilderness together without the distractions of television or other activities offers a chance for those qualities to spark friendships as Scouts spend time with other Scouts. They learn to value simple conversation and the company of others. When that appreciation translates into relationships in the future, some of us realize how important Scouting was—and is—in our lives.

The traits that sustain millions of couples and families are rooted in the values and experiences of Scouting, even though many never realize it. Until I met these Eagles, I was part of that category. But then I saw how loyalty in a Scout troop or hiking treks with friends or a girlfriend can lead to richer relationships. Yet another lasting gift that not everyone might recognize but that is nevertheless shaping our world.

OLYMPIC DREAMS

With very little apparent effort, Morgan House paddled his kayak across the finish line of the 1996 Olympic kayaking course. It was December, and the lakeside trees were as empty of leaves as the grandstands were of spectators. Morgan rested his paddle across the boat and looked at the vacant stands and observation tower on his right. The tower still bore the laurel-leaf graphics that marked everything during the Centennial Olympic Games in Atlanta. The flat but still warm sunlight of a winter afternoon washed over Lake Sidney Lanier in north Georgia, chasing away the bitter wind and gray clouds present earlier. Sweat beaded on Morgan's forehead below his buzzed hair. In my own kayak, I rolled my long sleeves up to cool myself, although my legs were beet red from the chill of winter air and water.

"This is where it started for me," Morgan said when I'd caught up to him.

"Wow," I answered, preoccupied with the finger I'd just smashed against my kayak's side in a mad, futile effort to stay with Morgan during the last five hundred meters.

"I live fifteen minutes from here and I remember watching the 'ninety-six Games right in those stands," Morgan continued. "There were these amazing athletes from all over the world giving everything they had right in my back yard. Just seeing that, seeing people winning gold medals inspired me then, and it hasn't stopped. Now I'm friends with some of those medalists from ninety-six, but seeing those guys when I was nine really inspired me and that's what's kept me going." He fell quiet and looked toward the gradually setting sun, his kayak's stern gently eddying to the left from the waning momentum of his last stroke.

Since age nine, one goal drove Morgan: to win Olympic gold in kayaking. When he glided past the finish line that winter day, he wasn't just remembering the races he had watched in 1996. He envisioned himself crossing a similar line in a future Olympics. As a top member of the U.S. national kayak team, he had a shot. In fact, as the team's second youngest member, this twenty-one-year-old wonder would have several shots.

Morgan's kayaking career began on Lake Lanier more than ten years ago. It started simply—at age eight, he saw several friends paddling near his dock and thought it seemed fun. It also started inauspiciously—last place became his usual finish when he first began racing. "But I was also terrible at every other sport I played," he noted. "And I mean I've played basketball, football, baseball, and soccer, and I always rode the bench!" He kept kayaking, though, spending long hours on the lake, and eventually he started to finish mid-pack. Soon thereafter, he began claiming first or second place on a regular basis. Someone in the Boy Scouts noticed and interviewed the ten-year-old athlete for an issue of *Boys' Life* magazine. The interviewer asked Morgan what he wanted to do when he grew up. "Be an Olympic kayaker," came the response.

"I was just ten," he reminded me, "but by the time I was fourteen or fifteen, I thought I really might make the Olympics in 2008. I knew I couldn't make it in 2004, because I was too young, too weak, too slow, so I was looking forward to 2008, even though that was still early. Going to the Olympics is just incredible, I think. That's a huge goal in my life. To win a gold medal is my ultimate goal. I can't explain it; I just have to do it."

Among the goals Morgan had besides winning gold was earning Eagle in Troop 242, which his uncle started at Grace Episcopal Church in Gainesville. He spent his mornings and afternoons paddling across Lake Lanier, but he made sure he advanced toward Eagle all the while. In Scouting, he made lasting friends and learned how to lead. "Being a leader is about leading people, of course," he said. "But you also have to listen and see what they want to do. You can't just tell them what to do."

He never doubted he'd reach Eagle and learned to balance his life along the way. He not only balanced his time, he balanced stress and competition. Morgan loved backpacking with Troop 242, and not only because he enjoyed being in nature. He could relax. Aside from friendly competition within his patrol, he didn't need to race. He had nobody to beat, and he relished every quiet mile along the trails of north Georgia for that reason. His one regret remains that he could never afford a full week away from paddling, and consequently never hiked Philmont. I'd estimate that his success in kayaking has proved sufficient compensation.

In 2003, a sixteen-year-old Morgan traveled to Japan as the youngest member of the U.S. junior national kayak team. "Basically, I finished the race," he said dryly, summing up a self-described lackluster international debut. He arrived home undiscouraged, however, and focused on the next international junior competition in 2005 in Hungary. He worked doggedly; early morning and late evening practices on Lake Lanier were firmly established habits. So was Scouting, and he made time to complete the requirements for Eagle amid all of his training. In Hungary, just months after receiving his Eagle Scout medal, Morgan accomplished the rare feat of reaching the finals in both the thousand-meter and five-hundred-meter kayak events. He placed fifth in the five hundred, the best result ever for an American junior.

"That really got me set for making a run at the Olympic team in 2008," he explained. "My times were better. I was doing a 1:42 in the five hundred meter. That was my best time ever, my best race ever. Everything just clicked and I was only half a boat from getting fourth, but I could live with fifth in the world!" He laughed and shook his head, almost in disbelief of how far he'd come.

"I remember being out here growing up and I was always in front, I was always the leader," he mused as he rhythmically sliced his paddle blades through the water as we continued our circuit. He looked at the wooded shoreline, with its smattering of quiet homes. "Then when I moved out to San Diego to train with the national team, that's not the way it was. These guys were older than me, the same speed as me, and they didn't want to hear anything from this young guy. So I got to sit back and see how other people lead, learning from seeing their mistakes and their accomplishments. I also learned what to do when I get older and what not to do to hopefully be a better person when we have younger guys coming up.

"We're all competitive, but since I've been traveling around the world so much and we have a bunch of foreign paddlers training with us in San Diego, I've made friends with a lot of paddlers. When I was younger, I got on the start line and used to think, 'Man, who are these guys? They're huge and they're fast.' But now I know they're just normal people, regular human beings like myself. I used to be scared getting on the start line, but now I'm a lot more calm because I know those people and I'm just thinking I have to get from A to B the fastest way I can and not worry about what they're going to do. I have to keep my head in the boat and do my thing. It's very competitive but at the same time, before the race you're having fun hanging out with your friends—then you have to go race them."

By this time, clouds had covered the sinking sun and the temperature had dropped noticeably. The water had continued to chill my legs; I could scarcely feel my knees. Morgan and I pulled even to one another in our boats, and decided to return.

"Warmth sounds good," I said, "but first, I want to see what race pace looks like."

"Sure," Morgan said. A smile spread across his face. He began digging his blades into the water on each side of his kayak. His torso turned precisely, adding power to each stroke. One hand relaxed while the other strained against the paddle and water; then they switched roles as he plunged the opposite blade into the lake. He gained speed quickly and his body, arms, and shoulders accelerated in a synchronous flow. His head leisurely turned from side to side, almost showing a curious interest in watching the paddle pull through the dark water. The kayak surged ahead, its bow breaking the water easily. I witnessed a display of near perfection. As he neared the end of his demonstration, the paddle blades circulated through the air like propellers. His body's clockwork movements never misfired. The boat flew through the water.

Once he'd finished the demo, we talked about how he felt after sustaining that pace for a thousand meters, and he explained, "You're hurting at the end. Sometimes you're seeing spots. You get a lot of lactic acid in your arms and legs especially; you're hurting pretty bad. But it's a good feeling knowing that you gave everything. You never want to give any less. If I feel that much pain, I know that I worked hard."

Any heat remaining in the day had disappeared by the time we pulled our boats up to the dock. We slipped out of the fiberglass shells and sat on the dock, thankful to escape the water's icy grasp. We donned the jackets and sandals we had left on the dock and hefted the two kayaks. Carrying each by its bow or stern, we walked back to the hangar where the club's members kept their canoes and kayaks. Inside, rows of storage racks held beautiful, sleek shells of fiberglass, which reflected the fluorescent light falling from the rafters. We laid our boats on a rack near the door, then Morgan walked me through the aisles of boats, pointing out those he'd paddled in the past.

"I wish it were warmer," he said. "Then I could let you sit in one of the boats that I race. We could bet on how long you could balance! What you were in today was nothing; it takes forever to get comfortable in racing boats. You're almost sitting on top of the water, so it's really unsteady. I've won some bets with national track team guys in San Diego—they thought they could balance themselves in the boat. Nope."

We walked to one side of the hangar and Morgan showed me the training room, filled with rowing machines modified for kayakers, free weights, exercise balls, and an assortment of other contraptions for becoming a better paddler. As Morgan finished touring me around the gym, talking about the obscene amount of time he spends with weights or in boats, I wondered aloud where he found his motivation.

"Knowing I did the best I can do really drives me," he answered. "And that means being prepared—being in the weight room early, giving it everything in practice, and living like I'm on a mission so I *can* do my best and *know* it's my best. And hopefully my best will be the best in the world one day."

Several months later, Morgan took the next step toward the Olympics by winning a preliminary April time trial. Then in May, he won a gold medal at the Pan American Canoe Championships in Montreal. He kept training for a June showdown in Szeged, Hungary, at the ICF World Cup Regatta. There, he had to upset a renowned veteran for a spot on the 2008 U.S. Olympic squad. He prepared well and shot from the starting line, running even with the one paddler he had to beat to win a trip to Beijing. The twenty-one-year-old Eagle tore through the five hundred meter K1 (single paddler) sprint with his best time ever, but his thirty-one-year-old rival, a veteran of two previous Olympics, clipped him at the finish by 1.3 seconds. Morgan would have to wait until 2012 in London.

"I turned in my best results, my best times ever," he said, as we carried two kayaks from the Lake Lanier Canoe and Kayak Club hangar down to the dock. It was July now, two weeks after the race in Hungary and six months after our first excursion together. "It came down to one final race, and he ended up being faster than me. That's the way it goes. It's been a good year, I got my best results, but I was pretty upset that I didn't make the team. I was crushed that day, upset next week, but I'm okay now. There was some reason why I didn't make it. I believe everything happens for a reason. I'll go to school in San Diego full time . . . and keep training full time.

"Missing it this year makes me want it that much more in 2012," he concluded as we set the first kayak into the lake.

There wasn't much I could say, particularly since Morgan began teaching me how to paddle a notoriously unstable Orion racing kayak. Staying balanced in the narrow hull required all my focus. The weather had warmed considerably since our previous session in December, which was fortunate since I flipped the boat multiple times. Morgan's patience surprised me and he spent well over an hour sitting on the dock, teaching me techniques, and watching me slowly acquire them. We finally decided I was ready for a longer expedition, so we set off down the lake.

Next to me was one of the world's finest kayakers and best athletes, but on the lake, we were two Scouts and two friends. I knew thoughts of the time trial still plagued him, but he did his best to focus on the day at hand and enjoy the moment. I knew he'd trained hard and had a great race. Someone else was just one second faster. One second. Morgan had consistently paddled one second faster each of the past several years. He just hoped his times would continue to drop. Four seconds less would likely win a medal in 2012. What struck me was the consistency of his times. To clock multiple times consistent to the second requires the exact same effort: 100 percent each time. He had no margin for slack and gave his all in every race. "Leave nothing," he said. That amazed me more than anything.

When we first met, Morgan hadn't been thinking of anything longer term than the upcoming 2008 Olympic Games. Really, he was just thinking about the April time trial that would decide his fate. After the April race, he'd worry about June. After that? Well, now he'd have to see. But he generally seemed quite content to worry about each new decision point when it arrived, which was a bit surprising for a top international athlete. Now both the April and June races lay behind him and he remained quietly confident that desire and skill would eventually lead to the Olympics; he was after all, only twenty-one. As we paddled back to the club, he had begun to reflect on the future. He now recognized that there was life after kayaking. But when we carried our boats back to the hangar, he wasn't thinking farther than the coming weekend. He'd just scored two tents, two burners, and two lanterns on craigslist for $150. He was picking up the gear the next day and on Saturday, he and several friends were hiking into the Dick's Creek wilderness in the northeast corner of Georgia. He couldn't have been more excited.

Honestly, I wished I could add a shorter sighted and more relaxed perspective to my own outlook. I'd encountered many others who wished for the same. From day one, many from our generation experienced life as competition. Gone were leisurely summers and afternoon stickball games in quiet neighborhoods. After-school schedules piled event on top of event. Structured camps and various enrichment programs occupied each summer day. We competed in sports as soon as we could walk. As we progressed in sports, music, academics, or whatever interest we pursued, winning alone soon lost its appeal. We needed to fight for spots on premier teams, troupes, or ensembles. A higher level always existed, and we seemed compelled to fight for it. Then we battled for acceptance to the best college, one on the short list of acceptable schools *US News* seemed to have the sole power to determine. The message was that the perfect school awaited us if we worked hard enough.

That was a myth. In truth, as China Care's Matt Dalio and I had shared with each other, many good choices exist for us, but sometimes we find ourselves still futilely seeking perfection. The stress that accompanies that quest and the related competition can wear us down and obscure the truly important things in life: time with family and friends, time to relax outside, time to challenge ourselves in new areas. Along this trip, I had begun to relearn how to stop, breathe, relax, and trust that everything will turn out well—and perhaps even better without my constant fretting.

After he raced in the upcoming August Nationals, I hoped Morgan would take a deep breath and rejuvenate himself before returning to his Olympic pursuit, in which I had no doubt he'd ultimately find success. But even that couldn't last forever. I wondered about what life would be like for him after he'd won gold; once he no longer competed internationally. I began to wonder how Eagles who achieve dreams at such a young age cope with the afterglow. How did they move on from their near-term goals and quests for perfection?

I found part of the answer in another Olympian. He'd already stood on the podium where Morgan hoped so earnestly to stand. He'd already bowed his head to receive an Olympic medal, joining the world's elite athletes. Temperatures at his ceremony, however, were much lower than any ceremony Morgan would attend.

I remember driving to meet Joe Pack, leaving Salt Lake City, Utah, and ascending the steep grade of the Wasatch Mountains toward Park City. Several years had passed since the resort's slopes had hosted the 2002 Winter Olympics, but I still felt a certain aura in the cool air, the electricity that had filled the city as thousands of spectators packed the stands to watch a hometown favorite compete against the world's finest skiers. The competition they came to watch didn't involve slalom courses or long downhill runs, though. Instead, they saw Joe Pack speed briefly down a slope then launch himself sixty feet into the air. The then twenty-three-year-old athlete didn't fly with his skis spread and body angled forward like typical ski jumpers. Traditional skiing never matched Joe's spirit; he skied freestyle. Each time Joe's skis left the ramp, he began a dizzying succession of flips and twists, hurtling forward and downward, yet always under control. At the last second, he righted himself and planted his skis beneath him to land with a light *thwap* on the packed snow to the great delight of the gathered crowds.

He entered the 2002 Games having already medaled in the 1999 and 2001 Aerial World Championships. Everyone expected the former Park City High School football and soccer player to clinch a spot on the Olympic podium. Some athletes would say they feel the pressure; Joe said he felt the energy. During his runs, the crowds alternately chanted "Joe-y" and "Go Joe Pack!" His perfect jumps and landings prompted thunderous roars.

"At the top of the run, I could look down and it just felt like I knew half the people," he said. "That was just amazing for my first Olympics and it definitely helped."

Pack skied his best, perfectly executing successive flights, twisting, flipping, but always landing smoothly on the slopes below. All this to wildly approving cheers from his fans. When the competition finished Joe stood in second place. He had earned an Olympic silver medal.

"Winning a medal in Park City, at Deer Valley, in front of family and friends is a hard moment to top," he said. "Even not winning gold, it was electrifying and I had so much adrenaline pumping. I'd done what I set out to achieve; you just can't beat that feeling. Standing there on the podium was pretty intense. I was really happy to be there and be surrounded by lots of family and friends. Honestly, there was a little bit of disappointment because I wasn't on the first place block. Just a little more would have made the difference, but it was just the winner's day and he deserved it, but there's always this competitive drive in athletes that makes you want that first-place finish."

He supported the gold medalist because they shared the bond that exists among freestyle skiers, particularly aerialists. The danger and high risk fosters a special camaraderie, even when your comrade edges you out for the gold medal. The spirit of competition and sense of sportsmanship associated with skiing took Joe back to Scouting. "I learned lots about sportsmanship from Scouting," he reflected. "We'd be on long camping trips—going out camping and starting our hike at ten P.M. and hiking twenty miles. You're doing it at night and in the rain and you're cold and don't want to set up camp when you get there. But you have to look out for others and work together to get things done versus looking out for yourself. Even if conditions are straight awful, you've got to get business done and do it as a team."

Joe started his life in Eugene, Oregon, but soon moved to Hopkinton, New Hampshire, where his entire family became involved with Scouting. His mother ensured that all her boys became Eagle Scouts. "I've got to admit, Mom pushed hard," Joe said. "She really believed in the values of the Scouting world. She helped all of us get through and now she still helps with boards of review. She'll help Scouts develop ideas for projects and really affects lives in that way."

Many New Englanders tend to be outdoorsmen, Scouts or not, so to set itself apart, Joe's troop felt an obligation to spend exceptional amounts of time in the New Hampshire woods. Joe remembered great leaders who taught the Pack boys about the environment and respect for nature. He carried a lasting love for the outdoors away from Scouting.

Joe loved skiing, but still made time for Scouting when he moved to Utah as a teenager. He described it as a balancing act, but a worthwhile one. During the summers, he'd train incessantly. Then he spent his winters studying in school and competing on the freestyle circuit. All the while, he kept hearing a small voice from his mother: "Finish this up, finish that up, finish Eagle." Joe buckled down and let Scouting teach him a lesson in time management. He learned to set an agenda and stick with it. The result? Things work out, whether that's earning Eagle or winning an Olympic medal.

"When you tell people you're an Eagle Scout, they look at you differently," he said. "It's a lot of hard work and lots didn't do it, but a few of us decided to get it done."

Joe put more effort into earning Eagle than most, and for his Eagle Scout project he moved an entire house. He identified an endangered relic from an early Utah settlement. A farmer planned to tear down the nineteenth-century log cabin to gain more farmland, but Joe proposed an alternative. Joe and his friends—some Scouts, some not—mapped the home and tagged every piece of lumber before disassembling it. Then they set the cabin up in a new location, piece by piece.

"We kept a piece of history," Joe recalled. "I employed some of my buddies and bribed them with plenty of pizza, and we disassembled this entire cabin. It was very meticulous and we dealt with very fragile old wood, but we had a great time with a great group. We worked hard together and shared in the accomplishment of doing something fantastic."

After he finished his Eagle project, Joe focused on a new goal: the Olympics. In New Hampshire, he had become a formidable skier, his skills honed at the renowned facilities at Lake Placid, New York. He and his older brother spent hours together on the slopes and Joe became a nordic ski jumper. Then at age twelve, he discovered freestyle skiing. He did it in the summer, then the next winter. At thirteen, he nailed his first back flip. He had a new passion and skiing dominated every summer and winter thereafter. "Going upside down for the first time on skis? It's magical. You're controlling some uncontrollable forces. The more you progress, the more you get better, the more you want to push yourself."

Joe explained the basics of freestyle aerials: "You tear down a slope at forty miles per hour, hit a big jump and launch, and suddenly you're sixty feet above the snow!" The height skiers obtain amazed me when I first saw professionals compete in freestyle. Although they're moving at forty miles per hour, from a distance, the jumps seem to lift the skiers into the sky gently. They seem to float as they begin a succession of twists, spins, and flips. These maneuvers are not singular or even just consecutive. A skier executes them simultaneously. As skiers flip upside down, they're also spinning and twisting, keeping their balance and focus throughout. The number of tricks performed in a single jump can border on unbelievable. Their routine done, the skiers fall toward the snowy slope below with their legs miraculously under them, ready to land. Their skis slap the slope and they sail to the bottom of the run, most of the time. Other times, skiers miscalculate their rotations or lose balance.

They land in a cloud of powder. When the snow settles, skis, gear, and skier litter the slopes. But, as Joe noted, the risk creates the adrenaline and that's the hook.

"There's always an element of fear, but that's where hard work and training pay off. You can't let those nervous thoughts and negative thoughts get inside your head. Although having a few of them is healthy; it keeps you sharp, on your game, and focused. But doing a move for the first time? There's always an element of fear—you're fifty feet in the air and you can always hurt yourself. I've had my share of concussions, blown knees, and back injuries."

By age fourteen, Joe had realized that competing in the Olympics was an attainable goal, and he made the U.S. junior ski team, where he needed all the balancing skills he could summon. Five years later, at age nineteen, he joined the U.S. national team. "You looked at it like a job; it was also a nice way to stay really, really fit." The team would finish their season in March, ski for fun in April, then relax throughout the month of May. Then summer training began on June 1. "If you hadn't kept yourself in shape," Joe explained, "you really felt those first days of practice!" They spent their summers and early autumns on technical and strength training regimens, keeping their body's core strong to support their aerial acrobatics. Lots of squats, sit-ups, and stretching, Joe recalled. Three weeks on and one week off. In October, workouts intensified, more cardio. When the winter season arrived, Joe would be strong, fit, and focused on his goals.

By following the team's training schedule, Joe took first place in the Junior World Championships in Australia then won his first world cup in Breckenridge, Colorado, at age nineteen. "Hey, veterans," he remembered thinking, "I'm Joe, and I'm here."

Joe enjoyed a decade-long career that included his 2002 medal performance in Salt Lake City and competing in the 2006 Olympic Winter Games in Torino, Italy. Unfortunately, no medals were won in Torino, and after the Italian Games, several things happened. One, Joe decided to retire, leaving the Olympics for the next wave of aerialists. "It's just the maturing process," he explained. "I had mentors when I was younger, and I've been helping younger aerialists: 'try it like this, try it like that.' Now they're the real competitors. It's their time."

What else happened? Joe discovered surfing and got ready to start a family. When I next caught up with him in Hawaii—his new home—he had happily moved on from competitive skiing, although Mauna Kea, at 13,796 feet, offers a uniquely Hawaiian skiing experience when the spirit moves him. It's backcountry skiing with no lifts or jumps. Drivers take turns ferrying skiers to the summit in four-wheel-drive vehicles. But all around the islands, he can surf and enjoy life after the grueling Olympic circuit.

"I'm stepping away from the ski world," he said. "I'm letting my body heal up, living in Hawaii, and enjoying life. I'm moving on from traveling and skiing competitively. What I'm really looking forward to—and why it made sense to move on—is getting married and starting a family. I finally came to the point where that was the right thing." Joe got married shortly after we talked.

Joe had become comfortable in his own skin, welcoming the new experiences offered by this next phase of his life. While he'd always remember the adrenaline of Olympic competition, he was embarking on an adventure of a different type, and he was already appreciating its rewards.

"Being out here, it's a new challenge," he observed. "Particularly in how I interact with people. Most people have no clue about my skiing background which is nice for me. You get to know some fantastic people at a very real level. I'm just living what I've learned in the past, treating people with respect, trying to make a difference in the world by being a good individual and a good human being."

Joe and Morgan would both agree that you can't do much more than that. And while Morgan wasn't ready to leave international competition behind, he was beginning to glimpse life beyond sports. Joe provided Morgan and me with an example of how life changes, and how we can accept that gracefully. These two Eagles, one an Olympian of the past, another an Olympian of the future, showed me how Scouting can influence even the most successful athletes. More importantly, I saw that Scouting provides guidance for the inevitable life after competitive sports. The program seems to ground people—youth and adults alike. We may venture off to pursue glory, but when those glories begin to fade, we gently return to the idea of serving others and the fulfillment that offers.

Meeting these athletes, I was also reminded of a common lament I'd heard from parents: their children had to choose between Scouts or sports. They claimed that young men and women couldn't succeed at both. In Joe and Morgan, as in Deuce and John Beck, I saw that's clearly not the case. Beyond them, I had found a host of others who excelled in demanding areas of high school life but who also excelled in Scouting.

Scouting taught them to balance priorities and passions, and they shared a common dedication to an important goal: reaching Eagle. Setting goals in different areas of life, and going after them all, became a habit. As far as I could tell from being with Morgan, Joe, and many others, the habit sticks and helps to enrich each successive phase of a Scout's life.

FAMILY

When I first met Travis Amerine, he commanded the Brigade of Midshipmen at the U.S. Naval Academy in Annapolis, Maryland. He had been twenty-two years old, full of energy and optimism. One semester had remained before his graduation, and a Texas A&M senior named Lauren had just captured his attention. We spoke often after he graduated in 2005, and we became friends as he moved from Annapolis to graduate school at Stanford University and to flight school in Pensacola, Florida. Now, he had traded Palo Alto, California, and the beaches of Florida for the inland town and military base of Meridian, Mississippi.

As I began to near the end of this second journey into Scouting, I felt the need to visit Travis, who was one of four Amerine brothers who'd reached Eagle. I wanted to see, firsthand, where life had taken him since I'd recorded his story in my first book. Something told me that seeing him might hold more answers. So I rode into Meridian where several years earlier I had met Lee, Travis's older brother. Now, Travis had taken his brother's place in the navy's prestigious jet training program there. He spent his days inside flight simulators and in white and orange T-45 training jets, rocketing over the fields and forests of eastern Mississippi. Every other moment, he spent with his family in their three-bedroom ranch, set amid virtually identical homes of the other young military families living on the base. As Travis drove me into the neighborhood, I saw colorful bikes and toys in most every yard and carport. We parked in his shady driveway and walked into the modest Amerine home.

Lauren, the attractive Texas A&M Aggie that had captivated Travis years before, smiled and greeted us. She held a seven-month-old girl with short hair standing on end. Ashlyn Day Amerine squealed when she saw her father and Travis swept her out of her mother's arms, hugged her, and thrust her toward me. As I pressed the smiling baby to my shoulder with my left hand, I met Travis's brother Denver's strong handshake with my right.

Just as Travis had followed Lee to Meridian, Denver had followed Travis from Annapolis to Pensacola for flight school. That left him only 190 miles away from his baby niece and he drove to Meridian often, keeping the states of Alabama and Mississippi well funded with speeding fines.

All eyes were focused on Ashlyn, who still clung to my shoulder. "Did you see her when we walked in?" Travis asked proudly. "She has that recognition now. Whenever I walk into a room, she knows I'm her father and she gives me this little look. I got a squeal tonight as well."

"Everyone always says Travis has this love for life," Denver commented. "And it really is the truth. You can see it in Ashlyn; she absolutely loves life. She's always smiling and hasn't met a stranger she doesn't like. See?"

We spent the next half hour gathered together on the couch, just watching Ashlyn. As I had already started learning from my newly arrived nephew in Atlanta, babies occupy center stage. Ashlyn alternated her attention between her four admirers, until her bedtime arrived at 6:30 P.M. At the first indication of fussiness, Lauren scooped her up and said, "Okay, it's time for this little miracle to go to bed." Ashlyn seemed agreeable and quietly let her mother carry her to the nursery.

With Lauren and Ashlyn gone, Travis grew reflective again and explained more about fatherhood to the two bachelors in the room. "There's another part of being a father," he said. "I remember taking Ashlyn outside, watching the first time sun hit her face, the first time a snowflake hit her face. Imagine if you could share something with someone for the first time every day. That is a gift from God to be part of that. That's how a father develops a bond with his children, by being there and sharing all of those firsts. That's what's so hard, knowing I'll eventually be on deployment. I'll miss six months of firsts." A little mist had developed in Travis's eyes. He wiped them inconspicuously and went to start dinner.

We followed as Denver told me that he had no plans to marry anytime soon. Twenty-eight seemed like the right age—five years away—and he estimated he'd have his own children at thirty-one or thirty-two. I smiled and remembered a host of jokes about what happens when people plan their lives in advance. Life seems to happen irrespective of your plans and perhaps sometimes in spite of them.

As we walked into the kitchen where Travis rattled through shelves looking for pots and spices, Denver continued, "At this point, every child of my brothers' is a child of mine. I have a love for Ashlyn that far surpasses anything I've ever experienced. I'm sure it doesn't surpass the love of being a father, but she's my little niece!"

"Denver used to take offense to this," Travis said as he lit the stove and placed a saucepan on the nearest burner, "but people would always say he's the baby of the family. Then it became a pride thing for him: he survived three older brothers! Now, there's a new baby in this family. Denver is the best little brother in this world. Obviously, I'm biased; I know your brother Rob is great. But Denver's always wanting to be there and be that uncle for the first time. I think he feels like this is his opportunity; I can see it in him. He wants to have an impact on Ashlyn. He's never had a younger sibling, but having a niece is close, and Ashlyn can't beat him up like we can!"

"True, I do have a size advantage on her," Denver said, as he withdrew his hand from the refrigerator with drinks and snacks.

We moved aside and watched Travis set about preparing his specialty: spicy marinara shrimp. Next to the stove, a ceramic pig wearing a chef's hat held a chalkboard that read, "Welcome Alvin." I felt at home. Lauren returned and as her husband mixed ingredients on the stove, she slyly confided that the spicy marinara shrimp was also the *only* dish Travis knew how to cook. Her comment elicited a raised eyebrow from Travis but not much protest.

"Truth hurts, doesn't it, brother?" Denver joked.

Soon enough, Travis decided that his shrimp had neared perfection, and we filled our plates with pasta, sauce, and shrimp. Once at the table, we joined hands and Travis blessed the meal, earnestly saying each word of thanks. I always find something special about a family dinner. Especially when you're away from your own family, nothing compares to joining a warm circle like the one at the Amerine home.

Blessing said, we all plunged into our food. Within five minutes, red sauce had splashed predictably onto Denver's white shirt, my fleece, and Travis's gray sweater. Lauren, whose shirt never suffered a drop, just laughed.

The dinner conversation drifted to Lee Amerine, who was flying F-18 Super Hornets from the deck of the aircraft carrier USS *Nimitz* somewhere in the Pacific Ocean. As if their bond as brothers wasn't enough, Travis and Lee had married college roommates. After meeting Travis at Lee and Jen's wedding, Lauren had e-mailed her now husband. Sheepishly, Travis confessed to never responding. As brigade commander at the academy, e-mails inundated him daily and he doesn't remember ever receiving her note. "But talk about second chances," he said gratefully. "I am so lucky!"

Jen Amerine had sensed some potential between her friend and brother-in-law and invited Lauren on a trip to New Orleans; Travis would be there. A few weeks later, Travis and Lauren began dating.

"So how did you realize you'd end up together?" I asked.

Travis laughed. "What do you think whenever a girl says this to you, Alvin? You're laying around and she says, 'I have a confession to make.' For any guy, your heart hits the floor and you're waiting to hear that she's got four kids on four continents. You're sitting there with this woman you're crazy about, heart beating, thinking this was going so well. But now, you're thinking it's over. Then she says, 'I love you!' I was so relieved."

"Well," Lauren said defensively, "I didn't know how else to bring it up. I'd brought up the idea of dating exclusively, but didn't know what he was thinking at this point. He hadn't said anything."

"Anyway, I worked that into my proposal," Travis said. He explained that he had called in a favor from a friend and taken her to Texas Stadium, the home field of the Dallas Cowboys. Under the bright lights, he proposed at midfield.

"I told her it was my turn for a confession: I picked the biggest place I knew to ask the biggest question of our lives. Any Cowboys fan knows there's a hole in the roof so God can look down on his favorite team. I remember looking up and thinking, 'Okay, Big Guy, if there is ever a time I could use a blessing from You, this is it.' And she said yes."

"Well, not exactly," I said. I remembered Travis telling me the story shortly after it happened. "She said, 'Have you asked my father?' " Everyone laughed.

"But you know, marriage is just the best thing," Travis continued. "You never plan it; you can't. The great thing about Lauren and me was that it was such a surprise. The only thing I can say is never outthink love. You can't make plans. When it's there, it flows. And if it flows and you start thinking you'll plan someone else's life, it's not going to happen. The best advice is always to live in the moment and don't worry about what's around the corner. Even in the heartbreak times and low times, never try to outthink what is in store for your life and try to set it up yourself. It's just being ready, going with the flow, and knowing that something will turn out. Personally, I would never want to live a life that didn't have that aspect of adventure, that aspect of surprise."

By this time, everyone had finished dinner. We cleared the table and left the dishes to soak in the sink, which, from extensive personal experience, I spotted as a ruse for procrastination. At any length, it let us move back to the living room and continue our conversation.

"You see, that's fatherhood to Lauren," Travis observed. "When I asked her to marry me, she said yes, but also wanted to make sure it was okay with her father that we get married. If Ashlyn ever says that, that is going to make me feel so good; that at that moment she wants to know that this guy asked me for a blessing."

The couple had undeniably moved quickly. They dated only eight months before becoming engaged, and married one and a half years after their first date. On their one-year wedding anniversary, they brought Ashlyn home from the hospital.

"It was quick," Travis admitted, "and I remember my uncle doing the math, thinking back on our wedding date and the nine-month time frame. He spreads his arms like an umpire and called, 'Safe!' "

"Travis said himself that it was a fast-track plan," remembered Denver. "All the brothers in the early stages were asking, 'Are you sure you want to get married so fast?' Then we gave him a hard time about wanting a baby. But it was right for Travis and Lauren. And if they'd waited we might not have had Ashlyn! It might have been a different *form* of Ashlyn. Everyone goes through that at their own pace and it worked out just right for Lauren and Trav."

"But you know, Travis is just amazing so of course it worked out," Lauren responded. "He balances fatherhood, his job, and being a husband. His daughter loves life just as much as he does, and I think her joy in the world comes from him."

"That's not true," Travis interrupted. "Her mother—"

Lauren had no interest in his disclaimer and continued, "Just every day, he wants to love her. When she's asleep or waking up from a nap, the second he hears her cry he runs in there to pick her up. And also when she was born, it was overwhelming to him to see it happen. I saw how proud he was when he held her for the first time."

Travis sat on the couch, slightly embarrassed. Lauren squeezed his arm, then Denver spoke up. As the little brother, he'd watched his older brother traverse each phase of life. He observed that whether basketball, Scouts, or school, Travis always gave 100 percent. He never settled for doing just enough. Then he married Lauren and entered the grueling naval flight training program, but, his little brother reported, Travis somehow found 100 percent for the navy and another 100 percent for Lauren.

"*Now*," Denver almost exclaimed, "he's married, going through jet training, one of the hardest things you can do in my opinion, *and* he has a little daughter. Somehow he still manages to give one hundred percent to each aspect of what he's doing. It's pretty amazing and all the brothers recognize it, but I have to admit I get a little jealous sometimes because my priority on his list has gone down a few clips!"

"Everyone thinks fatherhood is such a huge responsibility, especially for someone who is twenty-six years old," Travis said, then emphasized, "and it is. But it's not that bad when you have a family's support and examples like Lauren's father, my father. Everywhere there are examples, all the way back to Scouting.

"I think back to these men who would give time out of their day to invest in us. From when I was ten years old through the time I was eighteen, this dedicated group of people just like your father and my father would come in there and take a personal interest in my development. It doesn't necessarily take blood to be a father; I know for a fact it doesn't take blood to be a father. It takes a real care, and that is what I saw in Troop 41, Paris, Arkansas. I had four fathers in that troop, including one who was blood. The other three just cared about my development. Two of them didn't even have any sons who were in the troop. You look at these great men and you learn what selfless means. That's what a father is; it's just giving of yourself."

Travis still views his Scout leaders as father figures and very real parts of the person he had become. He can't wait to teach Ashlyn the things those leaders taught him. "It's like handing off a torch," he said. "I don't know if there's a better phrase, but I was definitely handed a torch in a troop where the leaders really showed me that just because I wasn't their son by blood didn't mean they weren't there to help me. That's what every person in Scouting can look to."

The next morning, Ashlyn woke before seven, and her parents obligingly followed once her first cries escaped from the nursery. Denver snored on unfazed until I carried Ashlyn into his bedroom to wake him up an hour later. Shortly thereafter, Travis cracked fresh eggs into the frying pan and the sounds and smells of breakfast finally coaxed a groggy Denver away from his futon.

Lauren and I were already at the breakfast table, talking about the first time Travis managed Ashlyn for a weekend by himself. "Lauren left me a sheet of instructions," Travis called from the kitchen, making sure I knew he wasn't entirely without help. Then Lauren explained that the instructions apparently didn't cover everything. Travis had brought his daughter to church dressed in the clothes Lauren had laid out, but he'd put the outfit on backward!

"Speaking of dress," Travis said, "let me tell you something funny. When you have a baby girl, your view changes real quickly. There are lots of pretty girls out there and two years ago, I definitely noticed—everyone does. But now you'll see them, and some of them aren't wearing that much, you know? It doesn't offend me or anything, but I'm thinking, 'What does your *father* think of that?' That could be Ashlyn! It's funny, and I laugh about it. She's not even a year old, but you turn into that overprotective father and start to look for danger!

"But that's just part of the responsibility and again, that goes back to Scouts for me, and I think Denver, as well."

Denver agreed, sleepily nodding his head from his spot at the table.

"In Scouts you start hearing these words: *honor*, *commitment*," Travis went on, showing the insight that had kept him in top standing at Annapolis and Stanford. "At first, you don't fully understand what you're saying, but the correct meaning is something for which you develop an understanding. When you're involved in a program like Scouting, commitment and never quitting becomes a part of you. It takes commitment to get to your First Class rank. It takes commitment to get to Eagle. The chains of habit are hard to break. If you form a chain that has commitment and you develop the ideals of Scouting, you act in that way without even knowing it. It's what you come to know and what you've come to do.

"A young couple can be faced with the challenge of raising a kid and they have to rely on skills based on what has happened in the past. You need a foundation for your home and life. Scouting built that foundation, although I didn't know it at the time. We were thirteen, fourteen, fifteen, but those words became a little piece of us and our habits formed and so eventually we could commit to such a thing as raising a child."

Fatherhood and marriage aren't avenues that everyone will or must pursue. But millions will choose those paths and many will have been influenced by Scouting. Qualities like responsibility, mentoring, and sacrifice will again come into play, and Eagle Scouts tend to be well-prepared in those areas. All of the characteristics that Scouting teaches continue to reverberate throughout our lives, and into the lives of the *next* generation.

After breakfast, we returned to the living room where Ashlyn again became the morning's entertainment until Lauren put her down for a nap before church. When she left, Travis, Denver, and I began discussing a question that had begun to crystallize in my mind during this journey. With every mile, I'd realized the uniqueness of our generation; how our experiences and our mission differed from our parents and those who'd come before us. We grew up in a different time with more opportunities and new tools with which to pursue them. How were we unique as a generation of Eagle Scouts, and as a generation of young Americans? How were we meeting new realities and challenges?

Travis and Denver observed that the changing world has created new opportunities, but that younger generations should pursue them guided by the same principles that have been Scouting's hallmark for more than one hundred years.

"The world is so much smaller today," Travis said. "Alvin, you were just in Nebraska, Washington, and Africa! Our parents never imagined doing things like that at our age. That's an option for us and our perspectives are going to change so much. And this country is changing. We're so young, our generation, but we're built on a set of core principles. I'm not saying the morals are being thrown out at all, but there's a definite shift and I think it'll be up to us to define the new landscape of this country, keeping in mind those timeless principles we have: honor, courage, commitment."

I'd been discovering that many people in our generation interpret values in different ways than our parents and grandparents. Older generations often view that evolution as a threat, but I had grown to view it as natural. Obviously, a generation of people will have innumerable views of ethics and honor, but I had seen many of us developing a broader and less rigid understanding of the unfortunately overused term *values*.

Like Buey Ray Tut expressed in Omaha, the faces of Scouting and the faces of America are changing. Families from different cultures are influencing and enriching our communities. Their children bring new perspectives to classrooms and workplaces. News reports, air travel, and the Internet have brought the world closer together; we know more about the struggles and realities faced by people on every continent. And of course, fads and trends come and go, just as they have for all time. Ideas proliferate and change, but as Travis and Denver observed, our guiding principles should not.

"Just think about how many ideas our generation is constantly in touch with that our forefathers didn't have," Denver observed. "They couldn't be linked to people and ideas from all over the world. As we encounter these new ideas, it'll really be up to *our* generation to hold the line and retain the values that we hold dear. No generation has been faced with the information overload that we have. As we sift through everything at our fingertips, it's going to be up to us to remember our core principles and where we came from. Eagle Scouts especially have always had a certain charge to lead on that front. Even though they may not know us, Americans think we act on what's right, that we're torchbearers. They might not be able to quote the Oath, but they trust us to know what's right. They know we don't lie, cheat, or steal. They know we honor our commitments, we care for other people and our families, and we respect different types of people."

"As this world gets smaller and smaller, we just can't forget where we came from and what we stand for," Denver concluded.

"In our case," Travis agreed, "that's Paris, Arkansas, Troop 41."

Lauren called from the bedroom to remind the three of us to get ready for church. Thus far, neither Travis, Denver, or I had indicated any movement in that direction. But soon, we had strapped Ashlyn into her car seat and were caravanning to downtown Meridian for the service.

Half an hour after the minister gave the benediction, the Amerines and I still remained outside the church, enjoying the warm sunshine that springtime had brought to the South. Ashlyn seemed quite content on my shoulder. I had dinner plans in Birmingham that evening, Denver had to report back to Pensacola, and Travis had to fly, so we all said our good-byes in the parking lot.

"Having a family and kids is the ultimate adventure," Travis told me as I prepared to leave. "You can't pack a backpack for this. On a hiking trip, you may know there's going to be snow or other elements, but with our family and Ashlyn . . ."

"You never know what to expect," Lauren finished.

I realized that as a jet pilot, Travis controlled everything. As a father, he controlled very little. It seemed like a drastic transition and not the expected order of things, but he didn't seem to mind.

"It's completely unknown, Alvin," he continued. "You can't weigh a pack and say that's too much or not enough. You go into parenting with what you think, but every day is new and different and you just go with the flow. They say a parachute will break your fall, but you're the one who's gotta land on your feet. You get married, you pack your bags, and you're ready for these life challenges. But nobody is going to make you land on your feet. Like I said, we're blessed with great examples and support, but when it comes down to it, nobody can teach you how to raise a child and build a family. You never know what's around the corner, and it's up to you to be prepared and react. Every young person will face this adventure sometime—just wait.

"You'll find it's the real adventure and one that you'll always be on," he added, and I realized he was talking about me. "You won't always be writing this book and traveling the world. You're living an adventure, and this is your time for that. There'll be time for other adventures as well. We'll always be Ashlyn's father and mother and we'll always be on that journey. In a way, this is life's last but greatest adventure."

ALOHA

One evening in 2004, Pete Vincent prepared for his first nighttime spearfishing expedition. He checked his fins and gun one last time, then joined his cousin Nick and his girlfriend's father, Willie Ho'o-manawanui at Sandy's Beach, a popular spearfishing and surfing spot on the southeast corner of Oahu, not far from Honolulu, Hawaii. Willie was a native Hawaiian and excellent spearfisher. He assuaged Pete's nervousness about the local sharks who often take their meals at night by explaining that his family's guardian spirit, or *aumakua*, was a shark. That helped, slightly.

The three divers met just north of the beach and gingerly walked out onto the volcanic rocks near the surf before stopping to put on their masks and fins. Once ready, they slipped into the water and began a night of fishing. It went well until Nick noticed they'd drifted one hundred yards from shore, fifty yards too far. Then Willie said he needed to catch his breath. Pete shone his light toward his older partner and found Willie looking ill. He put Willie on the fish floater and he and Nick began towing Willie to the beach. But the forty-year-old man only seemed to get worse. Something had gone very wrong. As the three divers came closer to the beach, Pete waved his light at the other fishermen on shore, yelling for them to call 911. Once in the shore break, Pete held Willie's face above water and Nick pulled him to the beach. Willie weighed nearly three hundred pounds, making this no small feat. Nick and Pete struggled to carry their partner beyond the surf, stumbling over slimy rocks until they reached sand. With each heavy step, they felt Willie's strength weaken, his breathing grow more labored.

"He struggled for air with all his might," Pete recalled, "but it seemed that no air would go in. Then, like a scene from a war movie, Willie told me under his breath that he was going die. My heart sank . . . We'd been as safe as we could have been, but being prepared isn't always enough. Some things are out of your hands."

Other fishermen hurried to help, and they laid Willie on the sand above the waves and rocks. Pete was holding Willie's hand when he passed out. Just then the paramedics arrived, began CPR, and loaded the big Hawaiian into the ambulance. When they closed the rear doors, Pete could see the medics hovering over Willie, still performing chest compressions. Pete pulled himself into the front seat of the ambulance and called his girlfriend's mother. He told her to come to the hospital, but understated the problem. "I felt so guilty for not telling the whole truth," he explained, "but I knew that it was best to help her to keep calm."

Then Pete called his parents. "I was so relieved to hear my father's voice," he said. "At this point, I really just wanted to talk to my dad and tell him I loved him over and over."

Willie's wife, daughter, and son had joined Pete and Nick at the hospital when a doctor emerged from the emergency room to tell them what Pete had already suspected. Willie had died from a massive heart attack.

That night and in the coming weeks, Pete witnessed the real depth of the family's loss. Willie had loved his family as deeply as they loved him. He was a true Hawaiian and created a family full of love. Pete told me that Willie had embodied the essence of *aloha*, the Hawaiian word for love, welcome, and farewell.

"What I learned that night was that life does not revolve around me after all," Pete reflected long after that night at Sandy's Beach. "It revolves around our ability to express our love and appreciation every day to the people who are closest to us. I also realize now that our human nature allows us to value our loved ones only to a certain extent, and we don't know the true worth of our loved ones until they are gone. Life may not always be sweet. But I will always savor every minute of every day with the people I love."

That attitude of appreciating life seems to permeate the Hawaiian Islands. As Costa Ricans have *pura vida* ("pure life"), Hawaiians have *aloha*. Both terms refer to a spirit of enjoyment, care, and love, though I should admit that I originally associated them with surfing and little else. As I'd learned many times by now, however, impressions and assumptions made from across oceans are often flat wrong.

I had spent less than twelve hours in Hawaii, most of them asleep, when my phone rang. Pete Vincent was waiting downstairs. In my room, I hastily stuffed a towel and board shorts into my backpack, and hurried downstairs for my first day on Oahu. Sunshine bathed the marina next to the Hawaii Prince Hotel and Pete had his car waiting dockside. His relaxed air didn't betray the reputation I already knew: karate national title holder, team captain in two of Hawaii's top canoe and kayaking leagues, finalist in the international outrigger canoe World Sprints, and competitor in Tahiti's *Te Tama Hoe* long-distance open ocean race. But he would mention none of that himself.

We were soon driving down Kalakaua Avenue, with the windows of his white Crown Victoria down. Through the open windows, we enjoyed the perennially warm Hawaiian weather. Pete had been home for the past six days on spring break from the University of Texas, and the day's weather wasn't making it easier for him to return to school the next morning. He had missed Hawaii, and after only one night on the island, I already understood why.

We picked up one of his high school friends and drove east along the coast to Koko Head, a dormant volcano. There we walked to the base of World War II–era railroad tracks that ran up the side of the steep crater; they might as well have been a ladder. Pete needed to make sure his time on the plains of Texas hadn't atrophied his legs, and the three of us began a long assault on the summit. Part of a family line of Eagle Scouts, Pete viewed hiking Hawaiian peaks as ordinary. But Koko Head wasn't ordinary. Our quads were already burning near the bottom and never stopped during the sometimes almost vertical ascent. Eventually, we arrived at the sun-parched summit, pouring sweat and ready to pay twenty dollars for a bottle of water. We'd long since collectively drained our single bottle. Be prepared, right?

No vendors appeared, so we just made do and enjoyed the breeze that circled the ruins of the radar station that once guarded, ineffectively as it would turn out, Oahu and Pearl Harbor against America's enemies. We looked down from the summit at Maunalua Bay and the coastline that ran west and north from our corner of the island. Pete pointed to a strip of white sand and its breakers. That was our next stop; he needed to introduce me to the Hawaiian surf.

An hour later, we bounced Pete's sedan into an off-road parking lot and walked to Makapu'u Beach, where we found the local section, away from other tourists, and wasted no time before getting wet. I'd spent every summer of my life in the Atlantic Ocean just north of Charleston, South Carolina, and considered myself good in the surf. The Pacific, however, had nothing in common with the Atlantic's modest waves and murky water. Several steps into the crystal surf and the water hit my waist. I dunked my head and the cool water quickly became tolerable. Several strokes later, I'd forgotten about the temperature and concerned myself with negotiating the enormous waves that reared high above swimmers close to shore. Soon enough, I tried to body surf. Pete had warned me about this. This was not the Atlantic, he explained; waves will throw you straight down into the sand if you're not careful. Even if you are careful, there's a healthy chance you'll have a hard brush with the sandy seabed. On my first ride, that's exactly what happened. I started swimming, thinking I was catching the wave as it lifted me up. Instead it dashed me straight down. Luckily, Pete had stressed that you should roll sideways once you felt yourself being thrown toward the bottom. Then, the wave would roll you over the sand; painful, but better than a possible alternative. If you hit headfirst, the waves could flip you end-over-end, seriously injuring your neck.

Pete had a cavalier spirit and a love for his native surf, but he also respected the ocean. So typical of Eagle Scouts, safety was important to him. It wasn't nerdy, paranoid, or outdated, it was just smart. Surfing is a calculated risk and Pete knew it.

"Scouting is in the business of promoting consideration of others and of other things," he told me later. "Whether it's being smart surfing or chopping wood for a campfire. You have to know first aid before you can advance. Before you can cut wood, you need your Totin' Chip. The underlying message is about being prepared. Remember how I wanted you ready for those waves? You can't grow up to be a responsible individual if you're not safe. Scouting gives you tools to be discerning about what's safe and what isn't."

Some time later, we showered away the salt water and piled back into Pete's car. Returning to Honolulu, Pete pointed out Sandy's Beach. It was packed with tourists and locals; lots of surfers trying to ride the notoriously rough waves. I only knew of Sandy's from Pete's story about Willie Ho'omanawanui's last dive. I had imagined the place as dark and moonlit, slightly foreboding. The bright sunlight and throngs of sunbathers now covering the beach reminded us that life indeed goes on. The scene put Pete in a reflective mood and he remembered his dive with Willie. He reminded me that our generation would soon be facing a new challenge, the one Willie's family had confronted in its ultimate form: the aging of our parents.

"We'll all eventually have to deal with losing our parents," Pete said. "But we have to be prepared for that and the fact that life moves on. In a way, Scouting helps us do that. As a Cub Scout at age eight you're placing trust in your parents. They're doing lots of work—pushing you and nudging you. As you move through Scouting you're hit with more tenets of being a man, being more responsible. Parents can step back and kids become more accountable for their actions. You get weaned off your parents. In Boy Scouts, when you finally make Eagle Scout, you thank everyone for all the help they've given you: 'You put me in the car and took me to Scout meetings when I didn't want to go. Now I'm a man and I've been able to take on responsibility. I can go camping without you there. Thank you.' "

I hadn't considered the fact of my own parents aging, let alone them no longer being with my brother, sister, and me. But many people in our generation had already faced the realities that accompany that process, and all of us would confront it eventually. Scouting can never truly prepare you for the loss of those close to you, but it does teach you to appreciate them while they're here. It also teaches you how to live independently, as Pete observed. I'm sure that had helped many of us survive on our own as young adults without wearing out our welcome at home with trips for laundry and dinner.

Neither Pete Vincent nor I had lost a parent, but I encountered someone who had. Peter Crowe's mother was killed in a car crash in 2006, while the Pennsylvania Eagle Scout was attending Hampden-Sydney College in Virginia. Her death was a terrible shock, and one for which no program or organization could every fully prepare him. His younger brothers and sister, along with his father Bob, came together to support each other as best they could. Fortunately, they didn't have to endure the ordeal alone. Friends from their Scout troop helped however they could in the days after the accident, sometimes just by being there. The Scouting community came together around the family. After the funeral, the Crowes learned that their Scoutmaster's wife had organized meals every night for the next two months.

"The meals were an immense help," Pete said, "not just to my family, but to me, as well. I knew that after I returned to school, my family would have hot meals while they dealt with the shock. My mom had been the primary cook in the house, so cooking just brought up waves of emotions that made cooking pretty difficult, not to mention just how exhausted we already were with the shock of everything."

Pete's father has remained good friends with the Scout troop's leaders who, in turn, always make sure Bob is doing all right. "Even now," Pete said, "Scouting is a great help. It's a tight-knit community. Dad knows that people care and are there to help if help is needed."

The loyalty and friendship that exists among the Scouting community makes the program singularly unique and the Scouts of State College, Pennsylvania, helped carry the Crowe family though a painful time. The community teaches its members by example, and Pete will forever remember the selfless care the Scouts showed his family, and he will pass that kindness along if he ever encounters another family suffering as his did.

In Hawaii, Pete Vincent explained how that Scouting community and others also taught him to appreciate life and other people a little more. From his experiences, he knew nobody accomplishes anything significant entirely on their own. He grew to appreciate the ways others helped him advance and excel throughout Scouts and high school: parents, merit badge counselors, Scoutmasters, coaches. Pete always appreciated how much they gave him, and how little they asked in return—except, he joked, for several coaches who wanted big wins.

When Pete left for UT in Austin, he also took with him an appreciation for the simple things in life. Like other Eagle Scouts I'd encountered, Pete enjoyed getting by on the minimum. Campouts and treks made in weather of every type, where he slept on the ground and carried everything he needed in his pack, helped him appreciate cooking any kind of nonpowdered food in a real kitchen and just being dry at night. The idea of sacrifice and cheerful service behind Scouting's honor society, the Order of the Arrow (OA), furthered his appreciation for living with little and giving much to others. And while the weekend-long OA ordeal remains a secret, everyone generally understands that it involves sacrifice and going without things we usually take for granted. Pete had emerged from it more humble and with a better perspective on what he really needs.

"You live life at ninety miles per hour," he said. "But the happiest people can still appreciate things that happen on the micro level. Those bits grow into the bigger idea of happiness. You get more happiness by appreciating the smaller things that are around you all the time—that can be parents, sunsets, friends, whatever. Appreciate it all and you'll have more *aloha*!"

The idea of *aloha* had surfaced yet again, and I still didn't fully understand what it meant, as a term and as a way of life. Since Hawaii's entire culture (not to mention a multibillion-dollar tourism industry) seemed to revolve around it, I thought it was particularly important. So I asked another Eagle Scout to help me understand. He agreed, but qualified that he couldn't explain the spirit of Hawaii to me unless I was on a surfboard.

The lei-laden statue of Hawaiian icon Duke Kahanamoku, a renowned Olympic swimmer, pioneering surfer, and the legendary embodiment of *aloha*, watches over the most vibrant portion of Waikiki Beach in Honolulu. To Duke's left sits Hawaii Ocean Waikiki, an oceanside surf stand that offers endless rounds of surf lessons to tourists. From dawn until sundown, the shack hums. Beach boys—surfers who teach lessons and rent boards to fund their surfing habits—were already preparing for the day's first lessons when Hubert Chang and I arrived at 6:15 A.M. Hubert, a native Hawaiian Eagle Scout and local dentist, owned the stand and we selected two choice boards for the morning. Ka'eo O'Sullivan, another Hawaiian Eagle Scout, joined us minutes later. Since Hubert's first dental patient would arrive at his office at nine, he wasted no time in plunging into the surf as he did every morning. Ka'eo watched as I methodically waxed my longboard on the beach before we plunged into the famous Waikiki surf, me carrying my board, Ka'eo carrying fins and a bright yellow bodyboard. We found the water crystal clear, even the foaming of waves only obscured the bottom momentarily. The moon still shone to the southwest as we paddled out to join the flotilla of surfers that never seems to leave the break.

Ka'eo had plied the amateur bodyboarding circuit for several years and I watched him catch waves with ease, spinning and sliding as he rode the curling and breaking swells. One moment he'd be facing backward; the next, forward. He surfed along, guiding his board easily across the waves. I followed on my board, trying to glean as many secrets as I could from the surfers nearby.

Midway through our session, the waves suddenly died down. Not discouraged, we remained in place, eyes turned out to sea. The lull gave

Ka'eo and me time to talk, and the tranquil morning provided a reflective atmosphere. We discussed the term *aloha*, which I'd gathered had particular meaning to my companion. For him, the word was exceptionally important.

"Everyone here uses the word," Ka'eo explained. "But its real meaning can get lost. You can say *aloha kakahiaka*, which means good morning. You can say *aloha* as a greeting, you can say *aloha* as farewell. But it's also a spirit of camaraderie and brotherhood. It's serving and respecting others. It's valuing other people. It's a way of life out here. *Aloha*. It's just love, you know? Love for everybody and it's how you express and convey that feeling.

"*Aloha* has a big part to play in Scouting and what it means to be a Scout," he observed. "It's something that comes naturally. Once you understand the fundamentals of Scouting—the Scout Oath, Scout Law, the motto, the slogan 'Do a good turn daily'—you look at people and just smile. It's that idea of brotherhood and loving your brother Scouts.

"I remember how we'd always welcome new Scouts into our troop and how we'd always help each other with badges and on trips. We did service projects around the island. Small things like that sound simple, but they're important. Scouting conveys what *aloha* is. *Aloha* describes Scouting. They're both things that live with you and alongside you and bring out the best in you. It's more than something to live by. It's something that you are."

My journey had brought me to Hawaii twice, and each time I stepped onto the islands, I felt a spirit I couldn't label more accurately than with Ka'eo's *aloha*. The community of Scouts on the island hosted me as graciously as any I've ever encountered. Eagle Scout Chuck Sted generously ensured that nobody else had a louder Hawaiian shirt than I did. Volunteer Helen Shirota-Benevides guided me across her native Big Island for three days, showing me a genuine hospitality I certainly hadn't earned. The Scouts of Troop 101 adopted me during their hike through Hawaii Volcanoes National Park, and University of Hawaii professor Steve Seifried, another Eagle Scout, had shared his exhaustive knowledge of the islands' biology and geology as we trekked through rainforests and across volcanic craters that mirrored moonscapes. They freely shared their hospitality and their love for life in the islands.

It wasn't just Hawaii, however. I'd experienced the same with Scouts throughout America and around the world. Perhaps they didn't use the Hawaiian term *aloha*, but that didn't matter. They clearly shared its spirit. I sat quietly on my board, contemplating those memories and how *aloha* describes the brotherhood of Scouting. I could show up in Greenwich, Connecticut, or Riverside, California, or Columbia, South Carolina, and find strangers who would welcome me and quickly become lasting friends. When I said, "Thank you," I often heard "Of course" in response. My hosts wouldn't have considered caring for me in any other way. Those experiences reminded me how Scouting's spirit extends far beyond adolescence and our individual Scout troops. The spirit of these new friends encouraged me on my quest and kept this adventure alive.

I thought more about the concept and realized how many forms *aloha* takes. As Pete Vincent understood, it's appreciating life and the lives of others while they're with us, our parents in particular. For Pete Crowe and his grieving family, *aloha* became the care his Scout troop and neighbors showed his family in the months after his mother's death. For Ka'eo, it was simply enjoying the day at hand and loving his growing family at home. As for me, *aloha* became the spirit that simply helped me relax and enjoy a moment—in this case, cloudless sky, warm air, warm sea, good company, and perfect waves. Beyond that, it was the hospitality I'd encountered and the good fortune I felt at being able to pursue my mission, meet so many fascinating members of our generation, and sustain myself thousands of miles from home. I realized that *aloha* is a uniquely Hawaiian term, but it's a concept that all Scouts can understand. That same sense of enjoyment, appreciation, and care defines Scouting and marks our generation of Eagle Scouts, no matter how far they may be from Hawaii.

The swells finally returned and after catching several more rides, Ka'eo asked another surfer for the time. He had recently persuaded his manager at Hawaii Pacific Health to let him work from eleven until seven, freeing his morning for surfing and taking care of his daughters, Josephine and Juliet, aged three years and two weeks respectively. Now, eleven o'clock was fast approaching, so we agreed to ride a choice wave to the beach and end the morning's session. We saw the wave building and watched several surfers attempt to catch it too early. Ka'eo and I began paddling hard and felt the wave rise beneath us, grip our boards firmly in its curl, and carry us toward shore. After a long ride, my friend headed in as planned, but I decided one more wave remained for me to ride, and I didn't want to miss it.

I paddled back through the surf, pushing through breakers and dodging wave upon wave of inbound surfers. Fairly exhausted, I went just beyond the main pack of surfers to rest. I sat up on my board and floated where the waves swelled, but had yet to break. My board rose up and down gently. The morning was pristine—clear, sunny, and warm. Watching over the scene from the northeast was the Diamond Head volcano, majestic and brilliantly lit by the sun. I looked south to the far horizon, and I was surprised by what I saw: my ride home.

The USS *Nimitz* glided smoothly across the peaceful sea. Its superstructure and black mast rose proudly above its 1,092-foot flight deck, which seemed massive even from several miles away. I watched the aircraft carrier quietly sail closer to Pearl Harbor in an understated show of power. Then it disappeared behind Oahu's shoreline bearing its complement of five thousand men and women, one of whom was Travis and Denver Amerine's brother, Lee. Soon, I would join him on board.

TOPHATTERS

Lee Amerine descended to five hundred feet and the view outside his cockpit still hadn't changed. Raindrops traced the canopy of his F-18 Super Hornet, flowing in tiny beaded streams above his helmet and toward the twin tails of his fighter. Visibility remained zero and he was less than a minute from landing. A low cloud bank surrounded him completely and he could scarcely see past his plane's nose. He relied entirely on his instruments and the voice coming over his radio. The landing signal officer (LSO) directed him from the stern of the aircraft carrier *Nimitz*, which Lee knew lay somewhere one mile off. Massive by most standards, the carrier and its narrow landing strip seemed miniscule to pilots flying over the vast ocean, like a postage stamp on a football field. And on this approach, Lee couldn't see it at all.

"You're lined up a little right," the LSO reported via radio. Lee nudged his stick to the left. "That's a good correction. You're on glide slope." Fog still encased Lee's Hornet.

An altitude alarm sounded. Lee turned it off.

"Okay, you're a little high coming down," said the LSO, confirming what Lee already knew. He made another slight correction.

"Okay, now you're on centerline," said the LSO. "A little more power."

Lee still had no visibility; just haze and rain. Then the plane suddenly dropped from the cloud's bottom at two hundred and fifty feet. The carrier loomed in the rain and mist, suddenly filling his view. A strip of landing lights flashed before him and he had seconds to judge the rolling of the deck. A scant four seconds after he'd broken through the cloud ceiling, Lee sailed over the carrier's stern at one hundred forty knots, still descending.

In a single instant three things happened. The F-18's two rear wheels met the rising steel decking with a squeak and puff of smoke, the tailhook scraped the deck to snag one of four thick arresting cables, and the jet's engines throttled up in case the hook missed. In that event, Lee would need to get airborne before he reached the deck's rapidly approaching end.

The pilot felt the familiar strain of the jet against the cable however, and he eased back the throttle as the massive hydraulic system behind the cables slowed his charging plane to a stop. Relieved, he flashed a thumbs-up to a watching deckhand. He raised his tailhook and began taxiing forward across the rain-washed deck.

Pilots often describe carrier landings as "controlled crashes." I had watched this particularly harrowing landing on a screen. Lee actually lived it. He had long before lost count of the foul-weather and nighttime landings he's negotiated. For Lee, that landing was just part of a typical day at work on a shift that had begun nearly five months before. Now, the pilots and crew of Squadron 14 had arrived in Hawaii. As their carrier sailed in front of Waikiki Beach and entered the shallow waters of Pearl Harbor, they knew that only one leg remained before they reached their journey's end in California.

Green grass and trees still cover the hills over which 353 Japanese airplanes flew on December 7, 1941, on the surprise attack that drew the United States into World War II. The water in Pearl Harbor is no less clear and blue today than it was moments before the bombers' first torpedoes hit the USS *Utah*, whose rust-covered hulk rests where it lay at anchor that morning. The surrounding mountains remain majestic and retain that mysterious Hawaiian spirit. And the once-mighty USS *Arizona* still lies where she was moored on Battleship Row. More than one thousand of her crew members still lie with her.

Lieutenant Lee Amerine and I viewed this scene from the bow of the aircraft carrier USS *Nimitz*, sixty feet above the harbor but quite near enough to feel the weight of history. We looked down toward the USS *Arizona* Memorial, the distinctive white memorial that spans the surface over the sunken battleship. Rusted gun placements and mastheads broke the surface, and the dim outline of a six hundred-foot-long hull showed itself through the clear water. Tears of oil still seep up from the ship's tanks, a memorial to those who died on board the *Arizona* and her sister ships that day in 1941.

Our modern warship bore the name of the admiral who arrived at Pearl Harbor three weeks after the Japanese attack and orchestrated America's eventual victory in the Pacific. The *Nimitz* had been docked in Pearl Harbor for the past two nights and now tugboats were easing the carrier away from her berth, pushing *Nimitz* toward the open sea and the voyage home to San Diego. The tugs were turning the massive ship around in the harbor's surprisingly small confines, and her bow loomed over the *Arizona* Memorial momentarily before pivoting further to face the decommissioned battleship USS *Missouri*, where on September 2, 1945, the Japanese formally surrendered to Admiral Chester W. Nimitz and General Douglas MacArthur. The *Missouri*'s still unmatched twenty-six-inch guns silently watched over the *Arizona*, completing a circle of history, initial defeat to eventual victory.

When Japanese admiral Isoroku Yamamoto discovered that America's aircraft carriers had escaped his attack on Pearl Harbor, he was, with good reason, worried. The attack decimated the Pacific fleet's battleships, but Yamamoto knew that Admiral Nimitz would rely on carriers and their airplanes to press his campaign. From the war's beginning to its end, aircraft carriers were a determining factor, and so they have since remained. Today, carriers project American power around the world, their strength unrivaled. Whenever an international crisis erupts, America's leaders immediately ask, "Where are our carriers?" I could at least answer for one of them.

"This has always been one of the biggest cards that we have in international diplomacy," Lee told me from our new perch on a catwalk attached to *Nimitz*'s superstructure, the seven-hundred-ton, eighteen-story tower on the starboard side of the ship. He pointed to the tightly packed gray jets on the flight deck below us. Most were F-18 Hornets, with several EA-6 Prowlers and E-2 props mixed among them. "We can go anywhere and we have everything we need right here. We can park twelve miles off anybody's coast and be perfectly legal and conduct flight operations. The firepower we have coming from our strike group and the diplomatic impact that has is huge."

As the *Nimitz* sailed east past Waikiki and Diamond Head, I thought about how far Lee had traveled since we last saw each other in Meridian, Mississippi. Two years had passed from our first meeting, when we piloted flight simulators together and he first introduced me to his wife, Jen. I'd never expected that our next meeting would be on an aircraft carrier in the middle of the Pacific Ocean. Our arms hooked over the railing, Lee and I enjoyed the perfect weather and the timeless flicker of excitement and anticipation that accompanies going to sea. He used the time to fill me in on the past two years of living.

Months after we'd parted in Mississippi, he had earned his naval aviator's wings and qualified to pilot the F-18E Super Hornet—dubbed the "Rhino" by its pilots. Then he endured the most trying experience of his life in the Survival, Evasion, Resistance, and Escape (SERE) program, where he learned how to survive in the wilderness, evade enemy search parties, and endure interrogations. He assured me that nobody in that school learns from a textbook; staff push them to their physical limit. Not surprisingly, Navy SEALs were among the instructors.

"I barely ate for eight days," he remembered. "I dropped twenty pounds. All my buddies from Meridian went together. We bet who'd lose the most weight. I lost the most as a percentage and a total!"

After enduring SERE school, Lee experienced another test: carrier landings. He learned to land at night, in the rain, and in every other imaginable condition. One night, the weather was so bad and the deck was pitching so heavily, the LSO waved him off six times due to conditions. Several weeks later, he left for his first deployment: six months, from San Diego to the Persian Gulf and back. There, he supported American troops on the ground in Afghanistan and Iraq. This second cruise had already lasted nearly five months and now only the six-day passage to California remained. He was long past ready to return home.

"You have to realize that every day is the same out here," he explained, preparing me for what I could only partly experience—I would spend one week aboard; not twenty. "For me, for us in the squadron, life is on hold. Nothing really changes for us. Every day is exactly, exactly the same. Knowing it's pizza night on Saturday and wearing khaki flight suits on Fridays are about the only ways we know what day it is. Flying the missions may be different. We may be flying near Japan or down by Guam, but it doesn't matter. It's still the same thing day in and day out. Whereas for Jen, it's, 'Denver came to visit; I went to Acapulco and saw Lauren and Travis; Denver got picked for jet training.' There's a lot happening back there, and even when you read about it, it doesn't strike home. I don't mind being out here—I love what I do, but you're just removed.

"And there's so much back home that I don't ever really get to enjoy," he said. "Like my house. I've owned it for fourteen months and I've slept in it four months; I've slept here ten months!" He laughed, which was all he could do. He'd made his choice to serve years ago, knowing the sacrifices ahead. And like POW Ron Young, he'd readily do it all over again.

Lee was understandably glad to be heading east toward home. I would have welcomed several more days—or perhaps months—in Hawaii. But from our vantage point several stories above the flight deck, we watched the Hawaiian islands slip away astern as the *Nimitz* increased her eastward speed and her four screws churned through an ethereally blue ocean.

Two mornings after Diamond Head disappeared behind us, I woke up to the gentle rolling of the ship. I looked at my clock: 6:35 A.M. Two hours earlier than I'd planned. But I knew the sun would rise at 0651 according to the ship's weather report, so I pulled on a hat and made my way to the catwalk that girds the flight deck. Through the metal grillwork, I saw the blue ocean moving swiftly below me. I walked up four small steps and ducked under the tail of an F-18 to reach the flight deck. Once clear of the jet, I straightened up and surveyed the all-encompassing horizon. The lights of our two escort ships shone on our port and starboard beams. The sky had begun to brighten and all but the western-most stars had disappeared. The only sounds were the ever-present hum of the ship and the distant rushing of water parted by the *Nimitz*'s surging bow. Nobody else stirred on the deck.

I looked east, down the flight deck and noticed the ship gently rising and falling with the Pacific's swells. Two long rows of F-18s followed the ship's movement and formed an open avenue along the centerline of the deck. At the avenue's end, a solitary F-18 Super Hornet stood facing me like a predator observing its prey. Directly over its wing rose the sun.

I wandered down the line of planes toward the bow and the untouched sea it had yet to plow. When I reached the deck's end, I steadied myself against the Super Hornet. Its metal skin was cool and moist with morning dew. The dapper top hat painted on its tail marked it as a plane from Lee's squadron, the VFA-14 "Tophatters," the Navy's oldest.

Holding on to the jet, I peered over the edge at a glassy, cobalt sea. A brilliant orange streak traced from the rising sun on the far horizon to the carrier's bow. The 1,092-foot, 95,000-ton, nuclear-powered warship moved purposefully beneath me, slicing along the shimmering ribbon that marked the way like Oz's yellow brick road. Surveying the boundless ocean all around me, I felt the stiff and salty wind in my face and the muscle of a warship that had no equal in the world. I'd never known a more unbridled sense of adventure or a similar sense of power, privilege, and wonder. Once again, this long journey left me amazed. I looked due east to the open horizon and the coming day. Both *Nimitz* and I were heading home.

"Man, that's where you want to see the sun," Lee said ten minutes later when we met for breakfast in the wardroom. "It's not a good feeling seeing the sun rise over the stern. Three days farther east and we're home: *that's* a good feeling.

"And so is this," he added, surveying the spread of food the wardroom's cooks had prepared. Pilots are nothing if not well fed. In fact, the entire crew ate surprisingly well and food never seemed absent from either the officers' wardrooms or the enlisted mess. Food service began at 0530 and ended at 1930, to be followed by midnight rations, or "midrats," at 2300. I reverted to my college ways, grazing throughout the day and relishing every minute of it. Lee had long since adjusted to the ribbing he received for having the healthiest diet in the squadron, if not the entire air wing, and while I piled scrambled eggs, pancakes, and bacon onto my plate, he added small portions of eggs to his fruit-heavy platter. We joined a round table with several other pilots who were talking about the day's upcoming air show, while exploiting every chance for a good-natured verbal jab at one another. Lee took and dished out his fair share.

After a second round of breakfast, Lee and I left the wardroom for the flight deck, where he supervised a red-shirted ordnance crew. Stenciled on their long-sleeved shirts was "VFA-14," along with assorted nicknames and ranks. The young men and women were preparing to load eight one-thousand-pound bombs onto the number 201 plane, to be flown by Commander Dave Koss. Lee watched the team roll the bombs toward the plane in a line of three carts. Once the crew finished, he congratulated them and spoke with the chief petty officer, who would supervise the remaining preflight work. Lee then showed me other aircraft on deck before we returned to the 03 level of the ship, just below the flight deck. Lee left for the squadron's briefing, or "ready" room and I went for yet another round of breakfast.

An hour later, I walked into the ready room as the pilots were leaving for their planes, flight suits on and white helmets in hand. One pilot remained: Jack Hathaway. One of three junior VFA-14 pilots on the cruise, his lot was serving as the duty officer while the rest of the squadron flew. He appeared resigned to his fate.

The youngest Tophatter, Jack had finished the requirements for his Eagle Scout rank a scant two days before leaving for his first year at the U.S. Naval Academy. He had carefully calculated his decision to attend the academy: he knew the USNA produced more astronauts than any other undergraduate institution. Among them, Eagle Scouts Jim Lovell of Apollo 13, moonwalker Charlie Duke of Apollo 16, and William McCool who perished in the 2003 *Columbia* disaster.

"The first astronauts were all test pilots," Jack observed. "Not just adventure junkies, but guys with a lot of technical expertise and a lot of tactical operator ability. They wanted to take it to the next level; they wanted to keep doing something better. That's a driving force for me, too. The pinnacle of flying—to me—is being an astronaut. But there are a lot of different pinnacles. The more I've gotten into it the more I realize there are a lot of different routes and a lot of great people do a lot of different things—but what an adventure, what a great adventure."

For Jack, Scouting's adventure clearly did not end when he exchanged his Scout uniform for a navy one. He worked with the academy's National Eagle Scout Association chapter and for his sophomore summer, he convinced his superiors to let him spend one month serving as a guide at the Northern Tier Canoe Base in Minnesota. Several equally fortunate midshipmen had spent their summers at Philmont or the Florida Sea Base. When Jack arrived in Minnesota, he learned to guide crews into the expansive boundary waters region that straddles the U.S.–Canada border. After six days of training, the nineteen-year-old Eagle began paddling into the wilderness for weeklong adventures, bearing responsibility for Scouts and leaders from across the country. He suddenly found his crews looking to him for answers, and they fully expected him to have the right ones.

"You can take a group of seventeen-year-olds out and they look up at you and draw some inspiration from you," he said. "At the same time, you draw some inspiration from them. They have verve for life and excitement about being out there.

"It's a value-oriented lifestyle and you're leading small groups," he continued. "Especially when you're dealing with Scouts who are fourteen to seventeen, they look up to you. Sometimes it's easy to do the simple thing instead of the right thing, but you're standing in front of those guys and you can't do that. You've got to do it the right way. That's true now. It's pretty easy to take privileges as an officer; do something you could get away with but isn't necessarily the right thing to do. You learn the same thing in Scouts. You're around younger kids, so you can't give them the wrong impression: that you can do whatever you want when you're in charge. You've got to be a leader instead of just being in charge.

"One of the great parts about Scouting is that you get inspired by people who are two or three, maybe five years older than you. Your role models as you're going through the program are just a couple of years ahead of you. Your SPL [senior patrol leader] might be four or five years older than you. I had some role models a generation older than I was, but not nearly as many as I had going through the program who were two, three, or four years ahead. Even in the squadron, the more senior guys are eight or nine years older than you and not twice your age where it's hard to relate. You can see how you could be like them in a couple of years."

Part of leading involves making mistakes and helping others learn from them, and Jack explained how their executive officer (XO) would lead meetings where senior and junior pilots discussed their shortcomings and errors. "Everyone here is pretty proud and likes to do everything perfectly," Jack admitted, "but we'll have these meetings where we stand up and say this is the big mistake I made this week or this month. Everyone goes around and owns up to what they did. Hopefully everyone will learn from it or change something about what they do. People will say this is the mistake I made—senior guys, junior guys. You can learn from their attitude as well as their specific mistakes."

Alone with him in the ready-room, I knew Jack wished he were climbing the stairs to the flight deck with his fellow Tophatters. Trying to distract him, I asked about his most memorable flight from his first cruise. He recalled being on Alert Fifteen in the ready-room as a Russian bomber approached the task force. The loudspeaker had called: "Launch Alert Fifteen." Jack ran to his waiting plane. Within fifteen minutes he was airborne, flying to intercept the bomber.

"We'd sit off its wings, go behind it, and sometimes fly up front so we could see the pilots," he remembered. "We can see them and just like we're taking pictures of them, they're taking pictures of us. Between the aircrews in the two planes, we recognize that our countries are doing strategic things by having us out here, but we're just a bunch of twenty- and thirty-year-olds doing our jobs, flying our planes, having a good time. We'd be friends in a different circumstance."

Military uniforms may highlight differences between countries, but in many cases, the individuals who wear those uniforms value the same ideals, including duty and adventure. Wherever they are from, they all serve their country and their fellow citizens. Since Scouting exists in 156 countries, I felt certain many of those soldiers wore a Scout uniform before they ever wore a military one—yet another thing that makes the world a little smaller.

"I'm very drawn to the idea that something's bigger than me," Jack reflected as we discussed Scouting and the idea of service. "You read newspaper articles about what's going on in China or Taiwan and there we are in that part of the world helping our national strategic interest. I've also always wanted to be an astronaut, so this is a step in that direction. But we're jet pilots on an aircraft carrier. It's pretty cool. It's a mixture of a sense of adventure, patriotism, and doing something exciting with my life that most people don't get to do."

Time for launch had drawn near, so I left Jack in the ready room and headed upward to the deck where I knew the other Tophatters were conducting final checks on their planes.

Just inside the doorway to the flight deck, I met Brian Bradshaw, a yellow-shirted "shooter" who outfitted me in standard attire: a life jacket with "VFA-14" branded on its back, a "cranial" or helmet with sound-dampening headphones, foam ear plugs, gloves, and bulky goggles. Brian was taking the day off from being the officer responsible for each launch, and instead, served as my guide to the intricate world of carrier flight operations. With a friendly smile, he gave me his basic instructions: "Stick by me, and if I duck or hit the deck, do the same." Easy enough. He opened the hatch to the deck and we emerged from the dark interior into a realm of noise that my earplugs and headphones only partly dulled. The heat of jet engines added to the warm Pacific sun and the wind only partly diluted the exhaust. I looked up four stories to the tinted windows of the bridge, behind which the captain and admiral were watching the pageant unfold. *Nimitz* had turned into the wind to give her planes added lift and I could feel the steady breeze rushing over the bow and down the deck. The cruiser USS *Princeton* lay off our stern. The destroyer USS *Higgins* guarded our port side, only 150 yards distant. Two Seahawk helicopters hovered nearby at the ready, all part of the ritual of naval aviation.

Brian and I walked through the heat and the alternate rumble and scream of turbines until we reached the flight line, several yards clear of the catapult which would literally sling *Nimitz*'s airgroup off the deck and into the sky, plane by plane. There, we felt the air and deck vibrate from the thunder of engines as planes opened up their throttles, ready for launch. By the time we reached the middle of the four-and-a-half-acre airfield, Lee Amerine was maneuvering his F-18 into the number two position on catapult three. The CAG (commander, air group) had pulled his number 200 plane forward of the blast shield and onto the catapult track. The shield raised itself to a sixty-degree angle to deflect the jet exhaust. Green-coated airmen swarmed over the plane, performing final checks. A yellow-shirted shooter coaxed the plane forward until its nose gear touched the small metal catch of the steam-driven catapult embedded in the deck. A crewman secured the steel strut that connected the plane with the catapult then scampered away. At the shooter's direction, the pilot throttled his engines to a scream that seemed deafening despite two layers of ear protection. He saluted the shooter. The shooter knelt to the ground and pointed forward. At that signal, a crewman pressed a button and the sixty-thousand-pound F-18 shot forward as if it weighed nothing. Less than three seconds later, the steam-driven catapult stopped abruptly, sending the full-throttled jet off the deck at 170 knots, or 195 miles per hour. Steam rushed from the narrow catapult track and blew across the deck. The small shuttle sped back to take on another rider: Lee Amerine.

The blast shield lowered itself so Lee's number 212 plane could take its position on the cat, to use navy jargon. He eased the fighter toward the catapult and as it had before, the shield raised itself behind the plane. The greencoats locked him into place, the shooter flashed signals with his hand and Lee returned them with a thumbs-up. I tried to see his face, but his oxygen hose and the dark visor of his helmet obscured his eyes and any expression his face might have. He touched his bare right hand to his helmet in a salute then held onto the canopy. His two GE turbofan engines screamed and roared. The shooter's hand again pointed sharply toward the deck's end. Lee's head jerked back slightly as his Super Hornet thundered forward with its afterburners visible even in the daylight. His plane hurtled off the ship and he banked into a gentle climb to his left to meet up with the CAG and await the remainder of the air group.

When the full complement of planes had launched, the pilots

regrouped miles from the carrier and began a special air show for a crew weary from five months at sea. Crew members covered the flight deck for a chance to glimpse what most of them so rarely saw. These men and women faithfully supported the *Nimitz*'s pilots in every imaginable fashion: as mechanics, as cooks, as shopkeepers—basically any occupation found in a city of five thousand people. This city's purpose just happened to be launching aircraft. For the next thirty minutes, the pilots said thank you.

After a series of acrobatics, supersonic flybys that sent powerful booms pulsing across the deck, and aerial displays of every kind, the show ended with the performers flying slowly over the flight deck, grouped in diamond patterns. The crowd applauded thunderously.

Over the loudspeaker, the captain ordered the deck cleared for landing. The crew retreated below, and Brian escorted me toward the stern where the planes would arrive momentarily. We stood alongside the painted runway that ran from the very stern of the ship to an angled, secondary bow two hundred yards forward. A green light flashed from the bridge, indicating planes had been cleared to land. A group of F-18s thundered overhead from aft to bow in tight formation, and one peeled out to execute a wide 360-degree turn that brought him into the landing path. Another green light flashed beside the landing signal officer's platform near the stern and the officers began talking the pilot in to the carrier. This time, no clouds. Just sunshine and calm seas.

The landings continued until only two jets remained aloft. Number 212 finally peeled away from the CAG and banked along *Nimitz*'s port side. Once he'd positioned the fighter behind the ship, Lee gingerly aligned his plane on the glide path and descended toward the ship. His wheels met the steel decking dead even with my position. In a moment too quick for me to observe, his tailhook caught the wire. His engines throttled up and I felt their heat blowing down the deck. A black line of arresting cable trailed his plane down the runway, eventually drawing him to a halt. Lee raised his hook and taxied toward the bow.

By the time I arrived at Number 212, Lee had opened his canopy and stepped onto the wing. A small crowd of crew members had gathered to meet him and he thanked each one when he reached the deck. They seemed like teammates after Lee had scored a game-winning shot.

"Everyone in VFA-14 is part of this," Lee said after he made his way to me. He gestured to the crew behind him. "Fourteen is a team. *Nimitz* is a team. Everyone on this ship supports us in flying our missions.

From the galley to the radar to the crew chiefs, everyone here supports us in getting off this deck. I have two hundred twenty-somethings in the squadron who are dedicated to keeping twelve F-18 Echo Super Hornets fighting ready. And there's a cadre of fourteen pilots who go out and fight. Those two hundred young men and women bust their tails, work day in and day out, heaving one-thousand-pound bombs up there so that they get everything on this jet perfect. There's no way I could preflight this whole jet. I know that twenty-two-year-old kid [in the crew]. I've seen him progress from being in training at eighteen to being a full plane captain. I trust him. I know what he did. When Chief Palmer signs his jets safe for flight, I have complete confidence up and down the chain that this jet is ready to go flying.

"And the thing is, the parents of the guys who work pumping the fuel into these jets are just as proud as my parents. Everybody is proud to be out here and doing this. So it's very, very, very humbling. I get touched so many times when I'm on the flight deck and I look around and there are one hundred people dodging jet exhaust and things like that just to get me off the deck. And it doesn't matter if we're in the Persian Gulf where it's a hundred and twenty degrees on the flight deck or if we're off Korea and it's close to twenty degrees and snowing. Rainstorm? Doesn't faze 'em. It's unbelievable, it truly is. When I get out of the plane I try to shake as many hands as I can. To me, it's a big honor that I'll remember forever. These kids running around busting their tails so I can go fly. That's teamwork. It's awesome."

By sundown, the squadron crews had finished respotting the deck, arranging planes in an order that I couldn't quite decipher, but that seemed to make perfect sense to the directors in the tower. On a catwalk just off the flight deck, I met the man responsible for ensuring each VFA-14 jet had found its proper spot: Chief Petty Officer Rob Palmer. The chief had removed the white helmet that identified him as the lord of the Tophatters' aircraft. If anything went wrong mechanically, organizationally, or in any way whatsoever, the controllers above would expect Rob to have an immediate answer.

"If it's on the flight deck, it's my responsibility," he explained, looking west over our wake to where the sun had begun to sink toward the horizon. "That's planes and people for our squadron. Basically, it's a big Scout troop and I'm the senior leader."

Growing up in Peapack-Gladstone, New Jersey, Rob had learned about being a senior leader from his father, a Scoutmaster. When he was sixteen, Rob actually quit Scouts for that reason. He explained that everyone thought he was a Scout just because his father led the troop. So as a Life Scout, he walked away. A year later, at age seventeen, his father finally coaxed him back to Troop 7.

"I was halfway finished with the requirements for Eagle anyway," Rob said. "I had my project and a couple of odds and ends left. Dad said, 'Why don't you come back and finish it up?' I knew my brother didn't make it, so I was my dad's last hope to have an Eagle Scout son. So I went back, finished it up, and I got it pinned when I was almost eighteen.

"With rank comes responsibility," he continued, talking about both Scouting and the military. "There's a lot of responsibility to make sure the younger guys are led properly. I'm the older Scout that has to put the younger Scouts in my position. If I want to *stay* the senior leader, I'll make everyone else fail then I'll have no replacement. But I want to train each guy to do the next guy's job. I should be looking to do a senior chief's job where my first classes should be looking to do my job, a second class should be looking to do a first class's job. Essentially, someone should put me out of a job.

"And the higher you get in rank, the more of an example you are. If they see that the chief did it, they think, 'Why can't I?' We have to reflect what we say. It's not a 'Do as I say, not as I do' place. You gotta instill the proper attitudes and proper ethics if you want to help people better themselves."

Beyond responsibility for each crewmember, the chief ensures that his pilots step into safe planes. His crews prepare every jet then Rob signs a form that declares a plane ready for flight. Only then will a pilot accept a plane and take off. "I won't sign that sheet unless *I* would step into that cockpit," he said. "That's how safe it's got to be."

Rob knows each plane inside and outside, and has been working flight decks since he joined the navy after a stint as a carpenter and cabinetmaker in New Jersey. He spent his twentieth birthday in boot camp. He entered the fleet as an AD, an aviation machinist mate, and had now attained the rank of chief petty officer. Chiefs, who are noncommissioned officers, form the navy's leadership backbone and manage the more than four thousand enlisted personnel aboard the ship.

"I always love working with my hands," he said, recalling his background as a Scout and carpenter. "I've worked on cars ever since I was old enough to work on them. I used to hang out at the local gas station and do oil changes and things like that. It was basically free labor—the owner might give me five bucks after I'd put a few hours of work in. I didn't get any merit badges for it, but I liked tinkering with things. I always had a screwdriver and wrench in my hand as a kid. It was just fitting to become a mechanic. Then the background of the BSA helps you with the rank structure. I was at the top in Scouting and I'm aiming for the top here.

"But now I have to drop the wrench and let the other guys do it. That's been the hardest thing. Now I'm in a managerial position, where I'm not the first one to grab the toolbox. I have to make sure the seconds, thirds, and firsts are out doing it."

On this cruise, one of those doing it for the Tophatters was another Eagle Scout, Aviation Electrician's Mate (Third Class) Chris Poole.

Chris met me on the flight deck the following day when work paused and he could slip away from repair jobs. His team had finally fixed a nose-gear assembly that had recently grounded the number 205 plane. We talked about the repair job and I quickly became lost in technical terminology, so I asked the green-shirted electrical expert to show me. We ducked beneath a nearby Super Hornet and knelt by its forward landing gear, looking into the open bay that enclosed the gear during flight. The number of multicolored electrical and hydraulic lines overwhelmed me as much as Poole's terminology had. The twenty-one-year-old Eagle Scout patiently explained the complexity of his job and how each maintenance team worked together within itself and with other groups—rarely were problems independent and isolated.

"A few months ago, 212 had a severe wiring problem," he said, offering me an example. "It shorted badly and we actually had wires fry open in several places from the engines up to the avionics on the forward fuselage. That's a lot of area to cover. Every shop in the squadron was involved. We're not just a team in the electrician's shop. Everybody has to work together to keep the planes running. Our shop helps the other shops figure out their problems. On this jet, they had to pull every component out so we could get to the wiring. We ended up routing a new set of wires all the way through the belly of the jet. Two weeks of day and night work to get that thing fixed. Usually we relieve the next shift in the shop. For those weeks, we relieved each other in the hangar bay where we were working on the jet."

Reflecting the collective pride Lee Amerine explained earlier, Chris concluded, "When 212 came back on deck and flew with no problems, it really felt like something. I contributed to that. Lieutenant Amerine was flying 212 just the other day."

We stood up and carefully backed out from under the plane, then walked down the flight deck, heading to the hangar bay to escape the stiff wind that had picked up as the afternoon ended. On the way, I learned that Chris had earned his Eagle Scout rank with Troop 380 in Plano, Texas. He had bested both Chief Palmer and me by three years and received his badge in ninth grade. He entered the University of Arkansas, but decided he wasn't quite ready for college. I thought back to what William Thomas shared with me in Coronado at the SEAL base: all things in time. I was learning everyone has their own schedule. On June 15, 2006, Chris enlisted in the navy.

"I was nineteen," he said in his soft-spoken manner. "I've always loved aviation and wanted to fly. Basically my whole life has been trying to get there—and I've hit a lot of bumps. I seem to be doing it the hardest way possible."

Like it did for me, Scouting helped introduce Chris to naval aviation, and he remembered camping on the decommissioned aircraft carrier USS *Lexington*, now permanently moored in Corpus Christi, Texas. It lit a spark. Thousands of Scouts spend weekends aboard carriers like *Lexington* and *Yorktown*, as well as aboard other decommissioned ships around the country. Those nights, like so many experiences in Scouting, give us ideas about how many options we have in life and let us sample what those might be like.

Following the promise of adventure he'd first sensed aboard the *Lexington*, Poole entered navy boot camp three days after he enlisted. He spent four months in Pensacola, Florida, in technical training and then joined VFA-14 the day after he turned twenty. A short time later, he watched San Diego, California's skyline disappear as he sailed westward from *Nimitz*'s home port into the Pacific Ocean. His first deployment would last six months.

"In Texas, I was used to being a few hours away from home," he said, then looked around the hangar deck and laughed. "Now I've been halfway around the world and back! There's really something to helping out the world. We supported Operation Iraqi Freedom and Operation Enduring Freedom and I played a part in that. Pilots told us stories about helping ground troops and I like to feel I helped support those guys over there. They're a lot braver than I am; I just want to help them out."

Poole enlisted to help our soldiers, but he also aimed to make the navy a career. In two years, he hoped the navy would send him to college and from there, he hoped to reenter the service as an officer and apply for flight school. He mused, "Hopefully I'll come full circle and instead of standing on the flight deck, I'll be flying off the flight deck."

"You'd know a heck of a lot more about your aircraft than most pilots in the squadron," I observed.

"I'd fix 'em in midair," he answered.

The night before each squadron flew home to its respective base on the U.S. mainland, Lee and I talked together in the Tophatters' ready-room, sitting at aged desks of leather and steel. Lee wore shorts, a T-shirt, and running shoes—beginning the transition from boat life, he explained. It was late and the other pilots had already left for a good night's sleep before a 7:00 A.M. preflight briefing the next morning. The room was nearly stripped bare. The squadron had packed up everything into bags and boxes, which they'd hauled to the hangar deck earlier that day. There, they'd placed them in crates for shipment to their base in Lemoore, California. It reminded me of a fraternity house on the last night of college exams—nearly empty, awaiting summer break.

It's almost easy to forget the seriousness of the job these young men have: protecting and defending. That can mean dropping bombs and shooting cannons. It can mean taking the lives of others. Lee seemed genuinely relieved that on this deployment, he hadn't dropped any bombs or loosed any rounds from his guns. He'd helped keep the peace and contentedly reflected on past missions for which he'd been briefed in the ready-room where we sat.

He remembered flying over Iraq, locating hidden IEDs using infrared scanners and helping troops on the ground. He also described his first venture over Afghanistan: two hours to a tanker to fuel, into Afghanistan, back to the tanker, back to Afghanistan. Nothing happened. He laughed, and explained, "You're looking out there at your wings seeing bombs with yellow fuses, knowing they're live. Looking at your wingtips you have Sidewinders, and you know they're live Sidewinders and you have four hundred rounds in your guns. Nobody was shooting at us and there wasn't a lot of action—but that was fine! I wasn't looking for a fight. If the fight wanted to find me, I'd definitely swoop in. Some guys launch out of here looking for that fight. That's not how I am.

"But those bombs and missiles are precision-guided weapons and they give us a chance at virtual war—the ramifications of what you're doing you don't feel. I want to make sure that when and if I do drop that bomb, I don't take any joy in it; it's going to be real. You have to feel that; you're obligated to feel that so it makes war real, not just a simple tool of diplomacy. It's so easy for us: twenty thousand feet, autopilot, drop the bomb. It's a video game. That's not right. But don't confuse that for weakness.

"War becomes unjust when killing comes easy and one sided," he observed, harkening back to a senior military ethics class he had at the Naval Academy. "You almost forget that you're taking life because your own life is not in danger. As soon as you violate that moral code, you're going to have problems. It's more dangerous for me to land on a carrier than it is for me to drop a bomb in Iraq. War can now be an easy tool to use instead of the last resort. It can be easier than working a situation out diplomatically. We can send a section of Super Hornets into any country in the world and we can do some good work and we don't lose any of our guys.

"But duty is why I do all of it," he said. "I try to explain it to Jen and I try to rationalize it out here, but truthfully it's harder to rationalize it out here than it is back on the beach. You're stuck out here passing the time, but on the beach you realize what you do. I protect. I think it's almost like a priest's calling. Duty is why I do it," he reiterated, then smiled. "But then there's the adventure of it. There's not a greater adventure than this. There are guys who are jumping off cliffs in flight suits—that's interesting but this is different. Think about our purpose. And the fact that this is the job I wanted when I was eight years old means I never had to grow up!"

He at least grew up enough to marry Jen, however, and his thoughts turned to her as the evening grew later. He hadn't seen his wife in five months and would see her in just hours. "It's almost surreal," he said, motioning to the empty walls and boxes of equipment around us. "I see all this, I'm completely packed, I brief in seven hours, but it's still surreal. Am I really going home? When I get there, it'll be that same rush I got when I first got married. It'll be like scenes from the movies. I'll get out of the plane. She'll run out in a sundress. I'll be in my flight suit. Perfect." I sat next to a happy man.

Lee and I finally realized taps had arrived for us; it had long since been announced for the ship. We walked down the long, darkened hallway from the aft ready room to our forward staterooms. Red lights offered dim illumination as we stepped through portal after portal, opening and resealing water-tight hatches along the way. We met several pilots near Lee's room and all talked quietly beneath the glowing red lamps until each of us left for the wardroom's midnight meal or our bunk.

The next morning, *Nimitz* and her escorts again turned into the wind. For the last time on this cruise, aircrews fueled their planes and readied them for their pilots. For the last time, squadrons met in ready-rooms, briefed, then made the walk to their aircraft. I watched from up high as new friends pulled on their helmets one by one and shut their canopies. Not all of them were Eagle Scouts, but they all nevertheless shared a kindred sense of adventure and duty. They waited their turn for clearance from the tower then began their flights eastward. By the afternoon, the carrier had launched sixty-one planes and eight helicopters. The flight deck stood empty for my last sunset.

When I woke the next morning and walked onto the deck, I found the California coast waiting for us, low on the far horizon. I hadn't seen land since we left Hawaii a week ago, and I thought I'd be excited to find water no longer encompassing my entire world. Instead, the sight touched me with a sense of melancholy. My journey was nearing its end.

The thousands of men and women below the flight deck, however, did not seem to feel even a twinge of melancholy and clearly could not wait until their deployment ended. The previous day had been spent boxing gear and packing duffle bags, most of which were now stacked throughout the cavernous hangar bay. Walking through the maze of sailors and boxes, I came across Chief Palmer and AE3 Poole, both in dress uniforms and brimming with anticipation. I wished them well. The cruise was nearly over. It felt like the last day of college.

With her sailors and officers lining decks and catwalks in their dress whites, *Nimitz* eased into the channel that led to her home pier. Brightly colored flags flew on the ropes running from the signal bridge up to the ship's dark gray mast. Smaller craft played about on the water below. Excitement permeated the ship and crew like an electric charge. The military airfields of North Island passed to our starboard side and we turned slowly into the main harbor. Downtown San Diego rose squarely ahead of us; the largest yachts in its marinas suddenly looked insignificant as the massive supercarrier glided past them, majestic, powerful, and proud. Standing behind a line of sailors dressed in their whites, I felt humbled by their sacrifice. I knew that the pride in my heart matched the pride in theirs. Today, I was part of their moment, their homecoming.

As we moved closer to our pier, I saw *Nimitz*'s peacefully docked sister carriers: *George Washington* and *Ronald Reagan*. Then I saw our dock, covered with thousands of people who had not seen their loved ones in nearly five months. Some stood with new babies that fathers had yet to hold; others carried balloons, flowers, or posterboard signs. Tugboats nudged us closer to the pier and then we stopped. I could hear distant yells and cheers from the dock. The carrier's deep fog horn blared three times, booming over the gathered crowd. The PA system announced that mooring lines were now fixed to the dock, and a resounding cheer went up from all quarters, echoing throughout the hangar bay.

Minutes later, two gangways extended from the pier to the ship, and new fathers led an immediate exodus. From the railing of the hangar, I watched two waves collide below me: one of crew members surging from the ship, the other of families and friends pressing forward from the wharf to meet them. There were tears, smiles, and laughter. Over the scene loomed the mammoth warship that had safely carried these sailors across thousands of miles. The flags strung from the carrier's mast snapped in the steady wind blowing from the Pacific. At last, the great ship rested in the harbor, her engines finally quiet and still. *Nimitz* was home. So was I.

CONCLUSION

LIVING THE ADVENTURE

One year after that cold, cold night at Winding Stair Gap on the Appalachian Trail, my father and I hopped across the small creek that wandered beside our old campsite. Instead of experiencing snow-muffled silence, we heard sharp bird calls and the rustle of squirrels. Typical spring weather of warm days and steady rains had long since dispelled any remnants of the winter's snowfall. Dogwoods bloomed and trillium displayed their purple and white flowers, which still glistened with dew. New leaves on towering tulip poplars, sourwoods, and oaks created a canopy of light green above the forest floor.

The trail itself had already been conditioned with thousands of boot steps from the blitz of thru-hikers who'd left Georgia's Springer Mountain a month earlier, bound for Mount Katahdin in Maine, some 2,175 miles distant from the southern trailhead. The hikers walked north with the season. Likewise, as we ascended the mountain we watched the spring roll back. For every hundred feet we gained, the trillium were fewer, air cooler, and hardwoods increasingly bare. Even as we neared five thousand feet, however, I needed nothing more than my shorts, T-shirt, and sunglasses. Our luck had changed from a year ago; we'd picked a magnificent day.

My father and I passed the point where he'd stopped on our last hike and where my brother Rob and I had found him waiting after we summited Siler Bald. We hiked a spell farther and the trail opened onto a grassy meadow washed in sunlight. Remembering the stories Rob and I carried back from the top, he mused, "So that's the tree," and pointed to the still bare, solitary tree that marked the peak.

We both took a drink of water and began the final leg of the ascent. My fellow Eagle Scout had clearly resolved to reach the top this year. He talked a bit less as we climbed, but breathed steadily, intent on finishing. My brother and I had sprinted up the final slope; my father and I walked leisurely, albeit with purpose, and enjoyed the vista that opened around us. Dad had lulled me into complacency and as we neared the summit, he suddenly yanked my left arm from behind, pulling me back while slinging himself forward. With an unexpected burst of energy and speed, he took off for the summit. I raced after him.

Both winded, we looked out together from the 5,216 foot peak. Mountains still girded the entire horizon. From the valleys below us, we saw the inevitable progress of spring, creeping steadily upward along the flanks of the mountains. Soon it would reach the summits, as it has for eons. Seasons always change, and so do generations, as being with my father reminded me.

I suppose, then, that it was fitting that my father handed me several important symbols of my family's legacy. From a box he'd hidden in my backpack, he pulled three of my grandfather's greatest treasures. First, he handed me a green medal, with a golden key hanging from it, the Scout fleur-de-lis welded to its front: my grandfather's Scoutmaster's Key. Then, Dad gave me his father's Silver Beaver Award, which I think my grandfather treasured above all else. He'd received the silver pendant and its accompanying blue-and-white ribbon for his service to Troop 84 and the Atlanta Area Council of the Boy Scouts. Orphaned on an Alabama farm in the early 1900s, he never had Scouting while growing up. When his son, my father, joined in the late 1950s, my grandfather became a Scoutmaster and his passion for the program only increased throughout the rest of his life. Dad and I wished he could have seen where Scouting had taken us; we hoped he somehow knew.

The box wasn't empty yet however, and Dad selected another item that I remembered my grandfather showing me when I was young. Its place in his heart had ranked a close second to the Silver Beaver. He'd worked his way through school in Alabama, shoveling coal for student dormitories and working early mornings on his uncle's farm, before earning a place at Northwestern University in Chicago, Illinois. When he graduated from Northwestern in 1931, his pride must have been boundless. He bought a gold stem-winding watch to mark the occasion and attached to it still was a golden chain with his Northwestern Key; "NU Commerce" engraved on its front, "A.M.T. '31" on its back. With it was a note written in his shaky, aged hand that read, "Something for you to keep and pass along to Alvin III. I love you."

"I just thought it was time for you to have these," my father said reflectively. "I guess you've taken up the mantle now."

Silence lingered for several moments and a breeze picked up. I looked out over the valley below us. I thought about this journey, about where I'd been, what I'd learned, and how I too would contribute to Scouting's legacy.

Looking back on the trail that had led me from and to Siler Bald, I realized that the adventure of the past year was not only unforgettable, it was nearly unbelievable. I had never known exhilaration like standing on the bow of the *Nimitz* as she plowed through the open sea. Discovering the Great Barrier Reef alongside Eric Treml; venturing into Africa with the Peace Corps; climbing Red Rock Canyon with Josh McNary; surfing on Waikiki with Ka'eo; reading to little Chevai at Adamsville Elementary School, standing on Brownsea Island—I'd never known such a sustained rush. But it wasn't just the climbs, dives, and hikes that I relished. I also loved sharing a mission with other Eagles of our younger generation.

When I had arrived home after my cruise aboard the *Nimitz*, I wondered if the adventure had ended. Or rather, how could I enjoy that rush without standing on top of a mountain or diving on a reef? Lying awake my first night at home, I finally understood that the individuals I met had begun to give me the answers. I'd found that adventures of one type don't last forever. I knew Lee Amerine and his fellow pilots rarely flew from carriers for more than ten years. Peace Corps assignments lasted two. John Beck wouldn't always don helmet and pads for Sunday NFL games. Even Sean and Lenore O'Brien's adventure as a couple would soon change with the arrival of their first child. Due to varying combinations of rules, time, and priorities, the character of adventure inevitably shifts. And responsibility often has a role to play in that change.

My new friends had prepared me well for life's inevitable changes. I had seen many people rise gracefully to higher callings and new duties. Tom Campbell taught aspiring SEALs lessons from his ten-year career. In a reversal of roles, Deuce Lutui cared for his ill father. Travis Amerine suddenly placed his career second to little Ashlyn Day. Joe Pack traded freestyle skiing for the chance to start a family. I had seen change happen for others. I just hadn't realized or admitted that it might happen to me as well. As I hiked down the spine of Siler Bald, I knew a slightly different person left the summit that day than had arrived there the year before.

In innumerable ways across incalculable miles, I had watched our generation face new challenges and responsibilities. We didn't simply confront them; we met them with the spirit and passion we inherited from those who came before us. A new generation, we are living countless adventures, but we seem to pursue those paths with a sense of duty. As we come of age, our lives rise above adventure just for adventure's own sake. We want more. We seek out new responsibilities. We follow our passions to deliberate ends. What we ultimately seek, I believe, is purpose.

Often, true purpose becomes obscured by the hurriedness of life, by the thousands of details that clutter our vision and use up our time. The challenge is to learn to live deliberately, and constantly renew our commitment to something larger than ourselves. I reflected on my past months and asked myself two questions: One, how did I spend my hours and minutes, given my real aspirations? And two, which of my actions truly made a difference in the lives of others? I wasn't always pleased with the answers. The young men I met, however, served as reminders of how I should be answering those questions, and of how I could make life better for other people.

In the end, our service to others will be our only enduring legacy. No greater purpose exists than serving. Nothing else matters when we're gone, as we all one day will be. The people I met seemed to understand that already, and they judged their own actions by an exterior standard: how were they shaping the future? Their paths were rarely easy, but they were uniformly worthwhile. They treasured their experiences and found real value in their pursuits. They lived by those deeply held virtues that Scouting had instilled.

In their Scout troops, which were spread across the world, these twenty- and thirty-something Eagle Scouts had gained lasting skills and learned to lead, to sacrifice for a greater good, to press their limits, and to serve other people at all times. As I first began to discover at Philmont, Scouting helped them press beyond old limits and discover what they could become. It gave them the skills to attain those new, higher aspirations. Scouting had instilled in our generation a spirit of adventure: a drive to pursue our own path in life with passion and independence, guided by a set of timeless values. Our Scout leaders had made us good stewards and better human beings; they prepared us to take on the responsibilities of adulthood.

In many ways, Scouting shaped us just as it did our fathers and grandfathers. Scouts were earning merit badges for camping, first aid, lifesaving, music, public health, and swimming as early as 1911. Scouts earn those same badges today. For nearly a century, Scouts have been hiking and camping in wilderness areas throughout the country; they've trekked across Philmont's mountains since 1938. They still recite an unchanged Scout Oath and Scout Law, and Baden-Powell's boy-led patrol method still forms the core of the program. New merit badges have naturally come with advancing times, but Scouting's core has essentially remained the same.

Changes in our modern world, moreso than changes in the Scout program, have made our generation different from those that preceded it. We encounter more cultures and interact with more people from different backgrounds—consider the experiences of Collin and Dutch in West Africa, Matt Dalio with Shanxi's orphans, or Karl Brady with his students at Adamsville Elementary School. As a result of experiences like those and instant access to almost unlimited information, we tend to accept and respect viewpoints and ways of life that differ from our own.

And while many of us pursue traditional goals, I had found a growing number of people willing to strike out in less certain directions. Some choose futures that promise much less financial reward or stability but offer other meaningful returns. Many of us placed a premium on experiences instead of monetary compensation. Often those experiences held an element of service, as I had found in NOLS instructor Josh McNary and the cadre of Navy SEALs. As a generation, we seek the spiritual fulfillment that can only come with contributing to something greater than ourselves.

I also couldn't forget Head Ranger Sean Casey's comment: "We're told we can do anything, and I think we sometimes mistake *anything* for *everything*." That is one of our generation's challenges. When we look toward the future, we find more avenues of possibility than others did before us; we often have trouble choosing one road to follow. Sometimes that induces decision paralysis; other times it can lead us to jump from one track to another with alarming frequency. Viewing our options and choices within the framework of the Scout Oath and Law, however, seemed to help many Eagles bring steadiness to their lives, helping them pursue their purpose without the distraction of endlessly tempting options. They didn't lose sight of their greater goals.

But one characteristic defines our generation above all others: we represent the future. We'll soon inherit the mantle of leadership from our parents, and our example and actions will define the world for years to come. Thankfully, Eagle Scouts understand that coming responsibility and we are already creating our own legacy. It is a legacy born from Scouting's spirit of adventure, one that carries with it a duty and a noble purpose. I found its manifestation in countless acts of leadership, courage, and kindness that touch the lives of others. We are acting as leaders in war and peace, making sacrifices to pass our values to younger generations. We are stewards of the world's resources and institutions, upholding our responsibilities to family and friends, as well as others who may never truly know how we've served them.

As I thought back on my journey, I considered the individuals I met. Vince and Vance ventured into Afghanistan because they knew the country's people needed their help to survive. Buey and Jacob never succumbed to the violence of Wintergreen Apartments because they aimed to fulfill an obligation to their native country of Sudan. The servicemen I met at Walter Reed lived to serve their country in whatever way they could; Peace Corps volunteers and Teach for America members reminded me that serving our country doesn't necessarily entail carrying a rifle. The examples were endless, and I had found only a tiny fraction of them. But each individual that I had encountered led his life with a well-defined sense of purpose. That matters. We don't necessarily set out to change the world alone, but taken together, our generation's countless acts, performed in thousands of towns, cities, and countries, create a gathering force that is bringing about greater change.

I can only imagine how proud Lord Robert Baden-Powell would feel if he met these young men. They had adopted the spirit he first kindled and followed a charge he issued generations ago, one that has echoed across time and oceans. He issued it in 1929, as he closed the Third World Scout Jamboree in Arrowe Park, England. Fifty thousand Scouts had arrived from every corner of the globe to celebrate the Movement's coming of age. At the closing ceremony, Scouts filled the vast field around a podium of lashed logs, from which their Chief addressed them.

"Today I send you out from Arrowe to all the world," Baden-Powell said to the thousands gathered around him. "Each one of you my ambassador bearing my message of love and fellowship on the wings of sacrifice and service, to the end of the earth . . . Carry it fast and far so that all men may know the Brotherhood of Man."

Baden-Powell's charge now passes to us, Eagle Scouts or not, young or old. It's our turn to live our own adventure; to renew our mission to live with passion and purpose; to make our own mark on the changing planet. Our challenge is to understand where and how we can help, given our unique talents and concerns. Then we each must claim a part of our generation's responsibility.

The world's future is ours to create, and now is our time to lead.

Let's go.

ACTION AND ACKNOWLEDGMENTS

No chronicle of Scouting could ever be complete. The preceding pages capture only a fraction of the inspiring stories I uncovered, and they represent an even smaller fraction of the millions of people who are out there living the values and lifelong adventure of Scouting. While that proved daunting from a writing standpoint, I found it exceptionally exciting from another—the potential. Almost everyone I encountered harbored a love for the Scouting Movement and hoped to become involved, if they weren't already. They wanted to carry Scouting's story to—and be Scouting's story in—their communities and towns. Many, however, just didn't know how. I particularly saw that dilemma in those of us in our twenties and thirties, many of whom have difficulty making a weekly commitment to serve as a traditional Scout leader.

Well, Scouting is a true movement, not an organization, and as such, it relies on its alumni and volunteers to bring its promise to a new generation. So I'm very grateful to the cadre of Eagle Scouts in Atlanta, Georgia, who helped me start the Eagle Reserve initiative, under the theme of "One Weekend a Year for Scouting." We volunteered a weekend to help take a local troop camping and taught the Scouts of Troop 100 what we once learned ourselves. Now we're challenging you to do the same, and I hope that you'll dust off your boots and join us. Imagine what we can accomplish if we all give just one weekend, if not even more. Visit www.eaglereserve.org to get involved.

Speaking of getting involved, I want to thank those millions of parents and volunteer leaders who I found in every corner of the country giving so unselfishly of their time to help Scouts become better adults and thus make the world a better place. I saw what they accomplish in young lives, and I learned that they truly make Scouting happen; I admire them and am grateful. Many of those individuals, along with countless Scouts and Eagles across America, shared their personal stories and hopes with me during the past years, and they have left me in awe of this Movement's impact, legacy, and future. Thank you.

During my travels, I met Scout executives and professionals, volunteers, and Scouts from councils throughout the nation who understood what I hoped to accomplish for the Movement and warmly welcomed me to their cities and towns; thank you for your friendship and devotion to Scouting. Special thanks go to Ivan and Phyllis Seidenberg for helping me share my message, to Bob Mazzuca for his personal support, and to Rick Cronk for his encouragement and vision for Scouting in America and globally. Warren Young, I'll thank you on the squash court.

I basically traveled around the world twice to research and write *Spirit of Adventure*, and Delta Air Lines and the SkyTeam alliance carried me safely all the way. In particular, I want to thank the kind Delta agent who reopened the flight from Heathrow to Atlanta so this tardy traveler could make his flight home!

In Australia, Andy and Sally Young, along with Thomo, Emily, and the Sydney crew formed a quick circle of friends, and Eric and Renee were supreme hosts in Brissy. *Mahalo* to Chuck Sted and Helen Shirota-Benevides for showing me the spirit of *aloha* on Oahu and the Big Island, and to Hubert Chang for the surfboards and good company afloat.

Lieutenant Commander Kim Marks and Lieutenant Lesley Lykins, along with Rear Admiral Frank Thorpe IV and Secretary Robert Gates, helped me catch a carrier in the middle of the Pacific Ocean. Captain Michael Manazir, Lieutenant Jared Bergamy, and everyone aboard *Nimitz* and in Air Wing 11 were gracious hosts.

The Peace Corps, particularly Amanda Host Beck in Washington and Sheryl Cowan in Benin, made my trip to Africa a reality, and the volunteers on post made it a success. In country, Carlos and Victor guided me safely through an unknown land, and the Mitton family kindly hosted me during my last days in Cotonou. And thanks to Lauren Robbins for speaking French, braving the lagoon, and being herself.

In Great Britain, Kevin and Sarah Batteh took care of me in London, while Ken and Betty Parminter hosted me in Storrington and reminded me that it doesn't take blood relations to be a true grandparent.

John Gans and Jeanne O'Brien at NOLS, Mark Anderson and Gene Schnell at Philmont, Lieutenant Kimberly Brubeck with Naval Special Warfare, and Patrick Vassel and Samantha Cohen at Teach for America helped me uncover exceptional groups of Eagle Scouts within their ranks. Charles Dahlquist in Salt Lake City kindly and expeditiously opened several important doors; many thanks for your help and support.

In New York, my agent, Jack Scovil, shepherded me through round two, while Tom Dunne, Pete Wolverton, and everyone at Thomas Dunne Books made me feel like family. And how can I say enough about my outstanding editor and fellow Eagle Scout, Peter Joseph? He has smartly guided this book and me from the outset and always gives the right advice.

Spirit of Adventure truly belongs to the people whose stories it tells, and I deeply appreciate them lending me their time, stories, and thoughts. They took me into their lives—and in some cases homes—for a few hours or several days and treated me like a brother. I'll always treasure the time we shared talking, eating, surfing, climbing, diving, hiking, and doing every other activity under the sun. They made writing this book a truly worthwhile adventure.

During the past year, friends old and new, in Atlanta and coast to coast, encouraged, hosted, and supported me in numbers and ways too many to list; I have so many good memories of our time together, and you never let me take myself too seriously. My wonderful family has supported me every step of the way during this journey, even when those steps took me far away from home. I'm fortunate to call you my best friends; you made each homecoming particularly special and warm.

The preceding pages tell stories about people living with passion and purpose. Yes, they're Eagle Scouts, but their lives hold lessons for everyone, regardless of age or background. I hope that everyone will gain some inspiration from their examples and remember the duty we all have—to others as well as to ourselves—to find a purpose and pursue a lifelong adventure.

INDEX

Index